The Eloquence of Grace

LLOYD JOHN OGILVIE INSTITUTE OF PREACHING SERIES

The vision of the Lloyd John Ogilvie Institute of Preaching is to proclaim Jesus Christ and to catalyze a movement of empowered, wise preachers who seek justice, love mercy, and walk humbly with God, leading others to join in God's mission in the world. The books in this series are selected to contribute to the development of such wise and humble preachers. The authors represent both scholars of preaching as well as pastors and preachers whose experiences and insights can contribute to passionate and excellent preaching.

The *Eloquence* of *Grace*

Joseph Sittler and the Preaching Life

EDITED BY
James M. Childs Jr.
and Richard Lischer

CASCADE *Books* • Eugene, Oregon

THE ELOQUENCE OF GRACE
Joseph Sittler and the Preaching Life

Lloyd John Ogilvie Institute of Preaching Series

Copyright © 2012 Wipf and Stock Publishers. All rights reserved. Except for brief quotations in critical publications or reviews, no part of this book may be reproduced in any manner without prior written permission from the publisher. Write: Permissions, Wipf and Stock Publishers, 199 W. 8th Ave., Suite 3, Eugene, OR 97401.

Cascade Books
An Imprint of Wipf and Stock Publishers
199 W. 8th Ave., Suite 3
Eugene, OR 97401
www.wipfandstock.com

ISBN 13: 978-1-61097-647-3

Where indicated, Scripture quotations are taken from the New English Bible, copyright © Cambridge University Press and Oxford University Press 1961, 1970. All rights reserved.

"Called to Unity," *The Ecumenical Review*, 14 (January 1962), 122-131. Reproduced by permission. All rights reserved.

Material from *The Anguish of Preaching* copyright © 1966 Fortress Press admin. Augsburg Fortress Publishers. Reproduced by permission. All rights reserved.

Material from *Gravity and Grace* edited by Linda-Marie Delloff copyright © 1986 Augsburg Publishing House admin. Augsburg Fortress Publishers. Reproduced by permission. All rights reserved.

Material from *The Ecology of Faith* copyright © 1961 Muhlenberg Press admin. Augsburg Fortress Publishers. Reproduced by Permission. All rights reserved.

Material from *The Care of the Earth and Other University Sermons* copyright © 1964 Fortress Press admin. Augsburg Fortress Publishers. Reproduced by permission. All rights reserved.

Cataloging-in-Publication data:

The eloquence of grace : Joseph Sittler and the preaching life / edited by James M. Childs Jr. and Richard Lischer.

Lloyd John Ogilvie Institute of Preaching Series

xiv + 326 p. ; 23 cm. Includes bibliographical references.

ISBN 13: 978-1-61097-647-3

1. Sittler, Joseph. 2. Theology. 3. Preaching. I. Title. II. Series.

BX8080 S387 E45 2012

Manufactured in the U.S.A.

Contents

Foreword by Martin Marty/ vii
Editors' General Introduction / xi

PART 1: THE PREACHER AS THEOLOGIAN
Introduction: "Nothing Less than Everything" / 2
   1 Sittler Introduces Himself / 13
   2 Christology / 27
   3 Living the Given Life / 50
   4 Unbridled Grace / 63
   5 Ethos and Ministry / 84

PART 2: PREACHING THE WORD
Introduction: "Joseph Sittler and the Preacher's Calling" / 104
   6 The Word of God / 115
   7 Preaching and the Biblical Imagination / 159

PART 3: SERMONS
Introduction: "The Preacher as Theological Artisan" / 194
     The Care of the Earth / 201
     Remembering and Forgetting / 209
     How to Hear a Parable / 215
     The Unjust Steward / 221
     The Lost Sheep / 229

Contents

Epiphany, Glory, and 63rd Street / 236
Effort and Serenity / 243
The Nimbus and the Rainbow / 250
Suffering and Splendor / 256
Three on Romans 8 (Sermon 1) / 261
Three on Romans 8 (Sermon 2) / 266
Three on Romans 8 (Sermon 3) / 272
Maundy Thursday / 278
Easter: "This Is the Feast of Victory for Our God" / 286
The Passion of Christ / 291
The Haunting Allure of Jesus / 297
Post-Easter Sermon / 303
Sermon on Memory / 308

Postscript: The Last Lecture: A Walk around the Truth, Eternal Life, and Faith / 315

Index / 323

Foreword

"For Export Only"—was the tag attached to prime ecumenical theologian and preacher Joseph Sittler by the president of his church body. At least that phrase is what Sittler heard Dr. Franklin Clark Fry answer when the traveled professor asked why he was so regularly sent to represent his church overseas or in dealings with denominations other than his own. Why apply that limiting cautionary tag which his friendly and proud superior kept in mind, given that Sittler was such, like Fry, such a faithful Lutheran and American? Answer: he was too imaginative, too creative, too soaring to be confined to settings where people with his gifts could be rendered dangerous and suspect. As readers of the pages that follow can see, he was very much at home with the grand themes of Christian theology. However, he made connections where many others wanted to keep teachings disconnected, or connected them when they were often expected to be kept apart.

Nowhere will this be more obvious in these chapters than in his linking of "nature" and "grace." There was no logical or theological reason to keep them apart. Both have profound biblical rootage and, in the history of theology, ordinarily belonged together. Whether Sittler dealt with God as God or with God in Christ, it was clear to him that God is better served if "nature" and "grace" are treated and set forth together. A reader with a yellow highlighter who would explore this will be busy highlighting the many, many nature-and-grace passages and Sittler's rationale for them.

The long-time Chicago professor wrote several impressive books, but they were too few, too short for him to fulfill his promise. Senior theologians—and that is who is left with living memories of Sittler the speaker in his prime—who spot each other in crowds or convene to revisit his work immediately begin telling stories, quoting quips, or conversing about new meanings they found when reading him. For that reason numbers of them, as evidenced by the general samples in this book, have developed an archive of his journal articles, conference papers, occasional homilies, or almost any other oral remnant that they can transcribe and publish. We profit from their work.

Sittler could rationalize on Lutheran terms why he favored the oral rhetoric at which he was a master. With Luther he was devoted to the Word, which he addressed in the title of one of his books. Luther had said that the Word was to be *geschrieen,* "shouted," and not merely *geschrieben,* "written." The Church, he went on, was a *Mundhaus,* a mouth house, not a *Federhaus,* a [writing-]pen house. A problem with the legacy of a life like Sittler's, devoted as it is to the spoken word is that it disappears when its sound-waves have died. Sittler came along just in time to get to live on in many taped audio- and audio-visual presentations and thus to prolong his influence. Yet, this book by its very existence demonstrates, ironically, how valid and valuable "written" rhetoric is, can be, and, as books like this one live, *will* be.

I once asked Sittler why he enjoyed teaching theology and preaching so much. Answer: "Where else could I make my living reading *Moby Dick* or *The Education of Henry Adams* or poet Richard Wilbur?" Wait a minute: where is the Bible, and where are books of creeds and canons? Not a problem. Every page of this collection will show how deeply immersed in the Bible and in historical theology Sittler is. However, he argued that the preacher should connect the heart of the Christian message with *everything* "out there." Novels, poetry, essays, editorials, all helped mediate the world "out there" to the Christian theme. "To be a Christian is to accept what God gives in Christ" is Sittler's great digest. And God gave us cathedrals and games, banquets to enjoy and problems to solve. A moment ago I wrote that Sittler would connect to "everything," and these pages show him doing that, within the limits of finitude. The smallest and largest, the oldest and newest, the simplest and the most complicated, the sacred and the profane, are to be creative challenges and instruments for preachers.

A text for that, please? Sittler was sometimes ignored, shunned, or criticized for the generous reach of his illustrations and sources. He would be asked, "How can you include them? How *dare* you use the word 'everything?'" Sittler would answer citing the Apostle Paul, using the great Christological passage in Colossians 1:15–20, especially 16b–17. Let me

Foreword

emphasize, as if "shouting" the Word: ". . . **All things** have been created through [Christ] and for him, and in him **all things** hold together." Literally this is to be so, if you let the Word speak and take hold of you.

That Sittler was also an evangelist might surprise some readers, but we who knew him and his trail know of converts, whether gathered on campuses or retreats or in chance encounters, who can trace the awakening or profound enriching of their faith to his work. He could also stir conscience. One of the instances that comes to my mind—and I discipline myself to stop with one—occurred on the University of Chicago campus, where he would occasionally preach at Rockefeller Memorial Chapel. Those who have experienced campuses and their chapels on hot summer-vacation mornings, do not expect to see crowds. One August morning as Sittler was strolling down University Avenue before he turned to enter Rockefeller, he passed the high fence around a mini-field of corn behind the President's house. The President was George Beadle, Nobel prize-winning corn-geneticist, who, twenty-minutes before the bells rang, was in Nebraska-style overalls, working by the sweat of his brow. Till a smiling Joe Sittler leaned over the fence and tsk-tsked: "Twenty minutes until church time, Mr. President!" and walked on. Twenty minutes later Sittler spotted his president, all scrubbed up and black-suited, sitting expectantly in a front pew. I have no idea whether there was a follow-up to that conversation and act, but so many conversations and acts are part of the Sittler lore, that I have to believe that such invitations through the years had a yield. We who were and are influenced by that preacher-professor, don't merely start sentences about him with an ". . . of all things . . . " but we go on to connect him as he would connect us, with the **all things** to which his Christian message would witness.

MARTIN E. MARTY
The University of Chicago

Editors' General Introduction

Joseph A. Sittler (September 26, 1904–December 28, 1987) was a graduate of Wittenberg College and the Hamma Divinity School in Springfield, Ohio. He began his career in the ordained ministry as pastor of Messiah Lutheran Church in Cleveland, Ohio. For most of his life, however, he was a Professor of Theology, first at the Chicago Lutheran Seminary in Maywood, Illinois, then at the Divinity School of the University of Chicago. He ended his career as Distinguished Professor in Residence at the Lutheran School of Theology at Chicago.

THIS BOOK CELEBRATES JOSEPH Sittler's legacy as preacher, theologian of the Word, and teacher of the church. In the introductions and brief commentaries that accompany his sermons and essays, we have attempted to do more than take a historical perspective on his achievement. Clearly, his essays, sermons, and presentations bear the marks of a specific time and place. Though his time was not so long ago, both the cultural context and homiletical theory have undergone change since his day. Notwithstanding, it is our conviction that his is a living legacy. Theologically serious preaching, close attention to language, engagement with the best of sacred and secular culture, and a deep respect for the text, all characteristics of the Sittler's work, are the sort of features that continue to edify. They remain as benchmarks for good preaching even as styles and contexts evolve. In the bargain we are also rewarded with the experience of his eloquence and grace.

Many of the sermons and a number of other presentations have never been in print before. Most of these have been transcribed from

Editors' General Introduction

audio tapes kept in the Joseph A. Sittler Archives located at the Lutheran School of Theology at Chicago. Moving from oral presentation to written form requires a good bit of editing. Indeed, a number of these presentations, remarkable for their cogency and engaging style, were made after Sittler was in the process of losing his sight and needed to work without either notes or manuscript. The challenge is to provide an edited print version of his sermons and presentations that conveys as much as possible the qualities experienced by those hearing and seeing him in person. Things that sound good when heard in the living present may look odd if transcribed literally without attention to the grammatical and organizational demands of the print media. Extraneous comments referencing individuals and events that would have had immediate resonance with the audience would simply distract from the flow of the message if left in. Nonetheless, we have made every effort to be sure that, whatever editing was done, each piece is authentic Sittler.

We are thankful; first of all, to the Sittler family and to LSTC for establishing the JAS Archives, and to the many other donors who have contributed materials to make this collection of Sittler's work freely available, both at LSTC and on the website at www.josephsittler.org. We certainly owe a great debt of gratitude to Mel and Meta George of the Sittler Archive Committee, who assembled the archive and have kept it up to date. Without their enthusiasm and support for this project and without the resources of the archive, this project would never have been considered. We thank Robert Saler, who staffed the archive library, for providing us with the tapes we needed. Thanks are due also to recent graduate of Trinity Lutheran Seminary, Tom Pairan, for his excellent work in transcribing the audio files. Trinity faculty secretary, Nona Jenson, helped put previously published materials into manuscript form. Finally, we thank the Special Collections Research Center of the University of Chicago Library for their permission to publish the three sermons in this collection that were preached in Rockefeller Chapel: "Remembering and Forgetting," "Nimbus and the Rainbow," and "Effort and Serenity."

As indicated in the acknowledgments below, a number of the selections have appeared in print at various times throughout Sittler's career. However, this particular combination of selections is a new amalgam. Presented as they are in the frame of his importance for preaching, we believe they take on renewed significance.

"A Christology of Function." *Lutheran Quarterly* 6 (May 1954) 122–31.

"The Problems of New Testament Interpretation and the Task of the Preacher" and "The Anguish of Christology." Chapters 2 and 3, respectively, in *The Anguish of Preaching*. Philadelphia: Fortress, 1966.

"The Content of the Engendered Response." Chapter 3 in *The Structure of Christian Ethics*. 1958. Reprinted, Louisville: Westminster John Knox, 1998.

"Called to Unity." *The Ecumenical Review* 14 (January 1962) 177–87. Reprinted in *Evocations of Grace: The Writings of Joseph Sittler on Ecology, Theology, and Ethics*, edited by Steven Bouma-Prediger and Peter Bakken, 38–50. Grand Rapids: Eerdmans, 2000.

"Nature and Grace" and "Ministry: The Stewardship of the Mystery." Chapters 1 and 4, respectively, in *Gravity and Grace: Reflections and Provocations*, edited by Linda-Marie Delloff. Minneapolis: Augsburg, 1986.

"The Search for Theological Method and Its Requirement of Preaching," "The Role of the Imagination in Preaching," and "Maceration of the Minister." Chapters 2, 3, and 5, respectively, in *The Ecology of Faith*. Philadelphia: Muhlenberg, 1961.

"The Care of the Earth" and "Epiphany, Glory, and 63rd Street." Chapters 4 and 6, respectively, in *The Care of the Earth, and Other University Sermons*. Philadelphia: Fortress, 1964.

"The Haunting Allure of Jesus." *Trinity Seminary Review* 4/2 (Fall 1982) 32–35.

"The Last Lecture: A Walk around Truth, Eternal Life, Faith." *Religion and Intellectual Life* 4/2 (Winter 1987) 59–65.

JAMES M. CHILDS JR.
RICHARD LISCHER

PART 1

The Preacher as Theologian

Introduction

"Nothing Less than Everything"—Thoughts on a Sittler Legacy

Sittler provided a model for doing theology immersed in a vision of the graced interconnectedness of all things. I would even venture to propose that no aspect of the theological task was done outside that vision; it was explicitly engaged in major works and implicitly present in the smaller scale corollaries to be found in sermons and briefer musings.

IN ONE OF HIS earlier essays, Wolfhart Pannenberg defined what is arguably the essential task of theology.

> The quest for the ultimate unity which integrates and thus unifies everything is the question reaching for God . . . the way in which we must test any concept of God is asking whether it can account for the unity of all reality. If an idea of God fails that test, it does not comprehend the power dominating everything and is, therefore, not a true concept of God.[1]

Sittler, in his own style and with his own keen sensitivity to the evangelical vocation of theology, understood and pursued the task of theology in terms no less sweeping. The scope of theology is nothing less than everything. The grace of God, preeminently revealed in the Christ, suffuses everything. In the fragmentation of modern specialization that also characterizes much of theology and the fragmented structure of meaning that

---

1. Wolfhart Pannenberg, *Theology and the Kingdom of God* (Philadelphia: Westminster, 1969) 60.

marks our postmodern consciousness, Sittler's theological style has much to teach us. Moreover, it has the allure of blending dialectic and delight.

From Text to Trajectory

In his introduction to the 1998 reprint of Sittler's *The Structure of Christian Ethics*, Franklin Sherman provided this apt description: "Joseph Sittler may be said to have been a 'preacher's theologian,' both in the sense that his own theological development was shaped by that pulpit experience and that his understanding of the theological task remained forever after that of assisting the church to articulate its historic faith in such a way as to address the full complexities of the modern age."[2] It is appropriate therefore that we begin our journey into Sittler's legacy by taking as our compass insights from an example of Sittler the preacher-theologian.

On two occasions, once at a Catholic college and once at a Lutheran college, Sittler spoke on John 8:32 under the title "Knowledge and Liberation."[3] This verse, "you will know the truth and the truth will make you free," occurs in an important dialogue between Jesus and certain of the Jews. The burden of the exchange is that Jesus is the truth, the *logos*, who liberates from sin in contrast to his interlocutors' trust in their Abrahamic lineage and their messianic expectations of political liberation. Connecting with the academic *liberal arts* contexts in which he spoke, Sittler begins by talking of ways in which the quest for truth as knowledge and learning can be liberating. Truth through the expansion of our knowledge can liberate us from loneliness by taking us beyond our restricted time and place into a wider world of engagement. Learning also liberates from the tyranny of egocentricity:

> By egocentricity I mean a life understood and felt dominantly from the hot center of the tyrannical, demanding and stifling *self*. Learning disorganizes and complicates the stifling simplicity of the purely personal; it floods the self with a company of vital selves; it multiplies perspectives . . . Dostoevsky's Ivan—how he wrestles with me and for me in my frequent rebellion before God, and by expanding my solitary trouble to the dimensions

---

2. Franklin Sherman, "Introduction," in Joseph Sittler, *The Structure of Christian Ethics* (Louisville: Westminster John Knox, 1998) ix.

3. Joseph Sittler, "Knowledge and Liberation," in *The Care of the Earth and Other University Sermons*, The Preacher's Paperback Library (Philadelphia: Fortress, 1964) 140–49.

of a big and ancient problem puts me in my human place and makes me, if not at peace, no longer alone or egocentric in my dispeace.[4]

Knowledge and learning, so central to the academic world he was addressing, do take us beyond ourselves to a larger world. Even here in these rather mundane observations there is a hint of his expansive vision. But there is even more. One must turn to the incomparably more important meaning of Jesus' statement: "The flat and unmodified affirmations that God's truth is available, invasive, and adequate in Christ, and that this truth bestows absolute freedom is a statement which differs in kind from all we have been saying."[5] As Jesus needed to disabuse his hearers of their very limited political notions concerning truth and freedom, so Sittler distinguishes the liberating power of truth and learning as an enterprise of the mind engaging other minds—an operating premise of liberal education—from the liberating power of truth that Jesus' is talking about.

Jesus confronted his hearers concerning their trust in the freedom that is theirs as heirs of Abraham, who have been given the law. Sittler, in turn, confronts his hearers with the temptation to place their trust in their own quest for truth through the acquisition of knowledge. "We are always tempted to believe that if small knowledge grants small liberations, enlargement of knowledge works larger liberations, and up the quantitative scale, as it were, until one achieves sufficient knowledge to secure absolute liberation."[6] The foregoing, Sittler points out, is a good illustration of Luther's insight that our imprisonment is being subject to the tyranny of our own selves. Thus, "The truth [the Christ/God's love] makes us free from the illusion that *truth as knowledge* is redemptive!"[7]

I think we can see how Sittler captured the basic message that exegesis of John 8:32 uncovers but, as one who was more concerned with preaching and theology, he sees a trajectory in the language of the text that takes it directly into his context. He sees a larger message with a larger theological reach than what one might discern from the historically determined dynamic of his encounter with those Jews, but one that is still true to the basic message of that encounter.

---

4. Ibid., 143.
5. Ibid., 145.
6. Ibid., 145–46.
7. Ibid., 147.

Introduction

The distinctions made in this address concerning the liberating power of truth as knowledge and the liberating power of the Truth constitute an important insight into Sittler's orientation to the Scripture and its interpretation, which also is suggestive for his contribution in the present to both biblical interpretation and constructive theology.

In his 1948 Knubel-Miller lectures, published as *The Doctrine of the Word*, Sittler took on the tradition of Lutheran orthodoxy's equation of the Word of God with a verbally inspired, inerrant, and infallible Scripture. As one of the messages of John 8:32 was that "knowledge is not redemptive," so reliance on truth as sure "knowledge" of God's revelation guaranteed by an inerrant text supplants the dynamics of faith that Luther had captured so well. Luther's constant emphasis was on the "livingness" of the Word of God and its identification with the Gospel. "The saving activity of God in Christ is the theme that binds the scriptures together."[8] Approaching Scripture centered in Christ and interpreted accordingly, as Sittler urged, the interpreter is *set free* from the burden of scriptural authority as grounded in a theory of its truthfulness, free to treat Scripture as a living Word that continually reveals its truth in every new setting.

Following Luther further, and anticipating recent interest in the theology of the cross by decades, Sittler reminds us, then, that theology must be done with humility rather than the pride of certitude. Recalling Luther's *theologia crucis*, over against Rome's *theologia gloriae*, Sittler observes that Luther "meant by this distinction that his theology is a serving theology; it never claims fully to explicate, much less to deliver its holy content. It is a theology of the cross and it shares the ignominy of the cross."[9]

This same spirituality is evident in later years when Sittler engages issues of methodology in the interpretation of Scripture. In *The Anguish of Preaching* Sittler empathized with the preachers who found themselves caught in the debate between the contending hermeneutical theories of the day, which he characterized as a choice between *kerygma* and *narrative*. He disdains the notion that there is one choice that is the true choice to the exclusion of the other. One needs to employ both methods for their respective values. More importantly, one should not presume to know too much in these matters of biblical interpretation (truth as knowledge is not redemptive!).

8. Joseph Sittler, *The Doctrine of the Word in the Structure of Lutheran Theology* (Philadelphia: Board of Publication of the United Lutheran Church in America, 1948) 23–24.

9. Ibid., 64–65.

Part 1: The Preacher as Theologian

> Is it not possible that the nutcracker of twentieth century historical method is only modestly effective for the exposure of first century fact? Is empathy, actual feeling for fact, patterns of relation between fact and fact, so smoothly transferable from age to age?
> Indeed, there is something humorous about the solemn intensity with which we suppose that the twentieth century sense of the pathos of history, equipped with theological (and largely Teutonic) confidence can pull a single magic lever and open a jangling jackpot of certainty! . . . ways of knowing must be as supple and contrapuntal and various as history is—not as clear and clean and simple as philosophy hungers for.[10]

Operating within the rigid confines of methodological disputes—a situation that characterizes much of New Testament scholarship in today's academy—results in a far too narrow focus. *The interpreter needs to be freed from the constraints of seeking the one true method or the one true interpretation in order to allow the truth-making dynamics of the text to engender a fresh constructive theological message from the heart of the Word.*

Sittler certainly embraced that freedom to let the text take him on a trajectory into the wider contexts that confront both the preachers and the theologian. He saw in the work of his colleague Paul Ricoeur an important insight into the dynamics of texts that was quite congenial to his own expansive approach. Ricoeur argued that a text once written takes on a life of its own beyond the writer's intention in its original setting; "it takes off and establishes a trajectory." Sittler agreed: "It is the duty of the exegete or interpreter of a written text to follow the directionality of the text . . . to ask not only what the text says but what the text is about."[11] (We have here another instance of being ahead of the curve; he saw in Ricoeur what reader-response theorists were to pick up on decades later.)

This sense of trajectory was operative in Sittler's approach to Colossians 1:15–20 in what was probably his most famous speech, "Called to Unity," delivered in New Delhi at the 1961 World Council of Churches

---

10. Joseph Sittler, *The Anguish of Preaching* (Philadelphia: Fortress, 1966) 25–26. In *Essays on Nature and Grace* (Philadelphia: Fortress, 1972) 27–28, Sittler reflected back on those remarks with this additional comment: "I have in another place stated my conviction that the radical either-or's of the academicians are excessively rigid, and achieve their apparent demolition of their opponents by a strange humorlessness about the richness of the modalities of historical life."

11. Joseph Sittler, *Running with the Hounds: Conversation with Campus Ministry*, ed. Phil Schroeder (Chicago: Department for Campus Ministry of the Evangelical Lutheran Church in America, 2000) 16.

Introduction

General Assembly (The full text is included in chapter 4 below). In his interpretation of the text he discerned and proclaimed a vision of the cosmic Christ in whose revelation we can see that the scope of redemption and the scope of creation are one in the same. We shall return to a discussion of that speech, as every commentary of Sittler's work is obliged to do, but for present purposes we need to note what Sittler said in reply to the New Testament scholars who criticized his handling of the Colossians text. Paul could not have meant what Sittler says the text means, they argued. His rejoinder was, "You are perfectly right. I do not think Paul (or whoever wrote Colossians—it may not have been Paul) had that in mind at all. I do not think that was the intentionality of the writer, but that is what the text is about!"; and "what the text is about is a Christological question which is as important now, in fact, more interesting now than it was in Paul's time."[12]

Sittler's treatment of Colossians reveals the full implications of his outlook on the task of interpretation. When one is, as Luther was and Sittler was, focused on the Word (*the* Truth) one is freed from artificial dogmas of scriptural authority and artificial dogmas of method to let the trajectory of the text, powered by the Word, take you wherever you need to go. Indeed, as the interpretation of Colossians 1:15–20 displays, that is into no less than everything. Biblical interpretation and method in constructive theology are serious matters but they exist in the service of gospel and the various modes of its proclamation. This is a perduring principle of the theological task and Sittler was and remains as good a teacher in that regard as any.

Christology and Ecology

In an article entitled "Theology of the Earth" (1954) Sittler declared his uneasiness with Neo-orthodoxy's reassertion of an ancient dualism characterizing much of Christian theological history, "whereby the promises, imperatives, and dynamics of the Gospel are declared in sharp and calculated disengagement from the stuff of earthly life."[13] Against this theological neglect of the earth, Sittler affirms that the natural world of God's

---

12. Ibid., 18.

13. Joseph Sittler, "A Theology for Earth," in *Evocations of Grace: Writings on Ecology, Theology, and Grace*, ed. Steven Bouma-Prediger and Peter Bakken (Grand Rapids: Eerdmans, 2000) 24. The article was first published in *The Christian Scholar* 37 (September 1954) 637–74.

creation also bears the divine image. Then Sittler previews his later work on nature and grace with this comment on Psalm 104:27–30: "Here is a holy naturalism, a matrix of grace in which *all things* derive significance from their origin, and *all things* find fulfillment in praise."[14] God, "the undeviating materialist," who invented the material in the creation, loves the creation and makes that love plain in the incarnation.[15]

Later Sittler was to echo this early complaint against a theology disengaged from the world with this rather acerbic comment: "We are tempted to regard God primarily as a God for solitude and privacy and only secondarily a God for society. We have a God for my personal ache and hurt, but no God for the problems of human life in the great world."[16] Certainly Sittler sought to remedy such truncated theological vision by advancing his own comprehensive outlook.

Perhaps there is no other writing in the Sittler corpus more profoundly indicative of his conviction that theology be concerned with nothing less than everything than his 1962 New Delhi speech mentioned above. On that occasion Joseph Sittler captured the universal scope of God's redemptive promise in his discussion of Colossians 1:15–20. The text invites us repeatedly to see "all things"(*ta panta*) in and through Christ. So, Sittler wrote,

> God's restorative action in Christ is no smaller than the six-times repeated *ta panta*. Redemption is the name for this will, this action, and this concrete Man who is God with us and God for us—and all things are permeable to his cosmic redemption because all things subsist in him. He comes to all things not as a stranger, for he is the first born of all creation, and in him all things were created. He is not only the matrix and *prius* of all things; he is the intention, the fullness, and the integrity of all things: for all things were created through him and for him. . . . A doctrine of redemption is meaningful only when it swings within the larger orbit of a doctrine of creation.[17]

---

14. Ibid., 28; emphasis added. The twice-repeated phrase "all things" in this quote anticipates what was to become virtually a hallmark of his New Delhi speech and its treatment of Colossians 1:15–20.

15. Ibid., 29–31.

16. Joseph Sittler, *Gravity & Grace: Reflections and Provocations*, ed. Linda-Marie Delloff (Minneapolis: Augsburg, 1986) 35.

17. Joseph Sittler, "Called to Unity," in *Evocations of Grace*, 39–40.

Introduction

The scope of God's promise is nothing less than the redemption of "all things" (*ta panta*). This theological conclusion becomes foundational for Sittler's developing ecological theology. It anticipates in its comprehensive vision of the scope of grace the comprehensive promise of God's coming reign for the future of the world made so prominent by the theologians of hope. Jürgen Moltmann, for example, sees the fullness of God's coming future as the realization of the new creation (Rev 21:5); the transformation of all things, not their annihilation. Like Sittler before him, Moltmann sees this cosmic hope as the grounds for Christian commitment to ecological responsibility as an integral part of faith and ethics.[18]

Sittler was to observe later in his 1972 *Essays on Nature and Grace* how the entrance of the Eastern Orthodox into the Faith and Order discussions in the earlier part of the twentieth century opened up new vistas for Christology and the doctrine of grace. The Christ of the East is seen as *Pantocrator* whereas the Christ of the West is seen as *Savior*. Largely due to the prominence of Augustine's efforts in dealing with Pelagianism, grace was understood principally in relation to sin. For the Eastern fathers grace extends to all of nature. In an Eastern understanding of the broad scope of grace, faith active in love, engendered by grace, could be no less expansive in its concern for the good of all and for the good of all creation.

Sittler's pioneering work in the development of an ecological theology is certainly the achievement for which he is best known and remembered. It may also be the aspect of his work that some will regard as his lasting relevance given the present urgent concern for the environment. If that is indeed the case, as it well may be, we need to say more as to why it should be so. As Peter Bakken has observed, if Sittler were only one of the first theologians to work on environmental issues, his writings would only be of historical interest. However, Bakken points out, "Sittler deliberately cast environmental ethics in terms of highly charged religious doctrines central to Christian, particularly Lutheran, piety—namely grace and Christology—rather than in terms of teachings that are less central (but more commonly connected to environmental concerns), such as creation and stewardship."[19]

The importance of this distinctive approach is, I think, reflected in these words from Sittler toward the end of his "Call to Unity" speech:

18. Jurgen Moltmann, *The Coming of God: Christian Eschatology*, trans. Margaret Kohl (Minneapolis: Fortress, 1996) 27–279.

19. Peter Bakken, "Nature as the Theater of Grace: The Ecological Theology of Joseph Sittler," in *Evocations of Grace*, 4–5.

Part 1: The Preacher as Theologian

"The care of the earth, the realm of nature as a theater of grace, the ordering of the thick, material procedures that make available to or deprive men of bread and peace—these are Christological obediences before they are practical necessities."[20] Placing our call to care for the earth within the orbit of what it means to be "in Christ" is the logical corollary of his christological approach to environmental theology. As a result, environmental ethics for the Christian is integral to discipleship; it is not merely a subsidiary adjunct to more paramount concerns of personal faith and neighbor love. For Christians, then, an environmental ethic is driven by love grounded in God's promise for the redemption of the whole of creation; it is not simply a matter of calculation, important though scientific models and calculations are in this time of urgent ecological concerns. Christians may argue about facts, lifestyle choices, and public policies. However, if one accepts Sittler's legacy, there can be no argument about the fact that to be a Christian is to be an environmentalist. Such passionate concern fueled by the hope of faith is a sorely needed energy as we face the ecological challenges of our time.

Concluding Thoughts

- As the "preacher's theologian," Sittler approached the interpretation of Scripture with a clear understanding of current critical scholarship but in the freedom of the gospel at the center of Scripture and with the humility of a theologian of the cross. In following the trajectory of the text into the preaching situation he gave a lively, timeless, and eloquent expression to the fact that the interpretation of texts is in the service of proclamation. This remains a salutary counterpoise to the preoccupation with methodological disputes that has captivated much of New Testament scholarship.

- By grounding his ecological theology and ethic in Christology he presented to the global church an environmental ethic that was not simply a Christian perspective but an account of the Christian vocation. Nothing could be more relevant today for a global church confronting global environmental issues.

- His melding of nature and grace, of God's creative and redemptive intentions, revealed in Christ, provides a theological project that is

---

20. Joseph Sittler, "Called to Unity," in *Evocations of Grace*, 48.

a lively companion to present eschatological theologies of the kingdom of God. Like them it places our efforts in history within the horizon of God's promise for the whole of creation, providing both hope and positive motive for ecological justice and all efforts to seek and preserve the goods of that promise.

- His vision of the unity of all things in the cosmic Christ contributes to the church's ability to speak to a fragmented postmodern culture. It is a proclamation that enables us to order and cope with and give meaning to the diversity, contradictions, and confusions of our day within a structure of promise. As such, it stands in contrast to those reactionary religious movements that respond to contemporary cultural disarray by retreat into their own certitude. Sittler's theology would neither allow for such sectarian impulses nor would it ever permit the arrogance of dogmatic certitude:

> . . . the place of grace must be in the webbed connectedness of man's creaturely life. That web does not indeed bestow grace; it is necessarily the theatre for that anguish and delight, that maturation of longing and hope, that solidification of knowledge that can attain, as regards ultimate issues , not a clean, crisp certainty but rather the knowledge that:
>
>> We who must die demand a miracle.
>> How could the Eternal do a temporal act,
>> The Infinite become a finite fact?
>> Nothing can save us that is possible:
>> We who must die demand a miracle.[21]

Postscript

In Douglas John Hall's recent book of reflections on being a theologian, he tells the story of a conversation he had on an airplane with a businessman sitting next to him. When asked what he did for a living, Hall decided to tell the truth and say that he was a theologian. This prompted a request that he tell what a theologians does. Hall perceived that he really wanted to know so he gave about a twenty-minute account of what a theologian does. His traveling companion then replied, "My, it must be wonderful *to think about everything all the time.*" Hall goes on to say

---

21. Joseph Sittler, *Essays on Nature and Grace*, 94.

how delighted he was with that response; it was the sort of response he would always like to evoke when speaking of theology's vocation.²²
I think Joseph Sittler would agree.

James M. Childs Jr.

---

22. Douglas John Hall, *Bound and Free: A Theologian's Journey* (Minneapolis: Fortress, 2005) 25.

one

Sittler Introduces Himself

His God Story

1984

It may strike some as a bit odd that the first piece in this Sittler reader should be a presentation given toward the end of his life. However, these autobiographical reflections are a fitting introduction to much of what follows in the book, as well as starting us off with an interesting story. His narrative gives us a sense of Sittler as a person, his development as a person of faith, and as a theologian, from his childhood to his waning years. We see clearly his fascination with the power of language in Scripture, liturgy, and literature to evoke strong emotions and open up the depth and grandeur of divine revelation. At the same time, it is also evident that Sittler's profound respect for language is in the service of connecting the testimony of the Christian faith with the realities of life. Herein lie the seeds of his own gifts of eloquence and his capacity for seeing, with the help of Eastern Orthodox theology, that the scope of God's grace is connected not only to the human drama but to the drama of the whole creation.

Part 1: The Preacher as Theologian

BEING EIGHTY YEARS OLD may make you an object for some veneration, but it isn't much fun. On the plane coming out here, I did something and must report to you that pouring the Roquefort dressing in the coffee won't sell. The little tubs all look alike. The stewardess gasped audibly and brought me more coffee. I feel almost like I'm wandering in from another time to a group like this, and the things I am going to say I have really never said before. I haven't even thought about them before. I really think it's to my credit that I have not made my biography a sacred scripture. My own experience is not the one, holy, catholic faith. And I've never really done in public what I've been asked to undertake: to try to do a retrospective and cumulative account of the anatomy of one's faith. How one moves in childhood, adolescence, and maturity—in thought, in feeling, in experience. How one moves into a comprehensive effort to understand and exemplify the Christian faith. I've never tried that before, and so if this thing lacks certain contiguity, it's because it's the first time around.

I was born under Roosevelt—not FDR, but the Real McCoy, Teddy—in 1904. I try now to think back since that time and gather together experiences, images, occasions, persons, words, and remembrances, which are my earliest recollection of the allure of the life of the church, the celebration and the devotion of the Christian faith. I try to recover from that multitude of threads that which adds up to a kind of weaving into a person. That's a very complicated process. Certain little things—and there are really in life no little things—but certain memorable insignificant things gathered signification as I now recall them.

The church of which my father was pastor was in Lancaster, Ohio—St. Peter's, a lovely old neo-Gothic church—and I served as an acolyte. I remember just certain fragments of things and, as I think of them now, they constituted a kind of linguistic allure. The sound of the sentences. The things my father said from the Scripture and liturgy. They stuck in my head below the level of comprehension. I think it's very important, because we say children don't understand this or that. If a thing has fundamental magnificence, the language with which it is stated doesn't have to be understood completely. As we mature, we grow up to the understanding, which for a time comes to us only as a kind of audible, unforgettable language. For instance, when I heard my father reading from the Authorized Version, "And when the days were accomplished that she should be delivered," and moved on to the great, "My soul doth magnify the Lord, and my spirit hath rejoiced in God my savior." The magnificence, the beauty, the many dimensions and resonance of that language somehow communicated below the level of the intellect or the understanding that something big is going on here, that something very large is being reported. And if I, today, as a typical old duffer, lament the ceasing or the violent annihilation of that beautiful language in our liturgy, I know it's a dead fight. It's got to be changed. But I terribly miss it, because I know what I'm saying is true: that truth and beauty belong together, that big things deserve big statements. When, for instance, in the old liturgy I would hear my father at the altar intone, "And therefore with angels and archangels and all the company of heaven, we laud and magnify thy glorious Name evermore praising thee and saying . . ." I didn't understand, but I *did* understand: This is big. This is high. This is something that the mind has to open to and reach out for the dimensions of it. Therefore, as I try to account for one way of being a Christian, I cannot overstate the importance of the linguistic, the use of language for the kind of bigness which is appropriate to its object.

I'll move to another illustration—and this is almost a funny one. I asked someone, before we came over here, to look up an old hymn for me, because I recall that when the congregation sang, "They stand, those walls, O Zion, conjubilant with song," dear God, I didn't know what "conjubilant" was. I ran home to look it up; it sounded so good! I knew that anything that creates so resonant a language is worth having another look at. People sometimes say we must give children only the very best. There's one sense in which that's true, but there's also a sense in which anything that allures, that engages, that invites the mind or the feeling into a tradition, no matter what the level, if it gets 'em in, it'll do.

A teacher, a very uptight, classical teacher, once asked me, "You are a person who's always loved poetry." (She was right about that—I have and do.) "How did you get started into poetry?" And I began to search for a truthful answer, not just the answer she might want. I said that I started really in the basement. The earliest poem I remember was read to me by my primary teacher. She liked to open the class with a little jingle that we would remember. My inquiring teacher thought I would quote something from Shakespeare, or Dante, or Milton, or one of the biggies. [Sittler recounts having recited a humorous rhyme.] My point is, we must catch the mind and the imagination, not only with the great, the resonant, and the noble, but with the vivacity of the real—whatever is life.

Now somewhat in contrast: I grew up in a church that was more solemn, more somber, graver, and I think in some ways profounder than the church of this moment. Not in all things, but in its worship. When

Part 1: The Preacher as Theologian

I think of evangelism I ask myself, what are the forces with which the *evangel* came and grasped me and held me? Now that's what evangelism is: the proclamation, the invitatory word, the getting them into the family of God, the communion of the church. We usually think of all kinds of ways to draw people in. When I was a child, I don't think I ever heard the word "evangelism." But I know how the *evangel* came into my life. In the year 1917, which was the year of the great influenza epidemic, I was then thirteen years old. I had a paper route in Lancaster, Ohio. From 1914, the outbreak of the War, until the ending of it, I used to get my papers, the *Columbus Dispatch*, which came to our little town, and I would sit down on the curb or on the bench and read first, before I started to deliver the papers. I remember reading there words of horrible and bloody memory—the Seine, the Somme, Verdun—and I asked, "What's going on here? Why this murderous assault on one another by the people of the world?" Roman Catholics and Lutherans and atheists and black and white and rich and poor, people of all kinds and many places, engaged in the mass murder of one another. I asked that question, and if we think that children of thirteen don't ask that question, we're quite wrong. As I asked that question, a dialogue began in my mind, so that when I went to church and heard the old chorales, ["*O Haupt voll Blut und Wunden*"] "O Sacred Head Now Wounded," and that marvelous hymn, ["*Herzliebster Jesu, hast was du verbrochen*"] "Ah Holy Jesus, How Hast Thou Offended," there was a spark of insight: there is a living relationship between the evils of men and the infinite condescension of God. There is some relationship between "O Holy Jesus, How Hast *Thou* Offended" and all the offenses and the horrors that lay life waste. We might not think of that as evangelism. However, I would suggest that is the fundamental evangelism: that in the teaching, preaching, and worship of the church, we must set up this contrapuntal action in which the great language of faith crosses with a sharp impact the realities of ordinary life.

Now this leads me to my second point. As I grew older, I went deeply into the field of English literature. That's not some great heavenly gift. It's simply that I loved language that had engagement that was vivacious, that was fun, and that was beautiful. Well, I moved far beyond that and, by virtue of a fine teacher in college, I brought the main body of English literature under my attention—not under mastery, by no means. But I read great things: Milton and Shakespeare, up to the neck, John Keats, Emily Brontë, Charlotte Brontë, Hawthorne, Melville, right up through Joseph Conrad into the twentieth century. I knew the body of English literature in its great expression. So now, when the language of the Bible, which I heard in the liturgy, in my father's preaching, and in catechesis, intersected the infinite depth of the pathos of human life, as that comes to expression in the great masterpieces of our language, the truth of the Christian faith became attested from the inside. I didn't have to say, "I have to believe this because it's in the Bible." I began to see that what this biblical language is saying is the case. That's the way it is, when, for instance, we read, "Almighty God to whom all hearts are open, all desires known, from whom no secrets are hid." If we know that multiplication of our personhood that comes by joining in the experiences of people of all times and ages, then we know the secrets of the heart, the desires, the lusts, the hidden things, and if the gospel is not big enough to deal with that, it is not big enough. If God is not God of horror, and of death, and of pathos, and of bewilderment, and pitiable human wretchedness, if God is not God of that, God isn't God enough.

Now these discoveries began in college, but I did not set out to be either an ordained minister or a theologian. I had no such idea at all. I came in reluctantly through the back gate. I intended to be either a physician or a teacher of literature. On the way through college, I developed these two longings, along with a deep interest in the natural sciences, which has never ceased. In my last year in college, I still didn't know what I wanted to do. I thought perhaps medicine. I visited my older brother, who was then finishing medical school, and during those weekends I spent with him I found out that if you're going to be a doctor, you better give up everything else. The scientific work, the constant work with the new materials in pharmacology, medicine, surgery, and hospital care; all of this is so completely absorbing that if I became a doctor, I would have virtually to give up the cultivation of my concern with history, and literature, and music, and what we now call "the humanities." So, on the purely selfish ground that I did not want to give that up, I wanted to do a year that would not be wasted, by putting it in at seminary. Because they gave me an assistantship in language, I could make my way up there, and defer the decision. So I went into the seminary under false pretenses, to put in a year that my father would not think was all wrong. While I was there, I found that biblical language and literature, the history of the church, the marvelous intellectual structure of Christian theology began to engage me in such a way that it dawned on me that if one becomes a minister, you don't lose anything; you're going to need it all.

That literature then was not simply a kind of exterior adornment to find nice quotations for sermons, but it is a multiplication of each person's human life. Now just turn that one over a moment. To live oneself into the world of humankind as it's expressed in literature is to multiply your personhood. Students used to lay bets as to how long I'd get into a lecture before I quoted *Moby Dick*. Well, the guy who guessed it would be brief won. Why do I love that book? *Moby Dick* is a condensation of a whole human world: Captain Ahab, and Ishmael, and Queequeg, and the great ocean voyage with its perils, its dramatization of human pride and lust, and arrogance that shakes its fist in the face of not only the mighty sea but the Creator of both humans and the ocean. This is a kind of multiplication of my own little life, by letting it breathe widely and deeply in the life that is then celebrated in the great literature of the world.

When I finished seminary, I really had no "call." This idea that one must hear a voice in the night or be struck over the head, or have a deeply moving emotional experience—in that sense I never had a call. I asked my father about that. I said, "I've got some friends in the seminary who talk about their calling, and I feel a little guilty about this; I don't have anything like that." And I remember my father's very wise reply. He said, "If by disposition and some endowment, you can do what terribly needs doing, how loudly do you want the call to yell at you?" Well, that seemed to make more sense than anything that was said to me up to that time, so I went through the process, was ordained, and went to a little mission church. I was then twenty-six years old.

I was ordained during the first months of the Great Depression. The stock market fell in September/October of '29; I was ordained in the spring of 1930. My father was then the president of the Synod of Ohio, and he didn't want anything to do with placing me. He would catch it from someone no matter where he put me. So he had the mission superintendent look after me. And the mission superintendent put me in a tiny little mission in Cleveland Heights, Ohio. When my father heard where I was going, my mother reported that he said, "I wouldn't have wished it on my worst enemy." But it was exactly right for me. It was tiny. It was struggling. It was in the middle of a neighborhood in which the churches were so bad, I could only do good. It was so bad that when someone asked me once, what is the architecture of your church, I had to say, "American warehouse." But anyhow, it was just right. I was not married. I could live for almost nothing, and had to! My call in those days read, "For these duties, for these services, you shall receive the salary of $2400 a year," and then in back it said, "if we have it." And many times they didn't, up through 1937. But, unmarried, I didn't need a lot. And during those years, with 60 percent of my parish out of work, I remember going to the butcher, Mr. Crow's butcher shop where he filled a big cardboard box with bones, putting that in the back of my beat-up jalopy, gathering used clothing from one family to take it to the next; those wonderful years of the Great Depression, which to my own children is ancient history, were great formative years. I say they were great because no jazzed-up veneer, "clap hands for Jesus" gospel would do. It had to be at the level of tragedy, of deprivation, of the ultimate loneliness, of being unable to look your own children in the face. At the level of that kind of pathos, one had to say something on Sunday morning or shut up.

It was during those years exactly, when I was struggling to preach a gospel of hope and redemption, even in the midst of multiple damnations in public life—it was in the midst of those years—that the great theological work of Karl Barth began to be published. I remember that when the first book was translated into English, *The Word of God and the Word of Man*, I got the book and was stunned by the new profundity of biblical scholarship, the sheer insight into the biblical literature, because my seminary education had not been a very good one. I simply went to school for those thirteen years in this little parish every morning; study, study. Not in order to be a professor—I had no such intentions—but in order to get to the kind of depth of the understanding of the great message of the church that might intersect my people where they were. Unless an intersection takes place, unless that word has a trajectory, a target, the kind of precision which intersects the reality of our common human existence; the Word may do its work, but we ought to do much more than just putting all the load of effective power on the gospel itself. We must learn something about the people to whom this Word is addressed.

It was struggling with the Scripture that really constituted the best benefit for me, and I think for the later years of my struggling with the doctrine of the Word. What I did not know was the degree to which, for all of our Lutheran bodies, the Holy Scripture and the Word of God were identical terms. They meant the same thing. But I was already studying with Karl Barth and Martin Dibelius, Adolf Deissmann and the great historical critical scholars in both Old and New Testament, and I began to see that what we mean by the "Word of God" is prior to and more than just the Scripture, though it is the Scripture too. When, at the end of my parish experience, I accepted the call to the little, beat-up, and

Part 1: The Preacher as Theologian

tottering seminary at Maywood, Illinois, to be joined by a number of other younger colleagues, I was asked to do a lectureship on the doctrine of the Word. When you do a lectureship, you do as you like, but I thought I might as well dig into my own deepened understanding of the meaning of Scripture and the way to read Scripture. I did a series of modest little lectures, and as I once said to a church official, I didn't know the gun was loaded.[1*] When it went off, the head of Luther Seminary in Saint Paul told the students at the peril of their immortal souls not to read this book. And I was told by a number of less distinguished people that this is a most un-Lutheran and erroneous book! Well, it wasn't.

What I was saying then in all my youthful simplicity in 1945, I think it was, is now an accepted way of studying the Bible. But in those years it marked a momentous change for me—and, as it turns out, for the students that I later was to teach. It was to liberate them from this bibliolatry, this literalistic, mathematized understanding of Scripture, whereby we try to make bad geology out of good religion, or try to make bad chronology out of books that were not written for that purpose. So my first introduction into my theological career was going to a seminary to teach and making the principle object of my teaching to try to illuminate the Scripture, to drive the students deeper and deeper into the understanding of the Word of God, not just reading it and saying "*Gesundheit!*" but, "What is the text saying? What does this mean?"

This long trek leads me to what I now, upon recollection, think was the next phase. As early as 1935, for reasons I still don't understand, Frederick Knubel, then president of the United Lutheran Church in America, asked me to be one of five people to represent the ULCA at the Edinburgh Conference on Faith and Order. That's the theological cadre within the World Council of Churches, or what later became the World Council of Churches. At Edinburgh I had the privilege of breaking out of my provincial Lutheranism, or, if not provincial, at least personally experienced Christianity via the Lutheran way. I had the opportunity to meet wonderful churchmen, theologians, and biblical scholars from many parts of the Christian world. From that time on, I began to see that the Lutheran church is indeed a truly "catholic" church in the sense that it has the ancient meaning of that word built into it. It is a comprehensive church. It takes up all the experience of the Christian community from the first century, right on through. We are indeed a catholic, that is, a

---

1 * These lectures were published in 1948 under the title *The Doctrine of the Word in the Structure of Lutheran Theology*. See the discussion of these lectures on p. 5 above.

comprehensive church. I also learned to my (in the beginning) astonishment that one can be a great Christian without being a Lutheran. In order to be a good Lutheran, you had better not make it the principle item on your agenda. To be a Christian is the priority item.

The one, holy, catholic church is my home. The Lutheran church is my house, and I like that house. It's where I was born. I know where the kitchen is. I know where the bathroom is. I know where the bedrooms are. I'm at home in it! But it's only my house; it's not my home. It is very interesting that when we ordain a pastor—have you not observed?—we do not ordain them to the ministry of the Lutheran church. Furthermore, we are all, ordained or not, ordained into the ministry of Christ's church in baptism. And, you're not baptized into the Lutheran church, you're baptized into Christ's church and turned over to the Lutheran church to take care that you learn something about it—its devotion, liturgy, hymnody, and life of prayer. But we are baptized, as we are ordained, into Christ's church. Now this opening of the theological world never led to a diminution of the clarity and course of our Lutheran confession, or the majesty (as I understood it) of our Lutheran liturgical worship. No diminution at all, but rather an enhancement . . . appreciation of what my mother, the church, had taught me via the particular Lutheran inheritance that I received.

Those years in the Faith and Order movement, from 1935 until my resignation from it in 1970, took me every year to Europe or Asia or the Far East for the annual two-week conference of concentrated, hardheaded theological study. Each year the Commission set up a program of study for the next period. Those weeks and the years I spent preparing papers back home for my contribution were really my graduate school in theology. I remember those persons, now mostly gone: Franklin Clark Fry, the Bishop of Chichester, the Archbishop of Canterbury, Visser t'Hooft, Reinhold and Richard Niebuhr, Emil Brunner, Karl Barth, Paul Tillich; these are all my mentors, not directly, but through sharing in theological study with them. It was a very rich table that I was admitted to.

Now, I said a moment ago that to proclaim the gospel, the great invitatory to God's grace, means that we not only are clear about the ammunition we're shooting, we must be very sensitive about the target. To whom are you saying this? What are the conditions of their lives? What's going on below the surface of the life which each of us has in his span of given years? What's going on below the surface of manifestations that give us clues as to how to put our finger on the anxiety or the guilt or the ache or the emptiness or the meaninglessness of multitudes of our fellow men and women? How do you get this exercise in precision, whereby you not only aim good ammunition, but you also aim it with the kind of precision whereby the person hearing it will say, "Yes, that's the way it is. That is who I am, that's where I hurt, and maybe this thing that I'm hearing is big enough to deal with it."

This demand for precision in proclamation has never ceased for me. I wish I were twenty-five years old, starting all over again, because I am as troubled a theologian now as I ever was, in the sense that I'm always disturbed by the imprecision, the way our statements pass by or bounce off of or miss the mark, because we do not really find out what's cooking. A great writer in the history of culture said, "In every time, there are ripples, there are waves, and there are deep currents." The television, the radio, and popular music report the ripples with benumbing clarity and frequency. Some of it even gets a little bit deeper. Some programming in the educational channels reaches down to get a hold of the deeper waves that disturb a culture, that constitute the mentality, the emotional contour of a period, though very few really get down and lay their finger on the deep, deep currents that don't appear in the ripples.

John Updike is an expert at ripples and waves, but the great poets try to get the language that reports the deep currents. I'm trying to think of an illustration for this. Of the great modern poets that have been writing since 1930, including T. S. Eliot and Auden and Berryman and Wilbur, the daddy of them all I think is Wallace Stevens. He's written a poem—I wish I could give it to you verbatim—called "The Blessed Rage for Order."[2] He says, "The waters never gather to mind,"[3] that is, the waters of the ocean never interpret themselves; we have to impose upon the sea some meaning. What he's saying is that one cannot prove that God is. One cannot prove the reality of God. One cannot prove that Jesus is the very presence, the very physical reality of God become flesh and living among us in the Spirit. One cannot prove these things. The Christian faith is a profound act whereby we invest these things with the deepest, profoundest, most comprehensive catholic meaning of which they are capable. When I read "Ah Holy Jesus, How Hast Thou Offended" and ask what kind of a God has wanted to be God for us by becoming the Crucified One, I begin to see by the intersection of human wretchedness

2. The actual title of the poem is "The Idea of Order at Key West." "Blessed rage for order" is from the first line of the last stanza.

3. A paraphrase of the second line, "The water never formed to mind or voice."

and evil over which God makes the sign of the cross. He plunges into human life, really like a sword, and like every good sword the hilt has the form of a cross. Now this kind of an understanding, it seems to me, is a life process in Christian reflection. I'm not talking now as a theologian, I hope, but as an ordinary Christian. A theologian is a professional thing. It has its honorable place and its difficult duties, but I take no pride in being a theologian. I'm trying to talk to you about the process of a developing interior life of a Christian person—not an exemplary one, by any means.

How can I make all this concrete? I often hear pastors, bedeviled by work and many interruptions and sometimes by laziness, saying, "What are the texts for tomorrow, the appointed lessons? What are we going to say about it?" May I say so, in this holy place, that's a hell of a way to go about a sermon? My duty is not to say something about it, but to say more fully what it says. That's not always easy. That's my illustration. I have never preached until last year on what is for me the most difficult of the Beatitudes, "Blessed are the meek, for they shall inherit the earth." It seems to be simply not the case. The Bible is either just being pious or doesn't know its way around. General Motors, Exxon, Gulf, and other huge corporations seem to own big hunks of the earth. But the meek, the "blessed are the meek"—they shall inherit the earth? Just what can this mean? So, I had the impression that it is not foolishness; I simply had not stared at it long enough. I stared at it more closely, at the three words "blessedness," "meekness," and "inherit."

Blessedness: the word in Hebrew is *baruch*. And that is wrongly translated in our New English Bible as "happy are they." It doesn't mean that *at all*. Happiness has nothing to do with *baruch*. When the Old Testament says, "Blessed are they that sit by the rivers of water," it means the ones whose security and serenity is in their relation to God. That's absolute. That's at the fundamental core. Happiness is not like that. My happiness and yours may be very fragile. If I go home and find out that one of my children has a lethal disease, or is sure of death, or the child of which I've been very proud has done an evil thing, my happiness is shattered in a moment. Our happiness is like a glass ball. It's very strong if you don't drop it. You drop it, or the world drops on it, and it's gone. But blessedness is not like that. And Jesus didn't say, "Happy are the meek." He said, "Blessed." Okay, having learned that blessedness is a profounder thing . . .

"Blessed are the meek." Well that's from the old Authorized Version from 1611 so I looked to the Oxford English Dictionary, which gives the way words have changed. In the seventeenth century the word "meek" meant a strong, steady, and gentle spirit. Aha! We used to think as meek as a kind of sniveling, unsuccessful person. It's exactly the other way. "Meekness," in the King James Version, must be translated, "Blessed are they of a strong and gentle spirit," a kind of magnanimity.

It then came back to me—something that I learned when I was a child. My forbears were from Alsace and they know two languages over there: French and German. My grandmother used to write to me and to the other grandchildren little notes in French, because she loved the French language, along with her native German, and wanted us to hear a little of it. She was a very amazing woman. One of my cousins is in the room today. He'll remember *Großmutter*. She once said to me, when she was a very old woman, "Joseph, French is a beautiful language, but it's no language to talk to God in." She said when you pray, you say, "*Le Bon Dieu, O Seigneur*"; what kind of language is that? When I say my prayers, I say, "*Almachtige hast Liebste Gott*." Then you got a hold of something! But she's also the old lady who sent me a letter in which she wrote the Beatitudes in French, and I remember the startling French translation. Instead of "Blessed are the meek," it says, "*Heureux sont debonair*." "Blessed are the debonair." What a word! But "debonair" in French, in the time of the French Bible of John Calvin, meant a person who is not an idolater, one who hasn't gotten hooked on anything worldly, one who is so sophisticated as to know wealth for what it is and that it isn't everything. Such a one knows status for what it is and that it isn't everything and knows beauty and human acclaim for the promising and deceptive things they really are. This is a person who has a kind of centeredness that doesn't let the idols of this world capture it. It's a kind of debonair in which you sit lightly on the offerings and temptations of this world because you have a vision of something better. *Heureux sont debonair*. Blessed are they of a gentle spirit.

It doesn't say they shall own the earth, or control the earth, or have a real estate option on the big pieces. It says they shall *inherit* the earth. What's the difference between owning and inheriting? The difference is: what you own, you probably earn, or you make. An inheritance is something you don't own. You don't deserve it. It's a surprise. You live in the world with a gentle spirit, because the whole of creation is a kind of outrageous surprise, a gift. Blessed are they of a gentle spirit, because they live in the world not as ones who strut around as if they own the place, with their technological assaults upon it. Rather, their first feeling for the world is one of tender wonder, gratitude, and amazement. Like e. e. cummings' beautiful little poem, "I thank you God for most this amazing day."

The same time I was studying this beatitude, and began to see some light, I was what they call "Old Duffer in Residence" at a church in Salem, Oregon. There I went with the college kids on a trip, a big Saturday afternoon walk through the gigantic Douglas-fir forest in the lower slopes of the Cascades. I watched these sophisticated kids, high school and college age kids with their blue jeans and cassettes in their pockets and players in their cabins [the iPods of that day!]—all the marks of this generation. When they walked into the woods, they became quiet, silent. They would reach out and pat the big trees as they went by. The further we got into the woods, the quieter they became. Then the phrase came to me, "They inherit the world, *because* they don't own it." They don't think of it fundamentally as potential two-by-fours, though it's all right to use it that way wisely; if you love a thing, then you're prepared to use it wisely. Use it with prayers to God and not only chop it down. Now this kind of growing insight is the only contribution I can really make to your conference on evangelism, because for me there are better and worse ways of making the message of the church invitatory, alluring, winsome, and engaging. Fundamental evangelism is to create the intersection between Amazing Grace and the human condition. Therefore, as I look at my own deepening realization of both the mystery and the grace of God, I find that to be the only kind of evangelism which either "got me" or by which in some cases I have helped invite others.

It was partly this business of "Blessed are they of a gentle spirit, for they shall inherit the earth" that suddenly struck another major interest of mine, which is the physical sciences. I'm not well trained in science, but I went far enough in the biological sciences to prepare for medical school, at least, though I never entered. And I followed the biological sciences, particularly, with great interest all my mature life. I became aware of the vicious assault of modern industry—manufacturing practices, particularly petrochemicals and pesticides; pollutants—upon our earthly home with deadly and ever more deadly results. Early in the '50s, I began to smell the evil of this and feel the evil of it, and learn more and more about what has come to be called the crisis in the ecological structure of God's creation. And I wondered even then, where is a word that will illuminate man's relationship to the creation? How shall we encourage something more than to smash cans, gather glass, gather up the paper, recycle? Those are all right things to do, and we should do them. But how can we get something that has real punch? If anywhere, it ought to come from the Christian tradition. If we sing, "This is my Father's world," how can we act as if it belongs to the chemical companies, or belongs to an administration which wants to soft-pedal if not annihilate any effort to do something about this assault?

Where shall we find that word? Well, I found it deeply embedded in the great catholic tradition of the doctrine of grace. I'll use images from my town; you apply them where you live. I live in Chicago. That would be an intolerable city if it were not for the grace of that magnificent blue lake out in front of it; the lovely, cool lake, there all year round. In that crisscross city there are wonderful green parks that were laid out by far-sighted men long ago. Here is the world of nature; it is also a gift of God's grace. Therefore, the Christian church should be in the forefront of the environmental movement, though not simply on the ground of aesthetics or long-range economics, though those have their place. These are real concerns. But we should be in that struggle out of our fundamental doctrine, that Lake Michigan is a grace of God. We can destroy it, or pollute it, but we cannot create it. (I recall Rachel Carson's wonderful book of some years ago, *The Silent Spring*, in which she envisions what will happen to the animal life of the world, particularly the birds, if we continue the pollution of all that surrounds the habitat and the air they breathe.) Therefore, my last lunge into contemporary theology came out in my Yale lectures on the ecology of faith. I remember when I tried to build the ecological structure of God's creation into a major theological theme, the publisher said, "The book's okay, but you have to change the title. Nobody knows what that word means." This was in 1960! And the word "ecology" turned him off. I became blockheaded and said, "Take it or leave it. I'm not going to change it; it's the only right word." Well they took it, and it didn't fail.

two

Christology

A Christology of Function

1954

Sittler's "functional Christology" stressing Christ's work as God with us and for us, couched as it is in concern for overcoming the static and transcendent language of the Christology rooted in the historical development of the doctrine of the Trinity, anticipates and contributes to our thinking in connection with contemporary Trinitarian discourse. One thinks immediately of Rahner's focus on the economic Trinity (the triune God present and active in our world) and the depth of God's involvement in our world in Moltmann's Trinitarian theology of divine indwelling. As with all good theology, Sittler's is a faithful effort to preserve the faith by contemporizing it, much as he would later do in the discourse on nature and grace.

IT IS SIGNIFICANT THAT each commission reporting to Faith and Order in 1952 embodied within its report the conviction that the next endeavor of the movement must be in the direction of a vigorous restudy of Christology. Nowhere, so far as I know, did those who urged this step detail the grounds upon which they did so; but no great skill is needed to discern and state these grounds. Back of the church, within the church as the source and actuality of its life, stands the Lord. And within, and around, and out in front of the church stands the world that neither knows nor seeks this Lord. The church, under pressure from its Shepherd and under demand by the sheep, must confess the Lord, realize its obedience in the work of the mind, describe its faith in a continuing task of clarification and witness, and this entire task is the work of theology.

In the course of this confession, obedience, explication, and witness the church speaks of many things; our generation, at least as represented at Lund, was concerned with the reality of the church, the sacraments, Christian worship, and the authority of the Scriptures. When, in the course of inquiries proper to the explication of these themes, all concerned joined in a demand for fresh work on Christology, the recognition that shaped this consensus was surely this: that the church, on the frontier where new problems press and a new kind of mind inquires, is embarrassed in advancing its work so long as its Christology remains formally imprisoned in categories which are felt by the initiated to be inadequate and by the uninitiated to be irrelevant. This inadequacy and this irrelevancy are made the more painful because we recognize that the classical Christology of the Creed perpetuates formulations which operate with a way of speaking about God which is incongruent with our time and its ways of thinking.

Classical terms were expressive of bodies; ours must be expressive of functions. Nicaea operated with the discourse of *statics*; contemporary discourse is permeated through and through with a world view which is dynamic. For us, *persons* are not bodies, but units of force and will; all things are not bodies, but aims, means, and creations of these units. The classical relationship between bodies was positional; our understanding of relationship is functional.[1] Christology is therefore called upon to

---

1. "Modern physics has abandoned the doctrine of Simple Location. The physical things which we term stars, planets, lumps of matter, molecules, electrons, protons, quanta of energy, are each to be conceived as modifications of conditions within space-time, extending throughout the whole range. There is a focal region, which in common speech is where the thing is. But its influence streams away from it with finite velocity throughout the utmost recesses of space and time. Of course, it is natural, and for certain purposes entirely proper to speak of the focal region, thus modified, as the thing itself situated there. But difficulties arise if we press this way of thought too far. *For physics, the thing itself is what it does, and what it does is the divergent stream of influence.* Again the focal region cannot be separated from the external stream. It obstinately refuses to be conceived as an instantaneous fact. It is a state of agitation, only differing from the so-called external stream by its superior dominance within

transpose an entire theological vocabulary to conform with a thoroughly functionalized understanding.

Several generations of biblical studies assert in a rising chorus that the Nicene Christology comes under a second charge that the church's Christology is radically reductive of the amplitude and variety of the biblical witness to God's relation of himself to the world in the person and work of Christ. In view of the foregoing, this paper wishes only to submit, for further study, four propositions: (1) That the biblical, theological energies released by the Reformers operate with inward necessity to deplete the intelligibility of the Nicene Christology. (2) That modern biblical and historical understanding joins to supply us with a way of thinking which at once preserves the religious intention of Nicaea and avoids its categories. (3) That primitive-church and patristic evidence, either ignored or set aside by the fourth-century controversies as not appropriate to *their* way of putting the question, is strikingly relevant to *our* way of putting the question. (4) That to undertake a fresh explication of Christology in terms of functions is appropriate to biblical terms of discourse and congruent with what for better or for worse we now are.

I

The positive contributions of the Reformers were enunciated over against those themes which were thrust into the middle of things by the moral and religious concern of the age, and by virtue of the nature of the opposition. The necessary concentration was upon the righteousness of God, the justification of sinners, and the authority of the church. It was Christ in his work as Redeemer, and not Christ in his relation to the Father, which was the central problem. The Reformers' labors in the explication of the work of Christ resulted in a strange situation of which we are the inheritors.

---

the focal region. Also we are puzzled how to express exactly the existence of these physical things at the definite moment of time. For at every instantaneous point-event, within or without the focal region, the modification to be ascribed to this thing is antecedent to, or successive to, the corresponding modification introduced by that thing at another point-event. Thus if we endeavor to conceive a complete instance of the existence of the physical thing in question, we cannot confine ourselves to one part of space or to one moment of time." Alfred North Whitehead, *Adventures of Ideas* (New York: Macmillan, 1933) 201f. (italics mine).

Part 1: The Preacher as Theologian

The very religious realism of their biblical understanding, their recovery of the vigorous prophetic and kingdom-proclaiming immediacy of the Christ of the New Testament, generated biblical, realistic ways of thinking which were destined to transform the entire method of theology; and this dynamism, once released, cannot permit theology ever again to operate as if it had not been.

Furthermore, the Reformers' sense of continuity with the church of the first fifteen centuries, while it may have made them fugitively aware of the size of the revolution of which they were spokesmen operated also to permit them to speak of God in Christ in the church's given terms and remain quiet under a Christology which, outwardly undisturbed, was destined for radical criticism by virtue of the very dynamics with which they had invested *other* themes—God, the Word of God, the church, the sacraments. The result has been that when we in our day, inheritors not only of the theology of the Reformation but also continuing inheritors of critical biblical-historical studies, seek to administer the understanding of the Reformers, we are compelled to see the Nicene Christology in a way they did not and perhaps could not. We are more and more restless under the fact that this Christology operates to smother the dynamic energy of the biblical terms of discourse, prevents living and functional ways of speaking about God and Christ from expanding to their proper potential scope. Sixteenth-century veneration for Nicaea has descended to us as a twentieth-century frustration; the fourth-century settlement of Christology so massively overlays the sixteenth as to make the sixteenth stutter as it addresses the twentieth. It is not too much to say that our theological tradition, whereby we try to gather up and contain in the theology of our day both the fourth and the sixteenth centuries, constitutes an invitation to theological hernia.

An instance drawn from the history of Lutheranism will illustrate the point. The Lutheran Reformation did not *overtly* lay its hands upon the doctrine of God. Article I of the Augsburg Confession reads: "Our churches unanimously hold and teach, agreeably to the Council of Nicaea, that there is only one divine Essence which is called and truly is God; but that there are three persons in this one divine Essence equally powerful, equally eternal—God the Father, God the Son, God the Holy Ghost—who are one divine Essence, eternal, incorporeal, indivisible, infinite in power, wisdom, and goodness, the creator and preserver of all things visible and invisible." In the Apology of the Augsburg Confession, Article I dismisses any effort to expand the subject by saying that ". . . the adversaries approve

Christology

of the first Article of our Confession." In 1537 Luther composed the Smalcald Articles, and after a restatement of the principal teaching of the Augsburg Confession, concluded Part I by asserting, ". . . there is no dispute nor contention about these Articles, and inasmuch as both parties confess them, it is unnecessary now to treat further of them."

This is all very well. But overt acknowledgement of Nicaea was subject to covert reinterpretation. A consensus which is acknowledged with one hand is surely doomed to decisive modification on the other when, as Seeberg, discussing Luther, observed, ". . . the Gospel is in the historic Saviour and it is all there. Theology and Christology are no longer independent aspects of doctrine, they coincide. The Reformers knew no other God than the God who had manifested himself in the historical Christ and made us see in the miracle of faith that he is our salvation." This seems to be a true report of Luther, in any case, for he could declare, "I know no God, whether in heaven or on earth, . . . outside the flesh that lies in the bosom of the Virgin Mary." Luther never believed such a statement to be exhaustive of God as he is in himself—but he did hold that such a statement speaks adequately of God as we know him from below, which is the only place from which we can behold him. "Wilt thou go and grasp and meet God rightly, so that thou mayest find grace and help in him, then be not persuaded to seek him elsewhere than in the Lord Christ."

To be sure, Luther could write what he did in the Smalcald Articles about the received Christology, but his transposition of all theological themes into the key of dynamic biblical realism actually fractured the Nicene settlement. He developed his Christology in absolute religious attachment to what God's Christ, in his life, death, and resurrection actually *did* for man. All speculation was either set aside or quite burned away in the intense heat of this functional Christology of the office of Christ.

II

Modern biblical and historical understanding join to supply us with a way of thinking which at once preserves the religious intention of Nicaea and avoids its categories. In the Christology of the New Testament we are faced with several methods of expressing the mind of the church about the person of the historical Jesus of Nazareth. Of the belief that he was merely a great human teacher we find no trace. The Christology that prevailed was that which saw in him the incarnation of the divine

Word or wisdom, which was at once the divine and living pattern of the cosmos, the agent by which the cosmos was created, and the divine mind imminent in the cosmos, and more particularly in the mind of man. It was inevitable that this cosmology should triumph in the end since it was the only one which could, with whatever difficulty, be formally reconciled with Jewish monotheism; moreover, it transferred the Lord from the realm of eschatology, which meant nothing to the Greek convert, into the sphere of cosmogony, which was one of the central problems of the Hellenistic age as we meet it in the *Corpus Hermeticum*.

If, then, reconciliation with monotheism was, and is, the point, we are able to preserve that without employing the substance, essence, hypostasis terminology of Nicaea. And in so doing we can actually serve better both the Scriptures and our own time.

Biblical and other studies since Harnack have served to confirm his bold essay in which he makes the following argument: it is a Semitic idea that everything of real value that appears on the earth has its existence in heaven. It exists with God; that is, God possesses a knowledge of it, and for that reason it has a real being. And it exists with God beforehand in the same way as it appears on earth. Its manifestation upon the earth is merely a transition from concealment to publicity. In becoming visible to the senses, the object assumes no attribute that it did not already have with God; hence its material nature is by no means an inadequate expression of it, nor is a second nature added to the first. The Jewish theory of pre-existence is founded on the religious idea of the omniscience and omnipotence of God. As the whole history of the world and the destiny of each individual are recorded on his tablets or books, so also is each thing present before him.

Nicaea operated with quite different ideas. It is not necessary here to dilate upon the nature or the degree of that difference. The important step was taken when *Logos* was read in abstraction from the rest of the Scriptures, and even from the rest of the Fourth Gospel. Thus the way was opened to conserve monotheism in terms intelligible to Hellas. The result was that the relation of Christ and the Father was described in terms of pre-existence which were compelled to regard the body as inadequate, and necessitated the ideal ennoblement of the creature in terms of *assumption naturae novae*.

III

Primitive-church and patristic evidence, either set aside or ignored by the fourth-century controversies as not appropriate to *their* way of putting the question, are strikingly relevant to *our* way of putting it. Since the Reformation it has not been possible again to put the question of God in terms of substance and tranquil ideal essence. The problem of the knowledge of God must, with us, operate with the realities of energy, realizing will, purposive intention.

God as the doer of deeds proper to his will, "the mighty living active God" of the Reformers, has not only convulsed theological thought but has also informed and animated biblical studies. And some hundreds of years of thought, inquiry, and accomplishment in a dynamic description of life and the world have (although they do not constitute a revelation of God) built the theater in which the drama must for our time be presented. When, then, in an effort to articulate a Christology, we examine the understanding of Christ's work and his relation to the Father from this point of view, certain aspects of New Testament teaching, passed over by Nicaea, become of fresh interest. The Christology of the book of the Acts, for instance, is surely what we may call a servant-Christology. It is in virtue of his work as obedient, utter accomplisher of the will of God that Jesus is proclaimed Lord and Christ, "So let all the house of Israel understand beyond a doubt that God has made him both Lord and Christ, this very Jesus whom you have crucified" (Acts 2:36). "The God of Abraham, the God of Isaac, the God of Jacob, the God of our fathers glorified Jesus his servant" (Acts 3:12). "It was for you that God raised up his servant" (Acts 3:26).

While, to be sure, St. Paul, in his service to the church of the Gentiles, explicated this Christ in terms of pre-existence in spirit with the Father, that description is never the center of his proclamation. In the apostle's clearest trains of thought everything that he has to say of Christ hinges on his death and resurrection. What Christ became, and his significance for us now, are due to his death on the cross and his resurrection. He condemned sin in the flesh and was obedient unto death. Therefore he shares in the *doxa* of God, "who was born of David's offspring by natural descent and installed as Son of God with power by the Spirit of holiness when he was raised from the dead" (Rom 1:3).[2]

---

2. The studies of Lohmeyer, in which he seeks, by an analysis of the form of Phil 2:1–9, to establish this famous pericope as an early liturgical sequence, and hence

Part 1: The Preacher as Theologian

In some old writings of the New Testament from the hand of native Jews there are no speculations at all about the pretemporal existence of Jesus as the Messiah. These writings simply express the old Jewish theory, and they go beyond it only in the emphasis laid on the exaltation of Jesus, after death, through the resurrection. Such a passage is 1 Pet 1:18 ff., "You were ransomed from the futile traditions of your past by the previous blood of Christ, a Lamb unblemished and unstained. He was predestined before the foundation of the world and has appeared at the end of the ages for your sake; it is by him that you believe in God who raised him from the dead and gave him glory."

Here we find a conception of the pre-existence of Christ which is not yet affected by cosmological or psychological speculation. It does not overstep the bounds of purely religious contemplation. It arose from an Old Testament way of thinking, plus the living impression received from the person of Jesus. He is foreknown by God before the foundation of the creation of the world, not as a spiritual being without a body, but as a Lamb without blemish and without spot. That is to say, his whole personality, together with the work he was to carry out, was within God's eternal foreknowledge. He has "appeared at the end of the ages for your sake." That is, he is now visibly what he already was before God. What is emphasized here is not an incarnation, but a revelation. He appeared in order that our faith and hope should now be firmly directed to the living God, that God who raised him from the dead and gave him glory.

I am indebted to my colleague, Professor Arthur Vööbus, for directing my attention to an extremely interesting fragment of patristic Christology imbedded in the work of Aphraat. This man was probably a bishop. His homilies indicate that he possessed a certain authority, and his admonitions to the clergy have an episcopal ring. His life was coextensive with the christological controversies of the fourth century. Aphraat is a representative of Persian Christianity, a primitive type of the Christian tradition quite cut off from Hellenism. The archaic character of the community to which Aphraat addressed his homilies is revealed in his support of ascetic practices which were not common at that time in the West; for instance, only those were to be baptized who were willing to take the vow of celibacy and poverty. Christianity had reached Persia by way of Edessa and Arbela; the religious milieu of Aphraat was Jerusalem, not Antioch.

---

explain why Paul could appeal to its compressed and high Christology without explication, is an additional evidence of the proper center of Paul's thoughts.

The above is noted by way of enforcing the indigenous character of the teaching which Aphraat reflects. It goes its own way, paying no attention to the problems currently discussed in the West. The Nicene theology is not evident. We sense, rather, a Jewish-Christian development on Persian territory.[3]

Particularly interesting is the way Aphraat deals with the first chapter of the Fourth Gospel. He does not understand Logos as did the apologists of the Western church. It seems for him to be quite uninvolved with these considerations which so enriched and complicated the term in Western theology. For Aphraat Logos means simply the voice and utterance of God. "For the Word is sent out through the Messiah, who is God's utterance and speech, and returns to him in great might." "In the beginning there was the Voice, which was the Word. . . . The Word became body and dwelt among us, and this is the Voice of God."

Aphraat also deals with the relationship of Christ to the Father. There is no mention of the eternal generation of the Son, nothing of hypostasis or unity of substance. This man operates, rather, in the context of Oriental ideas which are quite strange to the West. In the West, for instance, the heir is such by legally acknowledged blood relationship to the parent; in the East, a child who is no blood relation, but who actually does the will and realizes the purposes of the father, may be acknowledged as legitimate heir by community consensus. "Therefore we also called this Christ the Son of God through whom we have known God. . . . Therefore we worship Jesus through whom we have known God. . . . We directly believe that Jesus is the Son of God and that through him we know his Father."

Very interesting is Aphraat's understanding of the relation between *vox* and *Deus*. Christ, as the voice of God, is to be understood as the one in whom the Spirit of God dwells in full and adequate measure. The distinction for Aphraat seems to be a quantitative one. In the prophets, to be sure, this Voice dwelt, but in Christ it dwelt with completeness and with constancy. Aphraat's use of the analogy of the life of the believer in Christ to explicate the life of the Son in the Father is a very significant device for illuminating Christology. His discussion, for instance, of the passages in the Fourth Gospel (John 14:10–11; 14:20; and 10:30) reveals that he understands these statements in a way that is non-philosophical, non-ontological, and non-substantial.

---

3. The source for the following citations is *Patrologia Syriaca*, vols. 1 and 2.

IV

To undertake a fresh explication of Christology in terms of function is appropriate to biblical terms of discourse and congruent with what, for better or for worse, we now are. My own conviction that a Christology set forth in terms of function is a sharp need of our time has not been matured by nursing my theological hernia. Strangely enough, it has developed out of a teaching concern with the Fourth Gospel, the very document which is commonly used as a club by champions of the adequacy of the Nicene Christology. In the course of these studies I have sometimes wondered if such persons advance beyond the first thirteen verses of the Gospel. For the moment one does so advance, one finds oneself in a complex of ideas which live in unquiet relationship with the Logos of the prologue. The Logos, as we watch and listen, is not the tranquil continuity of the imperturbable Deity operating in a mortal and temporal situation. His will is in absolute subordination to the will of the Father, whose will he calls in graphic language his meat and drink. His glory is the glory of the Father. He does not speak of his own accord out of some will-less lake of divinity; rather "the Father who sent me, he it was who ordered me what to say." This Logos in the flesh remains within his Father's love because he has kept and keeps the Father's command. Just as he does what he does because he is who he is, so he is who he is because he does what he does! The prince of this world has no hold on him. His coming will only serve to let the world see that "I love the Father, and that I am acting as the Father ordered." His oneness with the Father is an incomparable oneness of function.

The Fourth Gospel speaks about the life which the Son has in the Father to set forth the life which men may have in him and through him with the Father. This must be considered in any adequate study of Christology. And inasmuch as this oneness is presented as a perpetual interchange of love, decision, and obedience—terms which in the Scriptures are terms of existence, decision, and will—we are justified in requiring that Christologies of being recognize that in the Fourth Gospel, as elsewhere, a servant-Christology of function is taught with greater antiquity and with equal clarity.

The above discussion has been informed by no intention to bring under question what Nicaea sought to conserve, or to suggest that the oneness of the Father and the Son is other than a revelation inseparable from Scripture, catholic tradition, and Christian piety. The purpose has been, rather, to set forth the practical concern of a teacher, to ask how theology shall proceed in view of the general acknowledgement that formulations enunciated in one age are deepeningly unintelligible in another. The terms of discourse evoked by and addressed to one historical situation are no longer declarative of what they sought to say—a grammar of substance is alien to a grammar of function—and are therefore, for the contemporary church, neither adequate confession nor meaningful piety.

The Anguish of Christology

1966

Sittler calls to the attention of the preacher the urgent task of making the Christ of the New Testament and the tradition alive in the context of contemporary experience and the cultural expressions of human self-understanding. The task involves avoiding certain theological errors in matters of Christology as well as pursuing serious social analysis. The anguish of Christology comes with the full realization of the profound seriousness of the preacher's task in truly proclaiming the grace of God at the heart of Christology. Those who do not regard this calling with a measure of trepidation don't fully appreciate its gravity and their holy vocation.

THIS LECTURE BEGINS BY calling attention to a familiar verse of Scripture. The intention is not to undertake an exegesis of the verse but rather so to focus attention upon a powerful word in it that the strange title of this lecture and the kind of enquiry undertaken in it may be more clear.

In the twelfth chapter of the Gospel According to Luke our Lord is reported as saying, "I have a baptism to be baptized with; and how am I *straitened* til it be accomplished!" (12:50). The Oxford English Dictionary has two full pages on the verb *to straiten*. The principal meaning of the term, when it is used to describe a human feeling, is to be aware of great and relentless pressure.

Christology

The Greek phrase is *kai pōs sunechomai*. With what resonating precision the Elizabethan translation caught that in the King James rendering, *straitened!* Luther translates the phrase, "... *und wie ist mir so bange.*" In later versions the language progressively flattens out. From the "how I am constrained" of the Revised Standard Version which weakens but does not destroy the anguish of the cry, sensibility to occasion and language falls flat on its face in the New English Bible. There the rendering is "how I am hampered"—which is an instance of accuracy so concerned to be accurate as to be inaccurate. In that rendering more is changed than a word; the very sense is shifted. *Hampered* suggests a restricting force from outside, *straitened* is internal.

This anguish was in Jesus by virtue of his divine mission. It constitutes also a hard and unloosened knot in the spirit of any man who would listen to him, think and feel and imagine himself into understanding of Jesus. Participation in Jesus transfers what was an anguish for him into a bequest from him. That he was straitened haunts forever; and the same tautness characterizes the history of Christological reflection.

Let us try to elaborate from two perspectives what such straitened participation means for the preacher. The preachers' straitening is of a different level—for his vocation is not that of Jesus. But on the level proper to the *servant* of the straitened Word of God the anguish is as real. Let us reflect upon this matter from two perspectives. From the perspective of our own inner transactions with his abiding presence in the record, in the memory and tradition of the community that remembers him, in the intricate architecture of our *worship*, and in the round of the liturgical year. And second, from the perspective of our professionally commanded theological reflection upon the inexhaustible vitality of Christology as this relates to a specific issue that I shall specify in a moment.

First, then, the perspective from within. Recall the word and life of Søren Kierkegaard who often said that "the wound must be kept open in order that the Eternal may heal it; the cure depends on the wound being kept open." I know in my own experience that that is so. One is never a successful preacher; one is never a successful teacher—if the matter of his work be Christ. How one hopes, works to come to terms with the anguish that runs forever deeply under the incomplete and faltering efforts that one makes! And how incessant and beguiling the temptation to *settle* for a manly "I have done what I can—let me now have pity on myself and be joyful"! But just when one thinks himself on the way to a "professional" aplomb as preacher or teacher the figure of Jesus, expanded, made present and urgent by the entire Christology that ceaselessly flows out from him—that figure turns, as he did to pathetic Peter in the courtyard. And under that look everything is crumpled save the presence and the question and the anguish. Jesus is like a coiled spring in the mind; its holding-clips may give at any moment.

The anguish remains; and whether in fear that it will always remain, or in an understandable but evil hope that it may not, let us not suppose that it will ever change. A rigorous philosophical analysis of our day drives Bultmann's demythologization straight through to the end where nothing verifiable is left except Christ. Another, operating with language analysis, establishes that because no statements at all can be made about God, God is indeed dead, and then ends his argument with a curious chapter about the "contagion of Jesus"! Indeed, the wound is kept open—and how we are straitened!

There is a received Christology in the church catholic. It is ancient, magnificent, various. That is the Christology of tradition. But there is another meaning to Christology. Not tradition but pressure; not the given but the terrifying and hard pressure to be as grace about Christ who is alive now as our fathers were grace about the Christ who was alive for them, and the agent of their very aliveness. What he has meant is indeed tutorial to what he means, but is never sufficient for the sheer pressure of present meaning in one's own heart and mind, and for one's own time and place and instant vocation.

That that is so is a blessing and a wound, a promise and an anguish. The given Christology is the New Testament itself: rich, many-sided, not a harmony at all, spinning off from a fiercely burning center into multiple orbits of meaning. We are told both that he is who he is because he does what he does; we are also told that he does what he does because he is who he is. There is in the New Testament a Christology of essence become function and a Christology of godly function interpreted as essence. And the entire Christology of nineteen centuries is the long story of this anguish as faith has hammered out recalcitrant concepts in a memorable effort to contain life within language. "God of God, Light of Light, Very God of very God, Begotten, not made, Being of one substance . . ." And not only in authoritative creedal forms but in a thousand thousand wrestlings, rich in images, heavy with fecund symbols, in alliance with this philosophy and with that, the struggle goes on.

A part of the malaise, the endemic flatness that from all quarters is reported to infect seminary students is certainly related to this anguish.

Christology

For so much of our work has to do with the mastery of the historical evidence for and the reality of the anguish of unsilenceable christological pressure—and because we know that if we give ourselves over to it we shall never again be safe, never secure, never able again to put a professional suavity back upon that haunting face, we settle for *history*, what the church teaches, what has abundantly accredited force, that is confessionally acceptable. Both ways make one literally sick. To give oneself over to the problematic is a sickness that the glory might be manifest. But to dismiss, or bury, or flee from the problem is a sickness unto death.

So there is the given Christology, and here we are wishing to be fuller participators in the Christ who is alive, but alive in a world that is *not* Palestine, or Constantinople, or Nicea, or Augsburg. In the midst of rushing historical life we see, and are the children of, and make our contribution to ways of work that become ways of life that become ways of thought that are new in the world. And things seen and experienced beget freshly aware ways of seeing that become new modes of feeling and wondering and delighting and expecting that are new in the world.

Between these two worlds, the one that has enfolded men's thoughts and confession about Christ for hundreds of years, the other enfolding both a newness that is discontinuous with all that is past, and a continuity with it in the promise of God and the presence of the alive Christ—between these we must find a way, a witness, a word.

The acceptance in faith and joy of precisely this tautness is the way of the Christian. It is the particular vocation, ordination, interior life, and steady place of the preacher. He stands between the what has been and a presence whose present doing is a fact. But a fact unsecured by history. The preacher in a special posture stands between the "It is finished" and the tremendous word of the Apostle, "The whole creation waits with eager longing." Every Christian is indeed called to fill up what remains of the sufferings of Christ; it is the christological anguish of the preacher that he must *speak* of it!—speak it from behind, forward into the actuality of the day and situation that now is. To be a preacher is not only to know eschatology as a report and an agenda item in systematic theology; he is, in the anguish of his task, the *eschatological man*. The work of his mind is the intellectual form of his obedience.

The preacher by the burden of his office can have no authentic selfhood if he repudiates this way, or by acceptable forms of betrayal, seeks another. Other ways there are, to be sure, and the prestige and piety of them may mask for a lifetime he fact of the betrayal. The institution and the world want adjustment, not anguish. And one may even understand his theological education as tutelage toward acquiescence in non-anguish.

Martin Luther once wrote, "I did not learn my theology all at once, but I had to search deeper for it, where my temptations took me."[1] From our knowledge of Luther we may fill out somewhat the meaning of that cryptic statement. He searched deep, and the searching-place was pointed out to him by his temptations.

There is a clear temptation that confronts us. I should like to describe it. The very pride we have in the *objective givenness* of our theological inheritance invites us to a misunderstanding. For it is a misunderstanding to suppose that a theological tradition provides escape from struggle. The source of grace is objective; the realm and reality of grace is absolutely personal and intrinsically social—it is intensely the realm of our own experienced selves as persons among persons and in the world.

Our intelligibility to the world, as we address it in the name and according to the substance of the faith, is empowered by deep probing with the instruments of the really experienced, the really felt. Luther writes further—"A man becomes a theologian by living, by dying and by being damned, not by understanding, reading and speculating."[2] We may evidence the massive Weimer Edition to keep us from disparaging the role of reading, thinking, and speculating as part of the theological quest! But here we stress what Luther stressed—the driving into the center of Christ and the gospel with all the anguish, pathos, and imperious personal questioning that each of us knows as he sees older meanings and inheritances die, beholds the persona damnations that occur when the formally correct is unattended by that personally re-enacted passion which comes from probing prodded by temptation.

How painful for a teacher and how sad for a church to see what we so often see!—young men engaged in theological study who live in that encounter with the absolutely crucial without anguish! Well endowed, they come to the institution which occasioned this lectureship or places like it, with accredited academic preparation, impeccable ecclesiastical dossiers stamped with baptism, confirmation, in tranquil possession of the elements of a formal confession of faith—yet never repossessing for themselves, never re-enacting life dying in doubt and being raised in

---

1. Weimar Edition, Table Talk (TR 1.352).
2. Weimar Edition (WA 5.163.28).

Christology

fresh faith, never fighting back at the tremendous affirmations and perilous securities of actual faith.

But—and I speak as a fool but an experienced one—you may, in a sardonic sense, count upon the Christ who is alive. He means—and no repetition of past meanings is equivalent to present requirements; he intends—and no celebration of the purity and force of his historically experienced intentions is equivalent to what he now intends. Nor does ardor in reporting the past provide a substitute for depth and clarity in specifying Christly intentions for the world now. By the *anguish of Christology*, then, I mean the heart always restless and the mind always asking what the disclosure and concretion of the holy in the event of Jesus Christ means for the life of the world. And in accordance with the promise to illustrate this probing in one specific area we proceed to that task.

Recall the Luther citation in which he affirmed that he learned by searching where his temptations took him. The places and occasions of learning in things heavenly are seldom selected by us. Our will, our desires, our inclinations according to our self-assessments—these are seldom, as we look back, the occasions in which we have learned the most important things. We are pushed, or drawn, or dumped into growth.

An American poet, the late Theodore Roethke, puts it this way:

> I wake to sleep, and take my waking slow.
> I feel my fate in what I cannot fear.
> I learn by going where I have to go.
> We think by feeling. What is there to know?
> I hear my being dance from ear to ear.
> I wake to sleep, and take my waking slow.
>
> Great Nature has another thing to do
> To you and me; so take the lively air,
> And, lovely, learn by going where to go.
> This shaking keeps me steady. I should know.
> What falls away is always. And is near.
> I wake to sleep, and take my waking slow.
> I learn by walking where I have to go.[3]

Where, theologically, do we have to go? I want now to describe what I think that direction to be, and then point out a fault in the great christological tradition of the West that must be corrected if we are to go there.

---

3. Theodore Roethke, "The Waking," in Roethke, *Words for the Wind: The Collected Verse of Theodore Roethke* (Garden City, NY: Doubleday, 1958). Copyright 1953 by Theodore Roethke. Reprinted by permission of Doubleday & Company, Inc.

We have to go where contemporary man is. Because man's self-awareness is deeply influenced by his placement in time and space we had better be very accurate about where he is, know very surely the matrix of work, duty, daily operation, personal energy expanded in those tasks in which he *thinks* his reality. A colleague of mine once said, "Man's mind follows the fortunes of his body with an absolute seriousness." That is demonstrably true. And where is his body? What does representative contemporary man do with most of his hours and days, where does he do it, and as part of what procedure is he important—at work, a significant person?

This man is primarily *homo operator*! He is up to the neck involved in fantastically complicated, incessant transactions with some aspect of the life and productivity of nature. He is extracting, refining, fabricating, transforming, transporting, assembling, selling, redesigning, thinking about how to do something which has not been done before with the ever more abundantly available forces and products of a rationalized and managed nature.

You might well ask what is novel about that? Has man not always been so involved with the given structure and fecundity of nature? He has, indeed, but not at all as he is presently engaged. For in our time, in a completely new sense, he stands apart from, above, in a new and central position *over against* this reality. It is not too much to say that contemporary man's actual selfhood has been radically transformed by virtue of his theoretical comprehension and practical operations upon the naturally sustaining and environing world. He can literally do with it what he chooses to do!

This has not, until now, been true. It is not completely true as yet. But the spirit of our time is given in the fact that we live in a *not yet* of scientific methods ever more refined and pointed toward mastery, and no longer in a time of acquiescence in the given structures, rhythms, promises of things.

Man's sense of identity is not to be sought apart from steady reflection upon these actual engagements. We may choose to continue to define man in more general categories: essential man, reflective man, man as *imago Dei*; and these broader categories are necessary for ampler truth about him. But it is a penultimate truth I am after: how to keep theology pedagogically flexible to present fact, and faithful preaching appropriate to actual self-understanding. What man does is to operate as I have described. He is a digger of ore or of new equations, a fabricator and dealer with the stuff and possibility that pours out of research, experiment, sheer curiosity.

If we acknowledge the level of truth that is in this conclusion, we are ready for the second question. How does a man, so operationally constituted in his self-understanding, and in the hopes, projections, needs for supporting sanctions which are appropriate to that—how does he hear the traditional gospel of the grace of God? It is said to him that grace is the power and benevolent will of God active and always available for his restoration to true life, fullness, peace. That is how his question about grace is answered—and the answer is true.

But the self addressed by such proposals of grace, while recognizable as an aspect of the self of the hearer, can only receive such a powerful and a meaningful proposal if he pulls himself loose from, disengages his daily, immediate self-awareness out of that very transactional closeness to the world in which he lives and moves and has his most interesting being. Deep down, far back, and in the absolute nakedness of his privacy a man may be reached by such a proposal of grace. But his life in operational immediacy, meshed as it is with industrial and corporate and public reality is life unaddressed by a word of grace so restricted.

Such a word may be pastorally and homiletically uninteresting not because it is untrue (which it is not) but because its scope and promise is less large than the web of fact and relation within which man actually lives and is acknowledged as a person in the world. Man does not walk in a garden alone; he walks in a world with others.

I am convinced that contemporary lassitude under conventional preaching of the gospel of grace is commonly neither ignored nor repudiated because its power and claims are assessed as untrue. The word of grace is ignored because it is unreal and uninteresting, because it does not intersect actual man with promise, power, and possibility and with a bigness appropriate to the public, materially related, operationally actualized character of his living days.

It has recently been remarked that whereas we have a gospel for the alienated, the hurt, the depressed, the defeated, we have not a gospel for the well, the effective, the joyous, busy, engaged men of this world. And while, to be sure, a gospel that has no word to desolation is no gospel at all, it is more and more widely true that a gospel whose scope does not address man in his joyous, creative, constructive and effectual operations is unchallenging because uninteresting.

If, then, I have described with whatever lucidity and generality an actual situation, what defect or undeveloped aspects of our christological inheritance are germane to this issue?

What follows and concludes this chapter is but my own proposal for reflection. There is no assumption that other proposals would not be equally proper and promising.

It is precisely what I have called the anguish of Christology that has caused me to wonder if the celebrated center of our Reformation tradition has not developed into a confinement. We have received from the Reformers a powerful christocentric theological structure. That christocentrism achieved the place and power it did in fact achieve because nothing short of it would have been able to recover the gospel, renew the church, and do right obedience to the religious needs of the sixteenth century. But the price was enormous—and we in a different situation must reassess the Reformers' formulation according to the same biblical norms they honored if a polemical necessity of one time is to provide adequate guidance for another. For when the Christian faith is absolutely centered upon Christ, the second person of the Trinity, we are open, and have to some extent succumbed, to the following:

1. A conceptual reduction. By that I mean an understanding of Christ that claims fuller adequacy for the disclosure of the reality of God than Christ himself claimed. "Jesus only" is a phrase that conveys a theological error, for it postulates a christocentrism that Jesus himself repudiated.

2. An almost complete severance of the realm of redemption from the realm of creation.

3. A consequent formal inability to interpret the grace of God in Christ precisely within the operational theater of man's existence which so deeply forms him, which is so vividly the place of selfhood, and in which, with the neighbor, he is called upon to be light, salt, and exemplar of faith.

As, now, I attempt very briefly to give each of these points a somewhat fuller explication, I must acknowledge how much I owe to years of engagement with Faith and Order studies. During these years my mind has undergone a double movement: on the one hand an ever clearer and more grateful affirmation of the profundity and richness of the tradition of Lutheranism in the catholic Christianity of the West, and an ever

Christology

widening appreciation of the blessed fact that no theological tradition is identical with evangelical catholic truth. Even the great words of our Reformers—*Grace alone, Christ alone, Scripture alone*—so powerful in their ordering work for mind and devotion, may become a Protestant form of triumphalism, and in their unfolding career do damage both to the facts of historical faith and to the vast organic counterpoint of the biblical record. Reflect with me upon the three temptations.

First, conceptual reduction of Christology. The doctrine of the Holy Trinity is an effort to secure faith against that temptation. There is one God. We know him as God the Creator, God the Redeemer, and God the Sanctifier. And in knowing according to three foci of fact and encounter we but the more deeply know the cry of John Calvin, "Our business is with God!" The God encountered in the form of the Servant *is the Lord of the creation*; and it is no other than the Lord of creation who is the enabling and illuminating presence in the Spirit.

The moment the Old Testament was included into the Christian canon, substance was given to the claim of Jesus that ". . . he who hath seen me hath seen the Father"—and "he who believes in me, believes not in me, but in him who sent me." And recall how many are the biblical statements and images that ground Christ back into the eternal life of the Father and interpret him forward into the presence of the life-giving holy power in the Spirit: the prologue to the Fourth Gospel, the image of the Lamb slain from the foundations of the world, the Easter fact "raised by the glory of the Father," the remarkable statements in Colossians, Ephesians, and the letter to the Hebrews which, to a mind formed too exclusively by Romans and Galatians, introduce a christological anguish by the sober magnificence of an orbit of meaning that cannot be contained in a too single principle of the justification of sinners.

Second, almost complete severance of the realm of redemption from the realm of creation. It is not possible now, even if I had the competence, to detail the forces, theological, devotional, social which have tempted us to this severance. But a few may be suggested: the moralizing of dogma—and the consequent shrinking of its meaning to a circle smaller than characterizes the biblical speech; the centuries in the life of the Western church when, in order to purify a demonized and paganized world, it had to withdraw, repudiate, violently negate the vitalities and values of the creation *in order* to exorcize an idolatry of the world so that the world might again become a garment of praise; the peculiar course of the Christian community in the United States, where, by action of the founding fathers, Christian meaning and utility was regarded as a moral glue to hold a republic together. Such an understanding is still that of the generality of our people, and regularly the theme of political figures in their homiletical posture.

The result, however, is certain and it is theologically perilous. For it moralized Christian thought and seals within private piety and an individualistic understanding of obedience the world-restoring intention of the gospel of God. It encourages an understanding of church as a gathered coterie of the redeemed who now celebrate the benefits of their redemption, and thus it detaches the acknowledging company from positive stance and action within the world, exhausts the demands of faith in a view of the body of Christ that is congregational, a view of love that is eleemosynary or selected-personal, a view of nature which, neutralized by the absence of God the Creator, can now be turned over without peril to busy scientific and entrepreneurial hands. Sanctification is a program without proper scope if it is urged apart from a doctrine of the creation.

Third, when Christology is detached from a doctrine of creation we are left without motive, clarity, or guide whereby to designate the world of the creation as a realm of grace, the right use of it a holy demand, and our operation in it and with it, now technically astounding, as a fresh opportunity for world-making to "the praise of his glory." The primal joy of creation to which the morning stars responded with abounding joy must be translated over into atomic and astrophysics, now that the power and creative potency of the very stars themselves are available to the creature.

I have a modest estimate of the direct utility of a volume such as this. Because its limitation in size is so severe it should be used more to lure and trouble the mind than mainly to inform it. And if this discussion of the *anguish of Christology* is now livelier in allure than complete in substance I shall have succeeded in what I intended. And because there are always some for whom a vision realized in evocative language is clearer than a notion wrought out in propositions, I end with a sonnet from a man whose anguished reflection about Christ sprung him out to the furthest limits of speculation. Gerard Manley Hopkins came finally to regard all this factic world as the residency of Christ. He is not found there; but when by his work on earth *we* are found, his eyes become ours and this place of his finding becomes a Christic mystery, a veritable cosmic diaphany. The poem is "Spring."[4]

4. In Gerard Manley Hopkins, *Poems and Prose of Gerard Manley Hopkins* (London: Penguin, 1958) 28.

Christology

Nothing is so beautiful as spring—
    When weeds, in wheels, shoot long and lovely and lush;
    Thrush's eggs look little low heavens, and thrust
Through the echoing timber does so rise and wring
The ear, it strikes like lightnings to hear him sing;
    The glassy peartree leaves and blooms, they brush
    The descending blue; that blue is all in a rush
With richness; the racing lambs too have fair their fling.

What is all this juice and all this joy?
    A strain of the earth's sweet being in the beginning
In Eden garden.—Have, get, before it cloy,
    Before it cloud, Christ, lord, and sour with sinning,
Innocent mind and Mayday in girl and boy,
    Most, O maid's child, thy choice and worthy the winning.

three

Living the Given Life

The Content of the Engendered Response

1958

This chapter was originally published as chapter 3 of Sittler's book The Structure of Christian Ethics. *He stresses that the Christian life and ethic lived in the interplay of law and gospel shows the preacher how the moral life is a function of the gospel and thus integral to good gospel preaching. Therefore, preaching on matters of morality is not an exercise in moralism but a call to live the "given" life, the grace fueled life that is ours in Christ.*

THE SCOPE OF VITALITY is governed by its nature. Boyle's law of gases asserts that a gas tends to fill all available space. It is of the nature of the gospel of redemption that all space, all personal relationships, all structures of society are the field of its energy. The gospel of the Word of God made flesh makes mankind the object of the gospel; the gospel in the concrete figure of the man Jesus whose existence was filled out within our mortal conditions—born of a woman, betrayed, denied, crucified—makes the entire earthly life of every man the operational area of this gospel. The gospel as redemptive event on the field of history makes the configuration of historical events the matrix of this gospel's working. The thrust of the redemptive action of God is into the structure of mankind, society, the family, and all economic orders. The scope of that redemptive activity, restoring to God in faith and active in love, can clearly be no more restricted than its originating action.

These clearly biblical facts stand in contradiction to two dangers that have often crippled Christian expositions of ethics. The first is the practice of dividing ethics into the categories of personal and social. Aside from psychological and sociological facts which reveal the severe limitations if not the actual absurdity of such a division, it is clearly not biblical in its understanding of God the Creator and man the creature. Man is created in community, and for community. The proverb "*Ein Mensch ist kein Mensch*" (A solitary man is no man) bluntly puts a truth which is central to biblical teaching. God's covenant is with a people; one of Jesus' most impassioned statements of his mission is in the word "gather": and the obedience of primitive faith immediately understood its proper form in terms of a community of "the called" to "membership" in a "fellowship" which is "the household of faith" and which is "his body, the church."

The second danger that operates to delimit the scope of the Christian life in its ethical vitality is one that has existed from the first days of the Christian era but confronts the believer today with peculiar power. It is the life-situation of millions of Western men in their actual daily experience: the emergence and peril of the power struggle between conflicting ideologies; the destruction, as a consequence of the technizing of material existence, of symbolic forms in which men traditionally have actualized their individuality and significance; the permeation of the realms of value, meaning, and all self-consciousness by the relentless momentum-to-bigness that characterizes the huge collectivities of politics, social life, the economic order. The stuff that men make meanings of can become so mechanized, rationalized, and "packaged" that the natural facts and processes of nature are concealed by the transformation of technology. While the workings of nature continue to exist and determine, they are rendered too febrile to support symbolic weight. A bottle of homogenized, pasteurized, and colorfully packaged milk may be safer for the body, but it contributes little to a child's empathy with the suggested Creator and Sustainer of "the cattle on a thousand hills." Our generation is just young enough to know with immediate comprehension and delight what Dylan Thomas is talking about in the first stanza of his "Fern Hill":

Part 1: The Preacher as Theologian

> Now as I was young and easy under the apple boughs
> About the lilting house and happy as the grass was green,
>   The night above the dingle starry,
>   Time let me hail and climb
>   Golden in the heyday of his eyes,
> And honoured among wagons I was prince of the apple towns
> And once below a time I lordly had the trees and leaves
>   Trail with daisies and barley
>   Down the rivers of the windfall light.[1]

And we are old enough, and have lived long enough with apples packed in the State of Washington on Monday and consumed in Illinois on Friday, to know what A. E. Housman's lad is living through when he says:

> Into my heart an air that kills
> From yon far country blows . . .
> What are those blue remembered hills,
> What spires, what farms are those?[2]

This life-situation can be described in such a way as virtually to identify it with the demonic and hence exhort men to withdraw from any engagement with the very forms of society within which they are placed. Such a course is both futile and wrong: futile because it flees the facts, and wrong because it tempts men to suppose that both the power of the divine redemption and the power of human creativity are restricted to venerated ways of ordering the human community. It is ironical that certain proponents of this position nostalgically assess as better than existing structures of community life circumstances which are historical memories precisely because they failed to meet the needs of millions of men! Accurate descriptions of contemporary life which point out its perils and corruptions, its thrust toward the "thingification" of man, are to be regarded as challenges to the scope and creativity of ethical life, and not as excuses for failure or devout rationalizations for lack of positive effect.

There is a strain in Protestant piety which makes it particularly susceptible to the temptation to interpret the counsel to keep oneself "unspotted from the world" in terms of quietism. The very historical matrix within which Protestant Christianity arose guarantees that the actual situation of the solitary individual before God should be insisted upon as

---

1. In Dylan Thomas, *The Collected Poems of Dylan Thomas* (New York: New Directions, 1953) 175–80.

2. A. E. Houseman, *A Shropshire Lad* (New York: Shakespeare House, 1951) 62.

the impact-point of the message of alienation, forgiveness, restoration. Insistence upon the inescapable responsibility of the individual has both prophetic power and peril. Its power is in its truth; its peril is in its tendency to make a false stopping point out of a true starting point, to force a definition of scope out of a point of impact, to restrict responsibility to the dimension within which that responsibility was learned.

The gospel itself is the corrective of all restrictive distortions of the gospel. The same gospel which demands intense inwardness as the theater of faith points to the world as a field of faith. The same Lord who meets, judges, heals, and forgives, in the solitary and naked aloneness of the self, plunges that self into the actuality of the world as its proper place for faithful activity in love.

The content of Christian ethics is disclosed in ever new and fresh ways as men's actual situations are confronted by God's revelation in Christ. When this assertion is taken seriously, certain old problems which have confused Christian ethical teaching are seen in a new way. The will of God, for instance, declared to be supremely revealed in Jesus Christ, cannot now be identified with the Ten Commandments. The Ten Commandments are now seen to be disclosures of the Creator—creature structure of existence, of the holy Source of all that is, of the requirements that inhere in the human situation simply by virtue of its source in God and the structure which he has given it. Because God is Creator his reality is not to be denied by idolatrous substitution of any earthly source, good, value or purpose as ultimate. (I am the Lord Thy God, thou shall have no other gods before me.) Because God is the Creator the given structures of dual sexuality, marriage, family, the reality and needs of child-life are to be honored and protected. (Honor thy father and thy mother. Thou shall not commit adultery.) The integrity of personal life is not to be violated. Because God is the Creator, men's lives and those things which they fashion and use for support and delight are to be respected. (Thou shall not kill; thou shall not steal; thou shall not covet.)

The Ten Commandments, as the law of God, are a verbalization of the given structures of creation. They stand above all men, believers and non-believers alike, as an accurate transcript of the facts—that the world is of God, that ultimate relations among men and things are grounded in him. The Stoic-immanental concept of *natural law* with which many systems of philosophical ethics operate is not introduced here because it is not needed. The perceptions and needs that require this concept are, in Christian ethics, completely confronted, and their space filled by the doctrine of God the Creator. The deed of God in Christ, however, occurred in a world which had and knew the Ten Commandments. If the deed is redemptive in intention and in fact, that does not deny or abrogate the revelation of God the Creator, but rather fulfills in the strategy of redemption what man regularly fractures in the structure of creation. Redemption does not destroy creation but realized it. Grace does not destroy nature but fulfills it. This fulfilling and realization is generated in men who by faith in God's new beginning with them in the second Adam, Christ, are given what the New Testament calls a "new being."

This faith, this "new being" in Christ, is not only a restoration to fellowship with God in the forgiveness of sins, but an entirely new placement and activity in the midst of the world. Here and now in this living situation the believer is both forgiven and commanded. The forgiveness is of God's love, and the command is to actualize in history the same love which accepts, forgives, and restores the believer.

The content of this love is disclosed to the believer in his own obedience to it. "He that does the will shall know the truth." "If you love me you will keep my commandments." This does not mean that because the believer loves his Lord he has formal cause to keep the Lord's commandments; it means, rather, that the commandment and the actualization of the love of Christ are in organic continuity. To love is to serve; and to love Christ is to serve him where he presents himself in his identification with needy men for our service.

What then is the specific content of this faith-active-in-love at the point where Christ meets us in man? The moment the question is put that way (which is the way the New Testament puts it) we comprehend what is meant by the assertion that Christian ethics discloses its content at the point of God's revelation of himself in Christ. Only now are we ready for that concentration of content which confronts us in such a passage as Matthew 25:31–46. In this teaching Jesus presents himself for the service of faithful love in absolute identification with human need—loneliness, estrangement, hunger, thirst. There faith sees him, there faith must obey him.

Christian ethics is the actualization of justification. For justification, being certified or made righteous in the God-relationship, bestows positive liberation to serve. This liberation exists inwardly because, as Luther puts it, "God has taken care of my salvation in Christ," and I am henceforth free as before God. This liberation exists outwardly because the energies which men futilely devote to the pleasing of God are now called out and exercised where God's purposes and family require them. When the self is known, loved, forgiven, then the self is set free in disciplined service to the will of God. And this will of God is now confronted both as a known and as an unknown. It is known in Christ who is the incarnate concretion of God's ultimate and relentless well-to-restoration; and it remains unknown in the fact that the actual service of this will is presented to the believer not as a general program given in advance but as an ever-changing and fluctuant obligation to the neighbor in the midst of history's life.

Corollary to this known (which is the love of God as giver and restorer) and corollary to the unknown (which is the precise form the love of the neighbor requires in novel situations) is what Alexander Miller has called "An absolute element and an element of calculation." He comments,

> But Christian ethics differs from idealist ethics in that its absolute is an absolute loyalty and not an absolute principle. While the Christian calculation differs from typical pragmatism in that while there is always a hidden absolute in pragmatism, an unadmitted presupposition about what is good for man, in the Christian scheme the calculation is grounded in a very precise understanding of what is good for man, determined by the revelation of God in Christ: "Live life, then," says St. Paul, "not as men who do not know the meaning and purpose of life, but as those who do."[3]

It is not possible to speak somewhat more specifically of the dynamics of Christian ethical decision and to indicate how these operate. If not by appeal to principles, or in patternless dependency upon the mercurial stuff of one's chance observations and occasionally animated affections—then what alternative remains?

Christian ethical decision is generated between the two poles of faith and the facts of life. Each of these acts upon the other: facts act upon faith to reveal to it the forms available as its field of action; faith acts upon facts to discover their meaning and peril and promise for men.

Facts without faith are blind; faith without facts is empty. Facts are never *mere* facts. They are what they are plus an indeterminate, undetermined potential. And one aspect of faith is certainly this, that it bestows upon its child sensitiveness to dimensions of possibility that are not otherwise discerned. Faith does not diminish the facticity of facts; but

---

3. Alexander Miller, *The Renewal of Man* (New York: Doubleday, 1955) 44.

faith enlarges and penetrates the world of fact with its peculiar livingness. The quality of this creativity, Christianly known, is not disclosed when its source is sought in man's natural vitalities, or in the reason's power whereby old stasis is made malleable to the mind's vision; but ultimately it is found in the power of that love which "so loved the world" that it endlessly creates new fields for its realization in history.

The confused and often contradictory nature of the facts with which we are confronted presses obedience down to the operational level of faith. Faith interprets facts in terms of their specifically human content. That is why the facts of human misery in post-war Europe discovered to millions of Christians in prosperous America a contemporary field for the operation of their faith; and faith penetrated these facts with its unique dimension, revealing in this anguish not only men needing coats and calories, but human beings whose lives could be restored to meaning by nothing less than personal identification with them in their hurt by fellow children of the crucified object of the common faith. It is precisely the salvatory power of this uniquely faithful deed of love, whose content included the ancient word and the sacraments, which was not understood by those who would adequately treat all crucifixions with calories.

This means that the will to help must devise the means to help in ways determined by the actual collectivities within which men are deepeningly involved, and within which interdependency each man is related to all men by a thousand cords. Needs that are shaped by structures must be met by help that also is structured! The requirement of justice is not only not ignored by Christian ethics, but is in an even more urgent sense an actually effective way to bring the help of the group-concern to bear upon the needs which are created, in part, by the group way of life.

The faith should seek to realize its proper obedience in alliance with the struggle for and the use of the instruments of justice does not by any means constitute a distortion of the gift and primacy of faithful ethics; it is, rather, faith's realistic acceptance of the root-fact of collective life—that the quest for justice is a drive built into all human relationships. It is there, not primarily as an ideal envisioned by human reflection, but as a vision engendered by a dimension of man's self as a creation of the Creator.

There are, indeed, needs of the neighbor, uninvolved with patterns of group life; these confront the believer with a demand for concern which is immediate, simple, urgent. But deepening areas of contemporary man's need are shaped by and involved with his existence in the huge collectives of economy, politics, community organization. Love must grasp the kind of hand that need holds out. The quest for justice is, on the one hand, an effort to understand the peculiar requirements of human life in its mobile career, and, on the other hand, to create instruments of positive law to certify these requirements, set limits to forces that would ignore them, and order collective life toward a tolerable balance of goods.

This means that love and justice are not two forms of the obedience of faith; they are modes of life's responsibility for lives. The apparently impersonal arrangements which justice makes to serve a need may cover the face of the need with pipes, valves, and pumps. But the need, the stuff, and the arrangements are not thereby bereft of the holiness that all faithful obedience has. A cup of cold water for my neighbor's need can no longer be actualized by simply sensitizing mercy or multiplying cups. The town pump for a few dozen has been displaced by a gigantic water supply system for millions; and concern that justice should prevail in the procurement, distribution, availability, and price of water is the hard, pragmatic face that love wears. And justice and technical competence are the hands it must work with. Justice is not identical with love; and the potencies and ingenuities of love are not exhausted in the struggle for justice. But justice is a primary instrument of love and a field for its operation. This has always been so, as the prophets of Israel so passionately insisted; it is so now and with a heightened urgency.

Just as it is necessary to relate faith-active-in-love and the quest for justice, so it is necessary at the same time to assert that this relationship is not an identity. For while the God-relationship, which is both source and content of faith and love, acknowledges the requirements of justice as also from God, the nobility of the quest for justice can exist and trouble men's lives without such a recognition. Justice can exist without any acknowledgment of the God-relationship; but the God-relationship cannot exist without concern for justice.

A comparison of the terms *justice* and *righteousness* will clarify the point. Justice is a term whose referent is an ideal balance of goods, duties, satisfactions within the human community. This ideal, and some effort to realize it, is not foreign to any culture whose story is available to us. To account for the existence of the ideal of justice it has not been necessary to postulate a divine source. Vitalities operative within empirical society have been powerfully generative of the quest for and the creation of various structures of justice. With such accounts the Christian understanding of the Creator cannot be satisfied; and in its doctrine of God the

Creator and Redeemer, it has insisted upon relating justice to the creative and restorative will of God.

But the biblical term *righteousness* is grounded precisely in a postulate that justice need not propose. Righteousness is a term used to designate human life sprung from, determined by, and accountable to the life of God. It is a thoroughly theonomous term. That is why, although faith-active-in-love ought to relate itself to all in human life which seeks justice, this faith can never account for itself nor be at rest with the achievements of justice.

If, then, faith is to be active in love, and if justice in the huge and impersonal collectivities of contemporary life is love operating at a distance, how are the energies of love to be related to that practical ordering of life in community which is called politics? Preliminary to any effort to speak to this question must be a comment about the term politics. The term indicates the nexus of practical arrangements for the creation or order, the enhancement of community values, the protection of life, and the provision of necessary services that every community is absolutely required to bring into existence under one form of government or another. The tradition in Christianity whereby this function is held to be "ordained of God" is thoroughly biblical; and the frequent lamentations of the pious over the dirt in politics may constitute but a devout mechanism whereby one avoids coming to terms with the problem at all. While most Christians today, to be sure, would admit that the gospel is relevant to the realm of politics, they turn in revulsion from the actual operation of political parties and the devious devices required for the formation of practical policies. To involve themselves in jockeying, trading, calculation, compromise, baby kissing, and boodle splitting requires a rough handling of ethical "principles." And in avoiding this danger they successfully avoid any contribution to public order. This attitude makes a certain sense if Christianity and the duties of the Christian man are identified with loyalty to a set of principles; but such an identification is both a reduction and a perversion of the Christian faith.

The state may sometimes make pretensions beyond the finite and mortal end and function for which it is ordained; and these pretensions are in continuity with that general disposition to idolatry which tempts men always and everywhere. Nevertheless, the state, ordained of God for limited and finite ends, is the necessary means by which the will to the good becomes effective for the correction of collective injustice and the restraint of inordinate greed. Luther's view of the state, in so far as it was

Living the Given Life

tied to the peculiar political situation of his time, ought no longer be used as an adequate guide in our engagement with present problems. But he had an understanding of the function of state as a "mask of God" which far transcends his practical conclusions from princely-state circumstances of the sixteenth century, and is intrinsically more inclusive of the facts of human evil and political creativity than the state-view of either Geneva or Rome. For his call to men everywhere and in every circumstance to realize their vocation as the faithful service of God in daily work, shattered the false separation of sacred and secular, recognized the duties of the common life as valid structures for Godly service, and celebrated the entire creation as a field in which every believer is summoned to be a "little Christ" to his neighbor's need.

In this situation, in politics as in every other sphere, Christian ethics is given its content as it makes pragmatic selections among available alternatives to enhance and serve the common good, approximates ever more sensitively the demands of justice, and finds methods to allay tensions and curb inordinate desires. In this faithful process (which is the morally ultimate situation!) the believer never transcends the fact that he is *simul Justus et peccator* (simultaneously justified man and sinner). This is to say that ethical decisions are never delivered from, and ethical achievements never add up to, a position elevated above faith's obedient placement within, and joyful acceptance of, man's creaturely situation. Just as no achievement can place a man beyond the daily need of God's judgment, grace, and forgiveness, so that no ethical decision is ever wholly true, just, or good—so, also, men's efforts will forever stand under both the thrust and the limitation of the same situation. A particularly poignant illustration of this necessity confronts us as we consider efforts presently being made toward some kind of precarious peace among the nations. Here is the dilemma: because history—in this, like human life in general—can never wholly redeem, redress, cancel out, or compensate for past wrongs, the very efforts for present and future peace constitute a kind of "betrayal" of millions of men who are dead by the power of the evil, whose countrymen's torments remain, and whose loss of freedom may be permanent. But the present facts are of such a nature that the attempt to right what has been wrong would seemingly involve two caster terrors: a struggle more full of pain and death than the one whose effects the nations seek to redress, and world-wide acceptance of the fateful use of now available weapons which might well obliterate the very possibility of anything resembling normal human life and freedom for the entire planet. But in the very moment one so concludes, he is aware that this apparently "Christian," rational, humane concern represents also a pious façade back of which lurks a hope not to disturb prosperity, the securities of one's own career and family. It is in part a kind of highly commendable "long view" which permits one to have his ethical cake and eat it, too!

The heartbreaking choices which confront us too sharply in the affairs of nations are but the transcript of the situation which is structural in the solitary life of the believing individual. In a recent book *The Cruel Sea*, a dramatic instance of this is presented. The commander of a destroyer, convoying a fleet of merchant ships, has finally located the submarine which had sunk several ships and caused the loss of hundreds of lives. The sonar-device which located the hidden submarine indicated that it was precisely at the point where, on the surface of the water, some hundreds of men, previously torpedoed, were swimming about. To drop a depth bomb for the destruction of the submarine would at the same time mean the destruction of the men swimming in the water. There was but an instant to make his choice, and the commander made it knowing that no choices available could be anything but death-dealing. The subsequent tormented statement of the commander, "One must do what one must do—and say one's prayers," is an eloquent condensation of the ethical situation. "One must *do*"—for inactivity, refusal to do anything, is already to do something. And that something is not good. ". . . what one *must* do" is not an open choice; definite alternatives are absolutely given. Both are deadly. ". . . and say one's prayers" is an acknowledgment of deepest piety that no decision fulfills the will of God or releases man from that relation to God which dares to live only by the daily forgiveness of sins.

When the God-relationship is centrally informed by faith, then the actual situation of decision-pressed man is saved from the despair which would inevitably overtake him if this relationship were simply compounded of love. For love, no matter how deeply accepted from God, obediently directed toward men, firmly held to as the motivation of action, both reveals and compels the acceptance of pragmatic choices, *all* possible variations of which are fraught with inadequacy, pain, and denial. In this sense love is the tutor of faith! Even the "law of love," no less than the law of Moses, is a schoolmaster who leads the believer to Christ. For, in Christ, the believing lover of men-in-Christ now stands with his Lord and supreme Lover precisely in his crucifixion! "I am crucified with Christ" is a term expressive not only of the Christian recapitulation of the Christ-life in the large, but a symbol of the inner content of numberless ethical decisions in their actual heartbreaking character. A Christian ethics must, therefore, work where love reveals need. It must do this work in faith which comes from God and not as accumulating achievements to present to God. In this working it must seek limited objectives without apology, and support failure without despair. It can accept ambiguity without lassitude, and seek justice without identifying justice and love.

Ours is a generation upon which two forces from opposite directions are beating with such fury that we are in danger of ethical paralysis between them. From the one side we are the heirs of an ethical analysis which properly insists upon the will of God as transcendent to the relativity of all cultural life, reveals the ambiguity of everything human, the admixture of self-interest in everything human, the lurking demonic in every positive course. The result of this penetrating effort to speak the truth about man as sinner in his modern situation has been that decisiveness before gigantic evils and shrieking human injustices has been paralyzed by the sheer fullness with which every man's evil has been revealed, and ethical complexity has been so elaborately analyzed as to stun the conscience.

From the other wise, we are a generation before whose eyes every primal meaning of "The grace of the Lord Jesus Christ, the love of God, and the communion of the Holy Ghost" has been blasted by spirits organized into effective powers and threatening to reshape all existence into a one-dimensional denial of that God-relationship which constitutes humanity. Between these two forces—an analysis which reveals involvement and humble arrogance, and the fact of millions of men enslaved, betrayed, liquidated—the Christian believer is tempted to stand in horrified but inert repentance.

The repentance must remain, for it is the constant heartbeat of the man of faith in history; but the stasis must be overcome. We are sinners, to be sure, but precisely such sinners as are addressed by the word of St. John, that if a man see his brother in need and shut up his bowels of compassion, how dwelleth the love of God in him? Unless we can discover a way, both to acknowledge the facts, act in faith and love, and accept the consequences of our action, our generation will constitute a huge portrait of repentant believers with furrowed brows and inert hands.

The way of advance is to understand that it is a function of faith itself to discern the differences between facts and then act upon what it discerns. Faith without discrimination between facts is a sentiment that encourages brutality; faith without acts (works!) is dead. There is, to be sure, no human fact in which sin is not involved. But within some structures of fact there are alive, free, and operative forces of grace, insights of elemental justice, recreating energies of love. In politics, as in theology, freedom is a precondition of regeneration. It is a fact that the Negro community in American life has been exploited, contemptuously handled, overtly insulted by public law. It is also a fact that within American public life concerned men and institutions have been free to combat injustice, illumine ignorance, plead and work for equality of treatment.

The body of fact presented, for instance, by the Soviet reading of history and man, is a body of fact of a quite different order. It is a legitimate and necessary function of faith to discern this difference. For this closed matrix of dogma and force permits no operational space for the very forces which alone could corrode its idolatry, disintegrate its monodimensional dogma about man and history, and force its open to the powers of grace, justice, and love.

We began with the assertion that to be a Christian is to accept what God gives. We end with a reiteration of that assertion now so elaborated, it is hoped, as to disclose how the structure of Christian ethics grows organically out of the fact and the content of the endlessly giving God. The Christian man is to accept what God gives as Creator: the world with its needs, problems, possibilities; its given orders of family, community, state, economy. Each of these is invested with the promise and potency of grace, and each of these is malleable to the perverse purposes of evil.

The Christian is to accept what God gives as Redeemer: the earth and all human life as the place where God's glory became flesh and dwelt among us, and, therefore, the holy place for life in forgiveness, in the obedience of faith, in the works of love. "Man becomes man because God became man." God has given the form of himself and his will in a man; and the ethical life is the birth-pangs attending the new-being of man in history, ". . . until Christ be formed in you."

The Christian is to accept what God gives as Holy Spirit the Sanctifier. This acceptance includes the gifts that God gives from above; and the tasks which he gives in the world around. This gift and these tasks belong together. The gift is celebrated in the doing of the tasks; the tasks are undertaken in faith as witnesses to the gift.

four

Unbridled Grace

Called to Unity

1962

He is the image of the invisible God, the firstborn of all creation; for in him all things were created, in heaven and on earth, visible and invisible, whether thrones or dominions or principalities or authorities—all things were created through him and for him. He is before all things, and in him all things hold together. He is the head of the body, the church; he is the beginning, the firstborn from the dead, that in everything he might be preeminent. For in him all the fullness of God was pleased to dwell, and through him to reconcile to himself all things, whether on earth or in heaven, making peace by the blood of his cross.

—Colossians 1:15–20 (RSV)

THERE ARE TWO REASONS for placing these five verses from the Colossian letter at the beginning of what I wish to say about the unity of Christ's church. (1) These verses say clearly *that* we are called to unity, and (2) they suggest *how* the gift of that unity may be waiting for our obedience.

These verses say that we are called to unity, that the One who calls us is God, that this relentless calling persists over and through all discouragements, false starts, and sometimes apparently fruitless efforts; it is these verses that have engendered the ecumenical movement among the churches and steadily sustain them in it.

These verses sing out their triumphant and alluring music between two huge and steady poles—"Christ," and "all things." Even the Ephesian letter, rich and large as it is in its vision of the church, moves not within so massive an orbit as this astounding statement of the purpose of God. For it is here declared that the sweep of God's restorative action in Christ is no smaller than the six-times-repeated *ta panta*. Redemption is the name for this will, this action, and this concrete man who is God with us and God for us—and all things are permeable to his cosmic redemption because all things subsist in him. He comes to all things, not as a stranger, for he is the firstborn of all creation, and in him all things were created. He is not only the matrix and *prius* of things; he is the intention, the fullness, and the integrity of all things: For all things were created through him and for him. Nor are all things a rumbled multitude of facts in an unrelated mass, for in him all things hold together.

Why does St. Paul, in this letter, as in the letter to the Ephesians, expand his vocabulary so radically far beyond his usual terms? Why do the terms guilt, sin, the law, and the entire Judaic catalogue of demonic powers here suddenly become transposed into another vocabulary, general in its character, cosmic in its scope, so vastly referential as to fill with Christic energy and substance the farthest outreach of metaphysical speculation?

The apostle does that out of the same practical pastoral ardor as caused him, when he wrote to his Philippian community, to enclose a deceptive petty problem of human recalcitrance within the overwhelming therapy of grace. Just as selfishness and conceit in Philippi are drowned in the sea of the divine charity "found in human form . . . humbled himself and became obedient unto death, even the death of the cross"—so here. The Colossian error was to assume that there were "thrones, dominions, principalities and authorities" which have a life and power apart from Christ, that the real world was a dualism, one part of which (and that part ensconcing the power of evil) was not subject to the Lordship of the Creator in his Christ.

Against that error which, had it persisted, would have trapped Christ within terms of purely moral and spiritual power and hope, Paul sets off a kind of chain reaction for the central atom, and the staccato ring of *ta panta* is the sounding of its reverberations into the farthest reaches of human fact, event, and thought. All is claimed for God, and all is Christic. The fugue-like voices of the separate claims—of him, in him, through him, for him—are gathered up the quiet coda—"For in him all the fullness of God was pleased to dwell."

We must not fail to see the nature and the size of the issue that Paul confronts and encloses in this vast Christology. In propositional form it is simply this: A doctrine of redemption is meaningful only when it swings with the larger orbit of a doctrine of creation. For God's creation of earth cannot be redeemed in any intelligible sense of the word apart from a doctrine of the cosmos which is his home, his definite place, the theater of his selfhood under God, in cooperation with his neighbor, and in caring relationship with nature, his sister.

> Unless one is prepared to accept a dualism which condemns the whole physical order as being not of God and interprets redemption simply as release from the physical order, then one is forced to raise the question of cosmic redemption, not in contrast with but as an implication of personal redemption. Physical nature cannot be treated as an indifferent factor—as the mere stage and setting of the drama of personal redemption. It must either be condemned as it itself evil, or else it must be brought within the scope of God's redemptive act.[1]

Unless the reference and the power of the redemptive act includes the whole of man's experience and environment, straight out to its farthest horizon, then the redemption is incomplete. There is and will always remain something of evil to be overcome. And more. The actual man in his existence will be tempted to reduce the redemption of man, to what purgation, transformation, forgiveness, and blessedness is available by an "angelic" escape from the cosmos of natural and historical fact—and in the option accept some sort of dualism which is as offensive to biblical theology as it is beloved of all Gnosticism, than as now.

The Christic Vision of the Eastern Fathers

In our understanding of the vast Christic vision that informs the passage from Colossians it is Irenaeus, and not the Western and vastly more influential Augustine, who must be our mentor. The problem forced upon us

---

1. Allan D. Galloway, *The Cosmic Christ* (New York: Harper, 1951) 205.

by the events of the present decade is not soluble by the covert dualism of nature and grace. At a certain period in Christian thought and practical life, this dualism worked itself out in the dualism of church and world, of spiritual and temporal. But the time when Christian theology and Christian life could operate with such a view of things is long past. The view was never appropriate to the organic character of biblical speech; in the present state of man's knowledge in all areas it has become unintelligible.

But before that cleavage occurred, and strong with the vitalities of a Christology as splendid as our case is desperate, a unitary Christology prevailed in the church; Colossians and Ephesians are echoes of it. I recollect it here, and in connection with the theme "Christ the Light of the World," because it is now excruciatingly clear that Christ cannot be a light that lighteth every man coming into the world if he is not also the light that falls upon the world into which every man comes. He enlightens this darkling world because the world was made through him. He can be the light of men because men subsist in him. He can be interpretive power because he is the power of the Word in creation.

"Christ the Light of the World" has not had a career in the Christianity of the West comparable to the rich career of this doctrine of eastern Christendom. Nor has this image been expanded to address with lordly power the multiple energies of other images of light as these live and shape spiritual life in the religions of millions of men in whose midst we now meet. God is light. Men have in nature the bent light of God. Therefore Christ the Lord, who in our confession is named "Light of Light," must not be reduced to Light against light.

The church takes a large risk when she pulls into the center of her reflections the New Testament image of Christ as the Light of the World. For the holy meaning of light cannot be restricted to Christ, and cannot be separated from him. Creation is a work of God, who is light. And the light of the Creator-God falls upon and inheres with his creation. The world of nature can be the place of this light that "came" by Jesus Christ because, despite the world's hostility to that light, it was never without the light of God. Nature and grace are categories necessary to do justice to Christ the Savior of the World. But if they are absolute and contradictory categories they distort and reduce the doctrine of creation.

As we seek for a vision of Christ ample enough to draw us toward unity in his church we would do well to turn back the pages of Western theological reflection and attend to a father in the church whose understanding of Christ the Light was not able to settle for statements less majestic than the apostrophe to him in the first chapter of Colossians. From a recent and careful summary of the thought of Irenaeus, I quote the following paragraph:

> In Irenaeus . . . there are not two orders of goodness, but only one. All goodness, whether it belongs to this world or to the final consummation, is a manifestation of the grace of God. It is the same grace of God which sustains nature even in its fallen state and which confers salvation in Jesus Christ. The residual goodness in nature can even be regarded as an anticipation or foretaste of that salvation. The same . . . appears also in Irenaeus' attitude toward the sacraments as compared with that of the church of the middle ages. For Irenaeus the union of spiritual and material benefit in the Eucharist symbolizes the ultimate unity of nature and grace implied in Christian salvation. But for Aquinas that the sacraments are administered in a material element is merely God's gracious concession to man's regrettably sensuous nature (P.II.QI, A.8).

For Irenaeus, the incarnation and saving work of Jesus Christ meant that the promise of grace was held out to the whole of nature, and that henceforth nothing could be called common or unclean. For the church of the Middle Ages, on the other hand, nature was essentially common, and, if not positively unclean, at least seriously deficient in that shining whiteness of the saints in the empyrean heaven, and essentially incapable of sharing in such glory.[2]

The Split between Grace and Nature in Western Thought

The doctrinal cleavage, particularly fateful in western Christendom, has been an element in the inability of the church to relate the powers of grace to the vitalities and processes of nature. At the very time, and in that very part of the world where men's minds were being deepeningly determined by their understanding and widened control of the powers of nature, they were so identifying the realm of history and the moral as the sole realm of grace as to shrink to no effect the biblical Christology of nature. In the midst of vast changes in man's relation to nature the sovereignty and scope of grace was, indeed, attested and liberated by the Reformers. But post-Reformation consolidations of their teaching

---

2. Ibid., 128ff.

Part 1: The Preacher as Theologian

permitted their Christic recovery of all of nature as a realm of grace to slip back into a minor theme.

In the Enlightenment the process was completed. Rationalism, on the one hand, restricted redemption by grace to the moral soul, and Pietism, on the other hand, turned down the blaze of the Colossian vision so radically that its *ta panta* was effective only as a moral or mystical incandescence. Enlightenment man could move in on the realm of nature and virtually take it over because grace had either ignored or repudiated it. A bit of God died with each new natural conquest; the realm of grace retreated as more of the structure and process of nature was claimed by not autonomous man. The rood-screen in the church, apart from its original meaning, has become a symbol of man's devout but frightened thought permitting to fall asunder what God joined together.

It is not necessary or proper on this occasion to specify more fully the factors that have caused that unhappy divorcement. It is sufficient only to affirm that it has occurred, and to listen to the voices that lament its effects and to some, that, longing for a lost wholeness, celebrate the glimmering of its recovery. A representative voice of the lament is Mathew Arnold:

> The sea of faith
> Was once, too, at the full, and round earth's shores
> Lay like the folds of a bright girdle furl'd;
> But now I only hear
> Its melancholy, long, withdrawing roar
> Retreating to the breath of the night-wind down the vast edges drear
> And naked shingles of the world.[3]

And a seldom heard voice that celebrates the world as a God-haunted house is Gerard Manly Hopkins:

> The world is charged with the grandeur of God.
>   It will flame out, like shining from shook foil;
>   It gathers to a greatness, like the ooze of oil
> Crushed. Why do men then now not reck his rod?
> Generations have trod, have trod, have trod;
>   And all is seared with trade; bleared, smeared with toil;
>   And wears man's smudge and shares man's smell: the soil
> Is bare now, nor can foot feel, being shod.
>   And for all this, nature is never spent;

---

3. Matthew Arnold, "Dover Beach," in C. B. Tinker and H. F. Lowry, eds., *The Poetical Works of Matthew Arnold* (London: Oxford University Press, 1950) 211.

>   There lives the dearest freshness deep down things;
> And though the last lights off the black West went
>   Oh, morning, at the brown brink eastward, springs –
> Because the Holy Ghost over the bent
>   World broods with warm breast and with ah! bring wings.[4]

Claiming Nature for Christ

Is it possible to fashion a theology catholic enough to affirm redemption's force enfolding nature, as we have affirmed redemption's force enfolding history? That we should make that effort is, in my understanding, the commanding task of this moment in our common history. And by common history I refer to that which is common to all of the blessed obediences of the household of faith: Antioch and Aldersgate, Constantinople and Canterbury, Geneva and Augsburg, Westminster and Plymouth.

For the problem which first drove the church, as our text reminds us, to utter a Christology of such amplitude is a problem that has persisted and presses upon us today with absolute urgency. We are being driven to claim the world of nature for God's Christ just as in the time of Augustine that church was driven to claim the world of history as the city of God, for his Lordship and purpose. For fifteen centuries the church has declared the power of grace to conquer egocentricity, to expose idolatry, to inform the drama of history with holy meaning. But in our time we have beheld the vision and promises of the Enlightenment come to strange and awesome maturity. The cleavage between grace and nature is complete. Man's identity had been shrunken to the dimensions of privatude within social determinism. The doctrine of the creation has been made a devout datum of past time. The mathematization of meaning in technology and its reduction to operational terms in philosophy has left no mental space wherein to declare that nature, as well as history, is the theater of grace and the scope of redemption.

When millions of the world's people, inside the church and outside of it, know that damnation now threatens nature as absolutely as it has always threatened men and societies in history, it is not likely that witness to a light that does not enfold and illumine the world-as-nature will be

---

4. Gerard Manley Hopkins, "God's Grandeur," in W. H. Gardner and N. H. Mackenzie, eds., *The Poems of Gerard Manley Hopkins*, 4th ed. (Oxford: Oxford University Press, 1967) 66.

even comprehensible. For the root-pathos of our time is the struggle by the peoples of the world in many and various ways to find some principle, order, or power which shall be strong enough to contain the raging "... thrones, dominions, principalities" which restrict and ravage human life.

If, to this longing of all men everywhere, we are to propose "Him of whom, and through whom, and in whom are all thing," then that proposal must be made in redemptive terms that are forged in the furnace of man's crucial engagement with nature as both potential to blessedness and potential to hell.

The matter might be put another way: The address of Christian thought is most weak precisely where man's ache is most strong. We have had, and have, a Christology of the moral soul, a Christology of history, and, if not a Christology of the ontic, affirmations so huge as to fill the space marked out by ontological questions. But we do not have, at least not in such effective force as to have engaged the thought of the common life, a daring, penetrating, life-affirming Christology of nature. The theological magnificence of cosmic Christology lies, for the most part, still tightly folded in the church's innermost heart and memory. Its power is nascent among us all in our several styles of preaching, teaching, worship its waiting potency in available for release in kerygmatic theology, in moral theology, in liturgical theology, in sacramental theology. And the fact that our separate traditions incline us to one another of these as central does not diminish either the fact, or our responsibility. For it is true of us all that the imperial vision of Christ as coherent in *ta panta* had not broken open the powers of grace to diagnose, judge, and heal the ways of men as they blasphemously strut about this hurt and threatened world as if they owned it. Our vocabulary of praise has become personal, pastoral, too purely spiritual, static. We have not affirmed as inherent in Christ—God's proper man for man's proper selfhood and society—the world political, the world economical, the world aesthetic, and all other commanded orderings of actuality which flow from the ancient summons to tend this garden of the Lord. When atoms are disposable to the ultimate hurt then the very atoms must be reclaimed for God and his will.

The Setting for the Study of Church Unity

If now we put together that threat to nature and a Christology whose scope is as endless as that threat is absolute, do we, perhaps, gain a fresh and urgent vision of the call of God to the unity of the church, and some help toward its definition and obedience? Nothing that is affirmed here questions or slights the ways we have gone, or suggests that their continuation is not necessary and good. Incessant biblical study, penetrating theological analysis, the expansion of the scope and the deepening of our various traditions, and mutual acknowledgment in thanksgiving of the blessing s God has bestowed upon us all in our several ways and works—all of this must go on.

Just as Faith and Order acknowledged at Lund that cooperative ecclesiological studies are a prolegomenon to unity but no guarantee of our willingness to receive it or even to continue to long for it—so we must here acknowledge the profound studies of Christ and the church, while they show us clearly where our life and our center is, do not automatically furnish forth a common faith, or draw us toward a faithful ordering of the life of the church in history.

The alembic in which the dynamics of unity stir with life, fuse, give new forms to Godly vitalities, and have the power to generate new obediences amidst old recalcitances—is history. That is why there is such a discipline as history of doctrine. For this study discloses that doctrinal statement and development is confession-thinking to the glory of God amidst historical denials or pretensions which would usurp the glory. It has always been within the clutch of a definite historical threat, or necessity, or a sheer intolerable malaise that the church has found her teaching voice. Doctrines are not born out of doctrines in an unchanging vacuum. Doctrines are evoked, clarified, refined, given force and precision within the challenge of exact circumstances. The facts of history are the exciters o insight; the nature of the moment's need engenders the doctrine to serve and bless it.

This dynamism that characterizes the church's stance and movement throughout history, this momentum and promise inherent in the church by the spirit, furnishes us with hope as we try to construct a fresh doctrinal counterpoint between the *ta panta* of the claims of Christ and the facts of nature's pathetic openness to glorious use or to brutal rapacity.

But how does doctrine, addressing the necessities of history with its own interpretive unfolding of the life of God in the life of the mind of the church, bear upon the calling of God to the unity of the church? Just as the gracious gifts of God constitute and endow the church and sustain her toward fulfillment in history, so right doctrine drives toward unity in two ways: it constantly clarifies in intellectual terms what it is that sustains the church, and it calls the church to celebrate in deed what it points to as alone adequate to the world's need. This is but to say that the *telos* of doctrine is action, the fulfillment of right teaching is not right teaching but decision and deed. Clarity without the love of the brother who is luminously before us as the brother is the clarity of damnation. "He that loveth his brother abideth in the light." The church must think; but she cannot think herself into unity. The church must seek order appropriate to her nature; but she cannot order herself into unity. But the unity of the church may be given her when she thinks and when she worships, and when she reflects upon order—all in order to ethicality.

By ethicality is meant that actualization in the decision of the common life of those commands, calls, gifts of God which are affirmed and celebrated in theology and in worship. Clarity, obedience, unity—that is the interior sequence of the light. The church knows the light in deepening ethicality under the incandescence and guidance and judgment of that light. This it must do as a witness to the unity it now has and as the condition of the fuller unity it seeks.

It is the thesis of this address that our moment in history is heavy with the imperative that faith proposes for the madly malleable and grandly possible potencies of nature—that holiest, vastest, confession: that by him, for him, and through him all things subsist in God, and therefore are to be used in joy and sanity for his human family.

The church is both thrust and lured towards unity. The thrust is from behind and within: it is grounded in God's will and promise. The lure is God's same will and promise operating upon the church from the needs of history within which she lives her life. The thrust of the will and the promise is a steady force in the church's memory: the lure is clamant in the convulsions that twist our times in the church's present. The way forward is from Christology expanded to its cosmic dimensions, made passionate by the pathos of this threatened earth, and made ethical by the love and wrath of God. For as it was said in the beginning that God beheld all things and declared them good, so it was uttered by an angel in the apocalypse of St. John, ". . . ascending from the east, having the seal of the living God: and he cried with a loud voice to the four angels, to whom it was given to hurt the earth and the sea, saying, Hurt not the earth neither the sea, nor the trees . . . " (Revelation 7:2–3, KJV). The care of the earth, the realm of nature as a theater of grace, the ordering of the thick, material procedures that make available to or deprive men of bread and peace—these are Christological obediences before they are practical necessities.

Unbridled Grace

We live in a *kairos* where Christ and chaos intersect, a moment in which the fullest Christology is marvelously congruent with man's power-founded anxiety and need. Contemporary man expresses his hurt in terms of his broken or uncertain relationship to society and nature. We cannot, indeed, extrude from these the substance of his God-relationship. But it might be possible so to say to him that he entertain the possibility of its truth that the problems that appear in this earthy and societal relationship are not soluble in terms of it. For created life is a triad of God, and man, and nature. If we meet him where he hurts, we may be given new ears and eyes for that triadic Word from which the church lives in confessed acknowledgment, and under which all men live by creation.

The grace and truth which came by Jesus Christ, and which were celebrated in the Colossian hymn because ". . . it pleased the Father that in him should all fullness dwell . . . ," is alone a source and power and interpretive principle for a meaning adequate to the longings and needs of this cloven and embittered world. There are perceptive men in the world who glimpse this, even outside the Christian confession, and in the dark language of nature's pathos as it groans and travails in pain they set it forth. From many voices I chose one. His utterance is called, "Advice to a Prophet." The poet speaks of man's nature as it is formed in nature's net; of how the deer, and the sky, and the sun, and the patient, mute life of the animals accompany and enrich us as we live out our days. And then, reflecting upon the possible event by which all of these should be stunned, silenced, or obliterated, he cries of himself and his human fellows—

> What should we be without
> The dolphin's arc, the dove's return,
>
> These things in which we have seen ourselves and spoken?
> Ask us, prophet, how shall we call
> Our natures forth when that live tongue is all
> Dispelled, that glass obscured or broken
>
> In which we have said the rose of our love and the clean
> Horse of our courage, in which beheld
> The singing locust of the soul unshelled,
> And all we mean or wish to mean.
>
> Ask us, ask us whether with the wordless rose
> Our hearts shall fail us, come demanding
> Whether there shall be lofty or long standing
> When the bronze annals of the oak-tree close.[5]

5. Richard Wilbur, "Advice to a Prophet," in Wilbur, *New and Collected Poems*

The church has found a melancholy number of ways to express her variety. She has found fewer ways to express her unity. But if we are indeed called to unity, and if we can obey that call in terms of a contemporary Christology expanded to the dimensions of the New Testament vision, we shall, perhaps, obey into fuller unity. For in such obedience we have the promise of the Divine blessing. This radioactive earth, so fecund and so fragile, is his creation, our sister, and the material place where we meet the brother in Christ's light. Ever since Hiroshima the very term light has had ghastly meanings. But ever since creation it has had meanings glorious; and every since Bethlehem meanings concrete and beckoning.

(New York: Harcourt, Brace, Jovanovich, 1988) 182–83.

Nature and Grace

As we have already observed, a signature concern of Sittler's theology and preaching, present throughout his writings, is the expansion of the scope of grace beyond the matter of personal salvation into the whole of creation. The spirit of this rich and thoughtful presentation is capture in this quote from the text that follows: "What I am appealing for is an understanding of grace that has the magnitude of the doctrine of the Holy Trinity. The grace of God is not simply a holy hypodermic whereby my sins are forgiven. It is the whole giftedness of life, the wonder of life, which causes me to ask questions that transcend the moment."

HUMANKIND HAS BEEN HERE longer than my generation first supposed. Our history is yearly disclosed by research to be more and more complicated. But our existence on the earth as a small part of a single system of systems within systems that spin out into dreamlike magnitudes—this is the actual world of reflection in which the Christian faith must now ask after the relevance of its language. If we talk about creation, we mean more than the chrysanthemums and the bullfrogs and men and women. If we talk about redemption, we must ask if the ultimate meaning of redemption is confined to God's historical action for the human race in this place.

Theology is not only knowledge of human reflection about God; theology is also a constant doing, as well as a remembering, a transmitting, a refining. Theology is something that the church *does*, not only something that it *has*. Therefore a theologian is not simply a deep freeze in which the past is preserved and at certain times thawed out briefly for the attentive listener; theology is a vocation in which the accumulations of the past and the experiences of the present are always freshly attuned to the phenomena of the emerging, changing, frenetically racing world.

There are no logical, anthropological, psychological, or sociological definitions of *homo sapiens* in the Bible. But there are certain paradigms of where humanity stands. For example, in the very first chapter of the Old Testament there is a story in which human beings are spoken of from three angles of vision, as creatures with three dimensions, or as constituted by three enormous forces. First of all, we are from God. God is prior; he is the Creator, we are the creatures. God calls us into existence. As Calvin used to put it, "Man's existence is a subsistence." We subsist under God's eternal existence. So our God relationship is the first building block of this structure.

God made the first human not out of angelic substance or out of sheer gas or wind, but out of the dust of the earth. This is a symbolic and powerful way of saying that the human race belongs to the biological order. We are part of nature. We cannot lay aside our natural beginning, our rootedness in the same ecological system that characterizes the natural world. That is both a psychological report and a theological report.

The main point of the story of Eve is not that God made a woman, but that he made another human being. For a solitary person has not the possibility of becoming a person. The human relationship of one person to another, person to neighbor, is a determining factor of personhood. This aspect of relationship, then, is the second element of the human structure.

And the third building block is that God put his creatures in the garden. God places, thrusts, his creatures, roots them in nature. And the human relationship to nature is such that we are to tend it. The garden, the world of nature, is God's other creation, which stands alongside his creation of persons, not as neutral or mute, but as a living creation which has its own unique integrity and which defines the human place in the world.

Nature is never, for Jesus, simply a resource out of which we are to dig iron and copper and zinc, and pump oil; it is the theater of human life—the garden of our life—which it is our obligation to care for.

You can't solve the whole problem of nature's care by stewardship. That's a perfectly good word and a very powerful idea, but it's not a big enough doctrine; it's not central enough. For nothing less than the doctrine of grace would be an adequate doctrine to shape the Christian community's mind and practice in a way appropriate to the catastrophe in the environment.

Unbridled Grace

God creates his creation in grace. The creation itself is a realm of grace.

We must read the text very carefully: "The heavens are telling the glory of God" (Ps 19:1). But we must not go on to say that the heavens disclose the will of God. By going out on Sunday morning and looking up at the heavens from the seventh tee, one has not performed an adequate act of obedience. The will of God is not disclosed via the heavens—though the glory of God, according to the Scriptures, is.

Moralistic little essays here and there telling us to recycle the newspapers and smash the cans (and we should do both) are not sufficient efforts to care for our environment. There must be some primary theological reflection on this point.

What I am appealing for is an understanding of grace that has the magnitude of the doctrine of the Holy Trinity. The grace of God is not simply a holy hypodermic whereby my sins are forgiven. It is the whole giftedness of life, the wonder of life, which causes me to ask questions that transcend the moment.

I am interested in the reality or the presence of the grace of God in the creation, because only the doctrine of grace will be adequate to change the spirit of our minds whereby we deal with timber and oil, fish and animals, and the structure of cities, urban design, homes for people, places to work—all these mundane, concrete things that yet constitute the anchorage of our hearts, the home of our daily lives.

Nature is for enjoyment, in the profound meaning of enjoyment: to honor a thing for what it is, to consent to its being what it is and not another thing. Use nature, for sure, but use it only according to its inherent dignity.

Contemporary humans are diminished because our roots are not as deep or as widely spread as were those of our forebears into the field, the forest, the woods. They do not touch the flowers, the animals, the daily tasks on the farm. Contemporary people, contemporary children particularly, think that hamburgers come from McDonalds. They think that Bordens makes milk and Kraft makes cheese. The closest any of them ever come to a lamb is a wool jacket. This increasing distance from the natural world has made our vocabulary bereft of natural images, has almost stripped us of the possibility to talk of ourselves in relation to God's creation.

Part 1: The Preacher as Theologian

In the course of history the human race has not only sailed the seas but has pierced beyond its earth homeland. Now it is piercing into the deepest recesses of molecular life and cellular life. We are constituted by our transactions with nature—not just the cattle on a thousand hills or the molecules under a thousand microscopes. So deeply are we formed by our experiences of nature that if the gospel is going to be addressed to contemporary human beings, it's got to have a God who follows those probings, a God of nature thus understood.

When we turn the attention of the church to a definition of the Christian relationship with the natural world, we are not stepping away from grace and proper theological ideas; we are stepping right into the middle of them. There is a deeply rooted, genuinely Christian motivation for attention to God's creation, despite the fact that many church people consider ecology to be a secular concern. "What does environmental preservation have to do with Jesus Christ and his church?" they ask. They could not be more shallow or more wrong.

Several years ago I attended three conferences relating to this topic. The first was at Massachusetts Institute of Technology, and it dealt with the obligation of the scientific community for the environment. Attending were physical chemists, cosmographers, astrophysicists, physicists, agricultural experts, and others. The conference was characterized by carefully written, data-rich, and responsible papers on all aspects of the environment—its present state, its fragility, what must be done to preserve the ecological structure of our world.

At the end of the six-day meeting, a press conference was called, and a small committee that had been assigned to prepare a summary statement came to a remarkable conclusion. They said, in substance, "There is much that the scientific community can do, and much more that we propose to do about the care of the environment. But no conceivable enhancement of research methodology, no conceivable addition of public funds, no cries of warning will make any considerable difference unless we are all changed in the spirit of our minds."

I doubt if they knew they were quoting St. Paul in that last phrase, which is extremely important. We must not just change our minds. Minds are very fragile things; we change them almost daily. But they said something much more profound: we must be changed "in the spirit of our minds." With our minds we *look* at things, but in the spirit of our minds we *behold* things. The difference here is not only linguistic. To look at a thing is what the psychologists call an act of perception. To behold a thing means to regard it in its particularity—its infinite preciousness, irreplaceability, and beauty. This statement stimulated my thoughts on the problem of humanity and the natural world.

Then I went to another conference, one held at the University of Chicago and attended by teachers of the country's leading law schools. The topic was: "What is the role of public law in the care and protection of the environment?" The lawyers presented serious papers, but I read a news release at the end of it, and it was uncannily like the one from the conference of scientists. They said there is much that public law ought to do, and will do, for the environment. No conceivable operation of public law by itself, however, will provide any significant solution to human misuse of the earth. In addition, they pointed out, the role of public law is important, but its pace is very slow. For there to be a law there must first be information. Then a consensus must be forged; then a law must be pushed through to legislation, and whereas the degradation of our environment is proceeding at a gallop, public law advances at a crawl.

The third conference I attended was by no means as prestigious as the first two. It wasn't really a conference, in fact; it was a meeting of some clergy on the same topic. During the meeting, a well-respected clergyman uttered this particularly foolish statement: "This is my Father's world, this is God's world. And if God wants us to take care of the world in a certain way, and we don't do it, then God will certainly, in his way, look after things no matter what we do." I thought that a very strange reading of the doctrine of God and the doctrine of nature. It reminded me of some wonderful passages in the Old Testament: "And God gave them what they wanted and made them sick of it," or, "God led them home by way of the wilderness." The reprisals of God's creation against its abuse may be slow and invisible for generations, but God is just. Sooner or later nature reacts against its exploitation.

In my own Lutheran tradition, the development of our theology, our hymnody, our liturgical language, our ordinary preaching almost never intersects the problems of the natural world. Why is that? This is, indeed, my Father's world. We sing the hymn, but we do not preach the substance, nor do we get it very often in our prayers or our liturgy. Why is that? This question has bothered me for a long time.

Part 1: The Preacher as Theologian

I think the reasons Lutheran theology and piety are not known for any specific or any analytically delicate feeling for the problems of the environment are several. First, we use the Old Testament in our praises and in our liturgical actions with right gratitude, but we have quite sharply misunderstood the first chapter of Genesis. "And God blessed them, and God said to them, 'Be fruitful and multiply, and fill the earth and subdue it; and have dominion over the fish of the sea and over the birds of the air and over every living thing that moves upon the earth'" (Gen 1:28). The word *dominion* is a direct English effort to translate the Latin. In English *dominion* suggests *domination*, but that is an incorrect translation. The Hebrew statement is, rather, "And God said you are to exercise care over the earth and hold it in its proper place."

When one looks at that statement and considers the identity of the people to whom it was addressed, it makes considerable sense. The ancient Hebrews were surrounded by Canaanites who were nature worshipers, and God said to his chosen, "Nature is God's, but it is not God. Nature is not to be worshiped, but it is my gift, and you are to exercise care for my gift. You are to hold it in its proper place, and its proper place is very high."

In that same chapter is a discussion of the Garden of Eden. There is the root of the fact that when men and women want to express something that is the very profundity of their spirits, they reach for an analogy from nature: "Now is the winter of our discontent/Made glorious summer by this sun of York," or, "My love is like a red rose." Why do I have to use the language of nature to serve the expanded understanding of my personhood? Because my personhood is of nature, natural but inspirited by the breath of the Creator. We have not taken enough account of the nature images in the Bible.

The second reason our Lutheran understanding of this matter is inadequate is the perverse side of one of our greatest virtues: our radical christocentrism. That is, our theology is almost exclusively a theology of the Second Article. "I believe in God the Father Almighty, maker of heaven and earth" (Article One). "And in Jesus Christ, His only Son, our Lord" (Article Two). "And in the Holy Spirit, the Lord and giver of life" (Article Three). These three are ways of speaking of the activity and reality of one God. But we Lutherans have had a compulsive fascination with the Second Article. Jesus Christ, and him crucified, is the heart of Luther's, and hence our, theology.

Unbridled Grace

In the sixteenth century fundamental tilts and accents and statements of our theological tradition were given classical formation. In that century's Reformation, what was needed as over against the human authoritarianism, the sacramentalism, the sacerdotalism, and the monasticism of the church was a radical christocentric doctrine. And Luther was tactically right in putting forth the idea, "Unless I be shown that this is the gospel of Christ, I buy nothing else."

Luther was tactically quite right, and he was biblically quite right. But to be right at a certain moment is not necessarily to be completely adequate for all time. Luther is not always utterly adequate to every situation.

It is important that we understand our christocentrism at the point, as it were, at which God become historically present, radiant, incandescent, available for our knowing and historical reality. This is the doctrine of God in Christ. God was in Christ reconciling the world unto himself—but it is always God, God, God, in all three persons.

Against this background we must understand the doctrine of grace. Each person in the Holy Trinity points to and accents the reality and the activity of the one God. So we cannot say love belongs to God and grace belongs to Jesus.

We talk about the Old Testament in the same way. We often talk as if the God of the Old Testament were a God of law only; but then we go right ahead in our liturgy and use the Psalms, which have a magnificent rhetoric of grace. In sermons we keep on talking about the Old Testament being all law, but God is always a God of grace. The Hebrew word translated *charis* or grace in the New Testament is *hesed* or *hen*, and these two Hebrew words can only be translated to mean that one lives under a God of grace. David knew that and died in that faith. Abraham knew it, as St. Paul and the letter to the Hebrews both testify.

The manger child was the incarnation of grace, not the inventor or the origin of grace. Thus, if grace characterizes the whole of Christian theology—God the Father, God the Son, and God the Holy Spirit—what does this mean for our understanding of the natural world?

Christian motivation comes out of discipleship: understanding the will and the purpose of God. This reluctant literature that some of the denominations are issuing on stewardship is not wrong, but it isn't very exciting either. What we need is to relate back to the first point: the change in the spirit of our minds must come about by putting the grace of

God behind the eyes with which we look at the world and into the hands with which we touch the world.

And of course God's grace inheres in nature too. The early church fathers of the third and fourth centuries used two wonderful phrases that have almost fallen out of contemporary theology. They talked about "special grace" and "common grace." By "special grace" they meant that historical, incomparable appearance of the grace of God in Jesus Christ. But Augustine said that we were all born into the world of "common grace." *Common* does not mean low or moderate; it means available to everyone. By common grace the early church thinkers meant the grace into which everyone is born.

Before one is baptized, or even if one never is, such grace meets one in God's creation. There is a common grace in the pear tree that blooms and blushes. There is common grace in the sea (that massive cleanliness which we are proceeding to corrupt), in the fact that there was, before we laid hands on it, clean air. Our task is to appreciate that grace.

God's creations in the world are his voice, appealing to you and to me not only to join all people of good will in doing what intelligent things we ought to do about the creation, but one thing especially: to love the world and care for it to the glory of God.

The land is against large-scale changes. Nature is what it is in its ecologically intricate structure because of the long time in which small modifications have occurred and were absorbed into the whole. Recently I was talking with an Iowa farmer about the way intensive land use has changed from what we knew in our youth. Farmers then had a grassy corner of the field where they turned their horses and their plows, and later their tractors, around. My farmer friend recalled that his father taught him to call these unplowed margins "God's frame around the picture."

Now farmers plow right up to the edged of the fence or the ditch. As a result, what we used to call hedgerows—bushes or wild growth around the fields—have been destroyed in large part. This means that the cover for birds is taken away. And birds eat insects; they have them for breakfast, lunch, and dinner.

We have destroyed a situation of natural predation upon insects, and therefore we have to add more things to the land, the plants, and the air to control the insects. Nature is like a fine piece of cloth: you pull a thread here, and it vibrates throughout the whole fabric.

A working, joyful relation to the land has spirited, health-giving power. Around 1684 an old Puritan preacher, William Davenport, said in a famous sermon, "We have been dispatched by God and by history on an errand into the wilderness to create, on this land, a city on a hill, a light in the wilderness to all men." This is a marvelous statement about the promise and hope of the first people who came to this country. They came to this fabulous continent for a fresh opportunity. In some ways the American achievements have been great: we have exercised the American characteristics of goodness of heart, hard work, ingenuity, and cooperative adventurousness. Many good things have come out of the American experience, but we have paid a high price for them in the way we have assaulted the land. Our errand into the wilderness has tempted us to forget the message we were sent to deliver.

five

Ethos and Ministry

A theology for preaching involves not only what to do, the engagement of the Word with the context of culture and experience, and how to do it, the consideration of method, but also an ethos in which this vocation is grounded. Although Sittler did not speak explicitly about an ethos for the preacher, much of what he says in setting forth his theology for preaching amounts to just that. The two essays that follow are good illustrations.

Maceration of the Minister

1959

This well-known article admonishes preachers to avoid letting themselves get "chopped up" by largely superficial demands of parish and church. Instead it is important to be true to the preacher's vocation by maintaining a life of continual reflection and theological growth. The illustrations are dated but the message seems perennial.

THIS LECTURE IS NOT continuous with the preceding ones. It is related to them, however, because I have been aware in the preparation—with a clarity amounting to a sense of guilt—that urgings toward the kind of study and reflection presupposed for preaching to our situation have a bright and bitter sound to many who have done me the courtesy to listen. Bright because what I have called attention to is acknowledged as necessary for obedient preaching; bitter because the church, which might be expected to encourage and protect the minister in his cultivation of these conditions, does nothing of the sort.

What I have to say in this lecture might well come under an epigram applied to the Korean War: the wrong war against the wrong enemy at the wrong place! The situation I propose to describe is already and painfully well known to the clergy, and if a lecture to them has only an intramural value they are perhaps comforted in their pain by the knowledge that others know of it. It is nevertheless said here on the purely tactical ground that someone ought to speak up against what I call the maceration of the minister. He ought to do so with plain, reportorial force, and he ought to do it not as a psychologist, internist, or time-study expert—but as a churchman within the context of a convocation traditionally concerned with the practical well-being of the churches.

I have sought for a less violent term to designate what I behold, and maceration was the only one sufficiently accurate. Among the meanings of the term listed in the dictionary is this grim one: *to chop up into small pieces.* That this is happening to thousands of ministers does not have to be argued or established; it needs only to be violently stated. His time, his focused sense of vocation, his vision of his central task, his mental life, and his contemplative acreage—they are all under the chopper. Observation leads me to conclude, too, that this fact is general. The man who looks back thirty years to his ordination is in no better circumstance than the man who looks back three years. The man who is minister in an established parish and surrounded with a staff has substantially the same complaint as the mission minister with his self-propelled mimeograph. Nor does the church body in which the man is a minister, or the distinction or obscurity of the school which awarded him his bachelor's degree in divinity, make any perceivable difference.

The Niebuhr-Williams-Gustafson study[1] of several years ago makes it unnecessary to dilate upon this first point. Because these men are members of theological faculties their observations were related with particular force to the responsibilities of theological educators. They therefore

---

1. H. Richard Niebuhr, *The Purpose of the Church and Its Ministry* (New York: Harper, 1956).

made quietly and with becoming academic restraint a point that I want to make noisily.

What the schools elevate the actual practice of the ministry flattens. The schools urge to competence in the various fields of theological study. The canons of competence that determine the churches' practice are not only strange to what the schools supply and encourage, they are radically destructive of their precedence and nurture. There is something positively sardonic in a quick jump from a remembered student in a remembered classroom to the same man in his parish. I have done many such jumps and the effect is disheartening. In the classroom he was told that the *basilica tou Theu*, for instance, is a phrase of enormous scope and depth, and that his declaration of it should be informed by such studies as we could expose him to in class. It was further urged that such study ought persist throughout life. His teachers were concerned that he not become so insensible as to make such easy identifications with the kingdom of God as characterize the promotional theological literature of our burgeoning churches.

Visit the man some years later in what the man still calls inexactly his study and one is more than likely to find him accompanied by the same volumes he took with him from his student room. And filed on top of even these are mementos of what he is presently concerned with: a roll of blueprints, a file of negotiations between the parish, the bank, and the board of missions, samples of asphalt tile, and a plumber's estimate.

When one wonders what holds the man together, enables him to bring equal enthusiasm to his practical decisions and his pastoral and proclamatory function, one learns that he is held together (if he is) by his public role of responsibility for the external advancement of the congregation. The terms in which this advancement are commonly assessed seep backward and downward to transform his interior relation to his studies. Those studies become less and less an occupation engaged in or intrinsic to his role as witness to the gospel and pastor to people, and become more and more frantic efforts to find biblical, or theological, generalities which will religiously dignify his promotional purposes. The will of God has got to be simplified into a push for the parish house. The Holy Spirit is reduced to a holy resource which can be used as a punch line for the enforcement of parish purposes. The theme of Christian obedience must be stripped of its judging ambiguities and forthwith used as a lever to secure commitment which is somehow necessarily correlated with observable services to the current and clamant program. The message, in

Ethos and Ministry

short, is managed in terms of its instrumental usefulness for immediate goals. "Arise, and let us go hence" becomes a text so epigrammatically apt that it were a shame to lose it by the complication of context or exegesis.

Where are the originating places of this process, and what forms does it take? There are, I think, three that are so obvious and constant that they can be named and described. But even these are to be recognized as functions of a force that is pervasive, and underlies them all. This basic force is a loss of the sense of the particularity of the church, the consequent transformation of the role of the minister into that of a "religious leader," and the still consequent shift whereby the ministry is regarded as a "profession" and theological education has come to understand its task as "professional education." Had this shift in meanings not occurred the three specific forces I am about to name could hardly have been effective. But the shift *has* occurred—and the minister *is* macerated by pressures emanating from the parish, the general church bodies, and the "self-image of the minister."

The Parish: The very vocabulary that has become common is eloquent. The parish has a "plant," its nature or purpose is specified in terms of a "program" for which a "staff" is responsible to a "board." The "program" is evaluated in terms of palpable production which can be totaled with the same hard-boiled facticity as characterizes a merchandising operation—and commonly is. The minister, like it or not, is the executive officer. I know of a synod of a church body which, wishing to put the matter of financial support of the "program" of the church on a less obviously allocated basis than characterizes the property tax office of the municipality, came up with a "fresh" idea: each should give as the lord had prospered him—the synod called it the "grace system"!

This systemization of the holy betrays, if nothing worse, a peculiar atrophy of a Protestant sense of humor. Our theology of stewardship is pragmatically translated into terms and operational devices which deny the theology we affirm. The path to such practices is easily discernible. After a generation or two in which paid quartets, in the better-heeled parishes, praised God weekly as surrogates for the congregation, and professional organizations raised the money for "plant expansion" (all, of course, with a well-oiled unction that would have glazed the eyeballs of St. Paul) it is not surprising that the counsel to stewardship should be preceded, according to some church programs, by an inquisitorial scrutiny of the share of each of the sheep in the gross national product. The reply, of course, is that it works. There can be no doubt that it does. The same reply, however, if made normative for the truth of the entire nature and scope of the meaning of the church would indicate that the theology of prayer ought to take account of the reported correlation between petition and the growth-rate of potted plants.

The Christian community always walks close to the edge of superstition, magic, and the strange human desire to translate grace into nature by a direct and forthright program. There is a relation between an immeasurable gift of grace and the responding gifts of man to advance the institutional celebration of the gospel of grace. But it is the task of theology, as it ought to be a concern of planned parish preaching and instruction, to witness to this grace in such a way as to raise Christian eyebrows over every perverting proposal to mechanize it.

There is no evidence that policy preserves against perversion. A church in a surplice is as easily seduced as a church in a black robe, or one with neither of these. That the "business of America is business" has bequeathed to us all a vocabulary, a point of view, canons of evaluation that are so deeply rooted in our parishes that perhaps nothing short of a Kierkegaardian attack upon Christendom will suffice for renovation.

The General Church Bodies: What characterizes the mind of the parish is but amplified, solidified, and given enhanced authority in the larger world of the general bodies. Some years ago it became apparent to some large corporations that they had succeeded so well in fashioning the company man into symmetrical functionaries of an order that a danger was recognized. A few eccentrics were deliberately sought out, cherished, protected, and asked to give themselves to reflection uninhibited by charts.

Such sardonic maturity has not yet arisen within the churches. The fantastic rigidity, the almost awesome addiction to "channels," the specialization of concern and operation that characterize our structure have made us, in large part, prisoners of accredited mediocrity. "The wind bloweth where it listeth," but when it does a shudder of embarrassment racks the structure from top to bottom. If another J. S. Bach should occur in my church and succeed, as the first one did, in giving a new deep piety a new and adequate voice, he would have to plead his case before elected or appointed arbiters whose authority exceeds that of the consistory of Cöthen or Leipzig—and whose general cultivation is less.

The informing and edifying of the church through charismatic endowments by the Holy Spirit is not incompatible with the doctrine of one, holy, catholic, and apostolic church. But it is incompatible with the church

Ethos and Ministry

order that takes its model from the more banal children of this world. We affirm the charismatic in piety and imprison it in established structures in practice. It has actually come to pass that our churches maintain a disciplined cadre of inspirational operators. These persons are on call for whatever program the church from time to time decides to accent. They can blow any horn one hands them. If the program involves support for educational institutions they stand ready to declare across the broad reaches of the land in districts, conferences, and parishes that "the future of the church hangs upon the success of this venture in education." And when at the next general convention the scene shifts to rural missions, the same enthusiasm, now supplied with a changed terminology and directed toward a changed goal, is sent out on the road from general headquarters. One has heard this interchangeable vivacity vocalize so many and such various projects that he is reminded that the salesman is a category that can be defined quite independent of the produce he sells. Whether his sample case contains hammer handles or lingerie is nothing to the point.

Self-Image of the Minister: The transformation of the minister's self-image is the third force contributing to the maceration of the minister. The effects of this at the deepest levels of the man's personal life can hardly be spoken of in terms that are too grave. For this image is, strictly, not a professional or merely personal or even church-official image. It is rather an image given with the office of the ministry in and by a church in obedience to the command of the Lord of the gospel. The "Ministry of the Word and Sacraments" belongs to no man; all believers belong to it. And among these some are acknowledged as having been given a charisma, undergone preparation, and announced their intention to serve the gospel in this particular ministry. In the full gravity of this gift, task, and intention a man is ordained to this ministry, charged in specific terms drawn from the dominical imperative faithfully to fulfill it. The self-image of the minister is then more than a self-image; it is an image of the vocation and task of the self gathered up into a gift and a task that was before the self came to be, having a reality that transcends while it involves the whole self, and which will be bestowed upon the church by her Lord when this particular self is no longer of the church in history.

Fragmentation has become a common term in psychology and sociology. But what has happened to the ministry is all that term suggests and reports, but more painful and accusatory because of the gravity of that public bestowing and receiving of the Lord's Ministry of Word and

Sacrament. A vase can be fragmented; maceration is what a human being feels when fragmented.

It is hard for the minister to maintain a clear vision of who he is when he is so seldom doing what he ought. His self-image of a servant of the gospel has been slowly clarified, carefully matured, informed, and sensitized during years of preparation. At the time of ordination the church publicly and thankfully acknowledged a gift, a discipline, and a man's intention to assume a task.

All of this is under constant attrition in the present form of the churches. And thus it comes about that honesty in the fulfillment of the minister's central task is gradually laid aside in favor of sincerity. Sincerity is a term a man uses to enable himself to live with himself when he has uneasy questions about his honesty. There remain, however, deep down but insistent, voices and remembrances that tell the man what is going on, tell him that the exchange is not a good one. And the enthusiastic readiness of parish and church to accept, even to applaud, the shift makes the suffering of the minister the more acute.

There have been a number of studies, some widely publicized, in which attention has been called to the large number of crackups of various degrees of severity among the clergy. The supporting testimony is impressive. The reasons most often suggested are too much work, too long a day, too various a complex of problems and duties, too unremitting a drain on emotional and mental stores, insufficient opportunity to lift the clerical nose from the parish grindstone.

While these facts are present and powerful, the sum of them does not, I think, get to the heart of the matter. They are too obvious, too shallow; they do not designate what comes out—stumbling, embarrassed, and often gestured rather than stated—when one observes and listens with attention. From many hours spent with many former students I have learned that there is a constant fact in the variety of their confessions, overt or oblique.

These men are deeply disturbed because they have a sense of vocational guilt. This guilt is so strong, so clear, and so deeply sunk in their central self-consciousness that one knows with an immediate impatience that no diminution of hours or other rearrangements of outer life can have decisive effect.

This sense of guilt has an observable content. A minister has been ordained to an Office; he too often ends up running an office. He was solemnly ordained to the ministry in Christ's church. Most of the men I know really want to be what they intended and prepared for. Instead they have ended up in a kind of dizzy occupational oscillation. They are aware of the truth of what Karl Barth said in one of his earliest addresses, "Our people expect us to take them more seriously than they take themselves, and they will not thank us if we do not do so." Most ministers are aware that it is a tough and delicate labor to insert the lively power of the Word of God into the rushing occupations and silent monologues of men. They recall with a sense of joy the occasions when honest work and unhurried reflection gave a strange victory to their efforts. But these occasions are infrequent, set amid great stretches of guilt-begetting busyness.

What, then, is to be done? From each of the designated constituents of the problem a different response is required. These are the professors in schools of theology, the parishes, the officials in the general bodies, the ministers themselves. Upon professors in the schools of theology there rests an immediate and pressing responsibility. Our clear perception of the demolition wrought upon our labors with students, combined with the respect accorded us by our churches, urges us out of silence and toward articulate protest. We ought to be more courageous, critical, and noisy advocates for our students, more concerned protectors of their reflective future. Our intramural grousing has now the obligation to leap over the wall and seek to make itself heard among parishes and in the offices of church officialdom. For it is there that the machinery of maceration and the pounding of program is set in motion.

It is, I think, simply not true that the parish demands of its minister that he become simply an executive officer of multiple activities. It is likely to accept, support, and be deepeningly molded by the understanding of office and calling which is projected by its minister's actual behavior. It will come to assess as central what he, in his actual performance of his ministry and use of his time, makes central. And when this tightening and clarification of the minister's conception of his office discloses, in the reflective depth and penetration and ordering skill of the sermon, where his heart and mind are centered, the parish will honor this pastoral obedience to "take them more seriously than they take themselves."

The officialdom of the church, and how it may be penetrated by a knowledge of the plight of the minister, presents a more difficult—because more subtle—problem. When one beholds the staff-generated devices dreamed up by boards and commissions to focus the attention of the church-in-convention assembled upon their particular programs, one wonders if the motivation is exclusively either educational or evangelical. Have these members of promotional staffs not fallen under the sovereignty of Parkinson's Law, whereby whatever *is* tends to persist, whatever *does* is driven by dynamics strange to its purpose to do more and wider and bigger? Must not each "program" outshout the other in order to dramatize an urgency psychologically necessary for its own sense of importance, if not priority?

One does not have to operate at the top level of the ecumenical movement to suspect that the "nontheological factors" there exposed as powerful in church and theological history are operative along the whole front. It is no ingratitude toward my own family in Christendom that I take delight in the fact that there are about one hundred million of us! And the dynamics of this delight will not bear too much scrutiny in terms of the truth of the gospel, the obedience to Christ, and other such properly elevated rubrics.

We may and perhaps ought to be impatient about the world's quip that when a man becomes a bishop he will never thereafter eat a bad meal, read a good book, or hear the truth. But from within the family we dare a smile. For in the very generality that determines executive office there is a power that disengages from the common table of parish existence, from the direct and pathetic book of the common life, and from the moments of sudden truth that stun and depress and exalt the minister on his ordinary round.

Finally there is the minister himself; and in what follows I appeal to him from the same center as has informed these lectures on preaching. He, in his private and imperiled existence, must fight for wholeness and depth and against erosion. By a sheer effort of violent will he must seek to become his calling, submit himself to be shaped in his life from the center outward. He need not be slapped into uncorrelated fragments of function; he need not become a weary and unstructured functionary of a vague, busy moralism; he need not see the visions and energies and focused loyalty of his calling run, shallowly like spilled water, down a multitude of slopes.

Certain practical, immediate, and quite possible steps can be taken. The temptation to improvised, catch-as-catch-can preaching, for instance, can be beaten back by calculated ordering of one's study. The most profitable period in my own parish preaching came about because I did that. What I learned in seminary about Paul of Tarsus, Paul's Christology and ethics, was not sufficient either for the great subject or for the discharge of my preaching responsibility. In one memorable year I determined to bring together concentrated study and actual preaching. Surrounding myself with the best available to me from modern Pauline scholarship I literally lived with this man for six months, directed and taught by Adolph Deissman, James Stewart, Charles Harold Dodd, Robert Henry Lightfoot, J. H. Michael, and others.

Because the Philippian letter is the most direct, personal, and uncomplicated of Paul's letters I resolved to preach straight through it, informing and correcting exegesis from the Greek text by the findings and insights of historians, exegetes and theologians.

The result of this study and preaching—extending from Epiphany through Trinity Sunday—was the establishing of a love affair with this towering and impassioned "man in Christ." I came to know him with the quick and perceptive delight one has in a friend. Paul had been fused into an adoring, obedient, proclaiming, and explicating totality by the fire of his new relation to God in "this Son of God who loves me . . ." And the informing of all the parts of his writing by that rooted and vivacious new being in Christ, when beheld in concentrated study, opens huge new perspectives in every single verse or section. It is not necessary to add that such an exciting discipline makes quite unnecessary the weekly scrounging for a "text."

It was a sort of added dividend that when Holy Week and Easter came around, progress through the letter had landed me precisely at Philippians 2:1–11: "And being found in human form he humbled himself and became obedient unto death, even death on a cross. Therefore God has highly exalted him . . ." That section, explicated on Maundy Thursday, Good Friday, and Easter, had gained a momentum from the twelve preceding sermons on chapters 1 and 2 that was both powerful and full for the preacher and for the people.

The foregoing is an illustration; it is not a prescription. Each man must order his life from the inside, and each must order it according to the requirements of interest, nature, and parish situation. But order it he must.

The Stewardship of the Mystery

This essay continues the theme of the previous selection that preachers need to be faithful in their calling to be reflective and theologically alert. He goes on, then, to suggest that staying theologically alive also involves appreciation and nurture of the ministry of the laity and their witness to the faith.

THE PRINCIPAL WORK OF the ordained ministry is reflection: cultivation of one's penetration into the depth of the Word so that the witness shall be poignant and strong. Clergy have a particular responsibility to the discipline of the reflective life. But they are often negligent in this obligation. It's a terrible temptation to have one's life chopped up by what they tend to call administration, and the temptation must be resisted mightily so as to allow time for the real work of the job.

The contemporary church makes such demands on the minister that the poor individual must sometimes fight for his or her life. Those demands are for a series of virtues and activities that, compressed into one person, constitute an impossibility. One difficulty is in the area of education. If one is going to remain decently familiar with what is needed as a young professional scholar (I don't mean a research scholar), one must be like a good doctor. Most doctors don't do research, but they read the journals that keep them abreast of the research going on.

Most pastors will not do biblical or theological research, nor are they expected to. But most of them don't do what a good doctor does: subscribe to journals, take time to read, engage in programs of study whereby they keep abreast of information necessary to be professionally decent.

Sometimes when I go to a 25th anniversary of an ordination, or a church anniversary, I spend a few hours with the pastor in his or her study. I often see there the Levitical rule books that the student took away upon seminary graduation 25 years ago. But I see no evidence on the coffee table that the literature the pastor attends to is other than the most general reading of the American family. I find this very depressing.

A good teacher teaches her heart out trying to educate people about the excitement of biblical study or archaeology, for example, and then she finds that her students stash it all away and go out and preach sermons that are rich in piety and oversimplification—and the people love it.

At a conference of pastors, I sat for two and a half days with a colleague at my side who presented some beautiful, clear, and fresh New Testament studies; he was a complete master of contemporary New Testament scholarship. I was to follow with a theological reflection. We worked very hard.

But while I was at breakfast, lunch, and dinner with these 120-some pastors, never did the conversation turn to what the two of us had been talking about. My colleague was introducing some astounding insights, and I was not exactly unexcited either. But here these pastors sat at meals three times a day and talked about how the walleyes were biting and they were going to have to get a new outboard and their old boat was bad; they would have to put a new roof on their cottage, and the building program at the church was $10,000 behind schedule. Not a blasted word for two and a half days about the topic of that conference.

If I were to attend a professional meeting of gastroenterologists, I'd expect doctors to be there to learn what is going on in that field. At that pastors' conference, the pastors should have been interested in new developments in their professional field.

On the whole I find many pastors dull and soggy in the brain—and I do not apologize for that statement. Ministers are often dull functionaries. Ordination was their intellectual stopping place.

Part 1: The Preacher as Theologian

I was once asked to preach an ordination sermon for a favorite student. As I prepared, I wanted to avoid all past ways of talking about ordination, because many of them I thought were clichés, worn so thin by frequent usage that they slid through the mind like a gelatinous substance on a floor without a rug. I kept looking at the formula for ordination and thinking, "What in keeping the question going is the particular, non-sharable, absolutely specific job of this person? Why are we ordaining him to something that is not the same as being a faithful, baptized child of God in Christ's church? What's he got that the rest of us haven't got?"

My questions led me further to ask what actually constitutes the church. It is constituted by two things that do not come out of history, society, human religion, philosophical reflection on ultimate issues, or any human desire or intention. Those two things are Word and sacrament: the gospel as it is transmitted, and the gospel as it is celebrated in the dominical sacraments of the Lord's Supper and baptism.

The ordained ones—priests, pastors or ministers—also cannot be other than that which constitutes the church. Therefore I arrived at this conclusion: the ordained ones are the tellers of that story without which the church was not, is not, and cannot continue. They are those who tell the story of those events, promises, and mighty deeds of God that constitute the church.

But cannot others tell the story? The church must keep its story going and assure that there will never be a time or place where the sacraments commanded by Christ are nor proffered. Therefore the church insists on preparing a designated cadre to see to it that the constitutive story is told, and that the nurturing sacraments are administered.

This is a way of defining the ordained pastorate of the church that does not elevate it above the laity, but gives it a particular job among the people of God.

The notion that everybody has an equal right to authority on all matters is wrong—plain irrational. If I go to graduate school for three years, my judgment on relevant matters should be given a certain weight. My views need not always prevail, but they must be heard. That's my job. I do not have the same right to write a prescription for my dog's bellyache that the animal doctor has, and I can't tell the man who comes in to fix

Ethos and Ministry

the fireplace how to do it. But I don't think that's any denigration of the people of God.

There are varieties of gifts; and the ordained one is supposed to have been chosen by the church, or at least certified by the church, as having a set of gifts, and he or she must exercise these, while at the same time realizing their limits.

For reasons of good order, an ordained minister presides at the Eucharist. But we must not make a theological principle out of a provision for good order. My father, trained in the Joint (Lutheran) Synod of Ohio, began his ministry on the West Coast. He got to the lumber camps only once every three months. A couple of the congregations wanted the sacrament every Sunday, so old Mike Royce administered it. He was a lumberjack. On the frontier we were theologically very direct about some things; and then later we invented all kinds of ways to excuse what would actually be appropriate.

I come to the topic of ministry of the laity out of a genetically sound background. My father, a minister, had dignity; but my mother had the imagination in the family. I remember that she squirmed under the class structure in that old synod: there the laity were clearly the ground troops, and the clergy were the generals.

In the town where I grew up, my mother had great troubles with this. I remember that the district president, a particularly pompous man, came to preach at a conference. It was my turn to babysit (we had a large family) so my mother could go to church. When she returned I asked, "What did he say?"

She replied, "Nothing—for 30 minutes."

I also recall that when my older brother became a physician and began to practice in Chicago, he invited Mother to come and visit him. He thought he would shock this woman from a little town in Ohio by taking her to a big city show. So they went to the famous road show, the Ziegfeld Follies. On the stage was a great 12-foot frame like a book, and as the door opened, the scantily clad ladies came out one by one—to the apparent delight of the audience. My brother thought that my mother would be taken aback by all this. But she was completely unflappable, taking it in stride, and said, "Thank you very much. I enjoyed the show."

Then next spring when the children of the parish school in father's congregation had a program, Mother had the local carpenter build a big book, and out of the open book proceeded the little girls, each dressed like one of the women of the Bible. Now with the benefit of this imagination that could go from the Ziegfeld Follies to the Old Testament without batting an eyelash, I had a good early introduction to the ministry of the laity.

What does it mean that not only in the Lutheran church in the United States, but in various other bodies including the Roman Catholic Church, Christians are reinvestigating, reassessing, the meaning of the laity? What is the meaning of the rousing new life that is back of this topic emerging everywhere and with great energy?

First, we must consider the general world liberation movement that includes minority people as well as women. There is something happening in the twentieth century that is, as it were, the broad theater within which the phenomenon we're talking about is but one theological or ecclesiastical aspect.

A sociologist friend of mine was musing about this one night when we were having dinner. He said, "I think the deepest meaning of the twentieth century is that the baseline of the human is being enormously broadened." Think of humanity as a pyramidal structure. The baseline at the bottom of the pyramid is reaching upward. People in any culture we know about have always been ordered with very few at the top and then a layer down a few more, and so on. The baseline of billions had very little to do with what was going on at the top.

But what has happened in the twentieth century is that the baseline of the human is swelling economically, politically demographically, religious, intellectually. We tend to look at this general liberation as being an indubitable good, and there is a sense in which I think this is true.

But the clear justice of a more general participation in the events and decisions that constitute our lives does not automatically deliver at the top. Twenty million Iranians may be just as wrong as one ayatollah. The American voting population may regard issues with such banality as to end up in the same situation as if one person, a banal leader, made all the decisions. Liberation, as such, does not automatically mean that everyone will be wiser, more prudent, more responsible. It simply means that our stupidity, as well as our prudence, will be distributed among more people.

Ethos and Ministry

All of this is relevant to the ministry of the laity; for that theater is not simply an ecclesiastical box or a theological item, though it is that. But it is happening within a general context in which more and more people are joining this ever-striving baseline of human participation in running their own lives.

In think this means that for the foreseeable political future, another 100 years at least, we're going to have troubled times in the world. You cannot convulsively tear down and then slowly recreate more and more humane forms of human existence. You cannot do that without passing through a time of troubles. But what our late unlamented vice-president, Spiro Agnew, with great unconscious irony, used to call "the decay of our moral fiber" may be the confusion that accompanies all great creative moments in history.

In any case, the theater of our reflections must be broadened beyond simply ecclesiastical concern. My own background in this context is, of course, Lutheran. We Lutherans are not absolutely peculiar human beings, though sometimes some of us act that way. But there is something peculiarly to be perceived and specified about looking at the ministry of the laity from a Lutheran focus.

The Lutheran perspective can contribute to avoiding two pathetic blunders that are characterizing the discussion of the issue in many parts of Christendom. First is that the word *ministry* is an absolutely unqualifiable term. That is, if we say every baptized person is a minister in Christ's church, we are right. But if we become uncritically indiscriminating about that asseveration, we may refuse to recognize forms of ministry within the generalized gift; our demands of ministry will then be unrealistic. There are church bodies in which the word *ministry* is being used in such a way, with such breadth and enthusiasm, that it is almost impossible, without seeming gauche or unspiritual, to introduce any reflective efforts of definition to the various forms of ministry.

Certainly it is imperative to stress the ministry of the laity. As Gustaf Aulen points out in *The Faith of the Christian Church*, from about A.D. 900 to 1200, a legalistic and wooden theory of atonement was being taught in the schools and written in the theological texts. But all the time this thing was being elaborated from the formation of the church, the good people out in front were still singing the vital doctrine of the atonement that is characteristic of the Gospel of Mark: that a strong man enters the prison in which pathetic human life is held by the demons and cracks open the door and brings them out. Aulen notes, "The bishops and the theologians were saying one thing from the front of the church, and the good old laity were singing, 'Christ lag in Todesbanden.'" All of us in our churches rejoice in the fact that the laity are being admitted to all levels of discussion and are invited to all levels of participation in the life of the church. But sometimes we do that on a "professional basis." That is, the lawyers, the business people, the analytical people, the sociologists, the economists, the eggheads among the laity are being brought into the discussion of the church because we need their expertise. Then we rejoice in the liberation of the laity. But we are very selective about which laity we admit—and this is wrong.

Selfhood is not simply finding out and clarifying all the potentialities of the self as individual. There is no selfhood that is not at the same time a self existing in the grid of all selves. I have no self by myself—or for myself. I really have no identity that I can specify except the intersection point of a multitude of things that are not mine. They have been given to me. They are vitalities in history, in human life, and these all intersect at a point which is myself. And yet I know that that self is so richly intersected by others, not only those whom I meet personally but those whom I meet vicariously in the worlds of history and literature, that my self is only a point at which I acknowledge my own presence in the midst of so many things that are transindividual—more than myself.

Such a notion of identity is always in danger of a fateful reduction. I think of the notion of selfhood when I hear my students in their senior year talk about where they would like to exercise their ministry, and I hear them say that what they want most of all is self-fulfillment. There's something rather ghastly about that. I am not ordained to fulfill my precious self. One student had a list of things her first call had to have: it had to be in an urban setting; it had to be with certain kinds of Chicanos, blacks, and poor whites; it had to be in a cultural setting where she could enjoy theater and other activities. I said, "You know, it's as if the Bible says, 'Listen, Lord, thy servant speaketh,' instead of, 'Speak Lord, thy servant heareth.' The church is going to dump you someplace that may have little to do with your agenda. And it will offer the kind of challenge, humiliation, embarrassment, and opportunity that you didn't foresee." Our obedience in ministry cannot be calibrated with an agenda of clamant desires.

I think how in my own life my preaching has changed in the some 55 years I have been at it. Now when I preach, I no longer proclaim: "This is the Word of God and you'd better believe it. The church teaches it; therefore, get with it." In the first place, that tennis ball bounces right back at you. The Word of God has a thundering authority of its own. It must reveal its own reality; it must testify of itself. I cannot hold people to believe on my authority, or the authority of the church. I've got to preach in such a way that the messages of the text—the energies of the reality of God—are disclosed in episode, parable, miracle story, and so on. They've got to do their work by their own intrinsic force, by the truth that they reveal.

PART 2

Preaching the Word

Introduction

Joseph Sittler and the Preacher's Calling[1*]

WE PROPOSE THAT MUCH of what we can glean from Sittler's reflections on preaching are as relevant today for the preacher's calling as they were when first written or uttered. To that end the four sections that follow seek to map that contribution. In truth such sectioning is simply an organizing device for sorting thoughts that are actually woven together in a seamless vision of what proclaiming the gospel of Jesus Christ is all about, a blend of theology *of* preaching and theology *to be* preached. What he has left us is fitting for one who said after becoming a professor that he had ". . . never been able to have an immediate and lively sense of vocation save in relation to the church and its teaching and preaching obedience."[2]

Context and Content

Sittler is famous for his work with environmental concerns and ecology, but he could also speak "ecologically" of the preaching task as deeply and interactively embedded in the context of our concrete reality. In his book *The Ecology of Faith*, spawned by his Lyman Beecher Lectures on preaching at Yale, Sittler begins with an analogy from the ecology of nature. He

---

1. An earlier version of this article appear in *Trinity Seminary Review* 30/1 (Winter/Spring 2009) 31–40.
2. Joseph Sittler, *The Ecology of Faith* (Philadelphia: Muhlenberg, 1961) 11.

takes us to an imaginary river bank to observe for a moment the vital cycle of interdependence among beetles, birds, and trees and the damage that results when the cycle is broken. He goes on:

> Every situation in which the Word of God is declared in preaching is a place and a moment on the riverbank; and the permeability of that time and place to the declared Word is bound up with the forests, the birds, the beetles, and the waters of history. From Incarnation to culture is a straight line, for the determination of God to embody his ultimate Word places man's relation to that Word inextricably in the web of historical circumstances. The Word is not naked, it is historically embodied. The hearing situation is not naked either, and the culture is the name for that ecological matrix in which the embodied will and deed from above addresses the embodied hearer at every point along history's river.[3]

The preacher, standing on this riverbank, engaged in the ecology of faith, is also described as one who lives between two worlds of history's river: the world of tradition and its christological witness, and the world of constant newness that begs for an understanding and expression of continuity with that past as it comes alive in the present.

> The preacher in a special posture stands between the "It is finished" and the tremendous word of the Apostle, "The whole creation waits with eager longing." Every Christian is indeed called to fill up what remains of the sufferings of Christ; it is the Christological anguish of the preacher that he must *speak* of it!— speak it from behind, forward into the actuality of the day and the situation that now is. To be a preacher is not only to know eschatology as a report and an agenda item in systematic theology; he is, in the anguish of his task, the *eschatological man*.[4]

The anguish of preachers as they stand between two worlds, seeking to meet the urgent demand to connect faith's content with life's context, is not only anguish over a daunting task. For Sittler it is also a matter of the preacher's formation. The anguish of Christology, the anguish of preaching, arises when we recognize that repeating the formulas of the past, while still true, are no substitute for communicating in depth and clarity their meaning for today. That there is anguish points to the dimension of formation. There is anguish because the preacher is every bit as much

---

3. Ibid., 4–5.
4. Joseph Sittler, *The Anguish of Preaching* (Philadelphia: Fortress, 1966) 33.

in need as the hearer; she is "always restless and the mind always asking what the disclosure and concretion of the holy in the event of Jesus Christ means for life in the world."[5] Such a demand is shaping also because it leads preachers more deeply into their wrestling with their own doubts and struggles, even as their own doubts and struggles are a school for the task of discerning the connection of content and context. Thus, Sittler laments the prospect of those well-prepared theological students who aspire to preach but have no experience of faith's anguish in their own lives and therefore little prospect of that very real anguish of preaching.[6]

In the ecology of faith the dialectical interaction of faith and culture is both the ground of anxiety and doubt and the fertile soil of new awakenings; it is the common world of the preacher and the listener. In a video interview under the heading of "Spirituality"[7] but ranging far and wide—as was typical, given his fertile mind—Sittler recalled a conversation with a little girl in his University of Chicago neighborhood with whom he frequently talked as they both walked to their respective schools. One morning the little girl was carrying a new book. Sittler inquired as to what it was and she said, "It's my geography book..." Having liked geography as kid, he asked if he could look at it. He remembered his own childhood text as having a picture on the cover of a McCormick Reaper at work in the fields. However, this little girl's book cover showed a telescopic photo of the Milky Way. In the age of space and the ever-expanding scientific discoveries and theories concerning the makeup of the universe and our place in it, Sittler took this incident to be a kind of parable for our changing world and the need, he insisted, for theologians and preachers to expand the horizons of our understanding and communication of the Word accordingly. Expand them to match the scope of the Creed!

The age-old science-theology dialogue has resumed with vigor in recent years after what has seemed a hiatus during which theology was preoccupied with cultural issues of gender, ethnic diversity, and the impact of social location. These contextual realities continue to be engaged and that is certainly needful. However, the concerns of the environment and the expanding knowledge and impact of the scientific study of the universe are also exerting pressure on the Christian witness in ways that

---

5. Ibid., 34.

6. Ibid.

7. The video recording, "Spirituality Explored," is available online on the Sittler archives website, www.josephsittler.org.

go beyond the battles of earlier times. Rather than leaving it to the province of the specialists, Sittler saw the urgency of these matters for day-to-day Christian witness before most. He may well be still ahead of the curve when it comes to integrating the health of nature and the challenges of science into the context of Christian preaching.[8]

We are left to find our own way. He did not leave us a detailed map but he did leave us with a salutary ultimatum that we cannot dwell only in the past. We have a responsibility to know our world and respond to it in the present and in anticipation of the future. Lamenting preachers with lazy minds in this regard, he announced in one of his memorable phrases, "You can't do a cerebral bypass."

Of course, not all responses to the culture involve grappling with new ideas and worldviews. Sometimes the anguish of preaching involves delicate confrontations with long-lived sentiments of popular religious culture that threaten to obscure the real Christian message. And what could be more daunting than to address our inherited notions of heaven and eternal life? In fact Sittler was faced with the need to do just that, and the story he told of that encounter is instructive.

As a parish pastor, Sittler was called upon to minister to a devastated Mrs. Svenson at the death of her husband. She expressed her hope that they would be together again in heaven and asked if there she would again see him come through the front gate toward their cottage, knocking the ashes out of his pipe and asking what was for dinner. Sittler said nothing to disabuse her of this comforting image. But the experience also prompted a general pastoral-theological concern that we should not be casting God's future for us in terms of the desires and enjoyments of the present life as though eternal life was everything we like here, only more of it and without the problems. For Sittler such thinking smacked of egocentricity and unseemly concern for one's own "precious" identity. The search for one's identity and worth was at the time Sittler spoke and still is today a somewhat unhealthy preoccupation with self.

---

8. In his 1972 lectures on nature and grace Sittler gained much from his contact with Eastern Orthodox theologians through his work with them in the World Council of Churches Commission on Faith and Order. Sittler sought in these essays to overcome the Western dualism between nature and grace and to see, with the help of the Eastern tradition, God's grace permeating the whole of creation rather than being restricted simply to personal salvation. This expanded vision of the scope of God's grace meant that faith active in love engendered by grace is concerned with all things. Jospeph Sittler, *Essays on Nature and Grace* (Philadelphia: Fortress, 1972).

Part 2: Preaching the Word

This was really not the way of Mrs. Svenson in her tender expression of hope. Her hopes were grounded in a loving relationship, not concern for self-fulfillment. Indeed, he goes on to speak of her great faith and humility. Nonetheless, her comments opened a window to culturally fed projections onto God's promises. Thus, he recounted that he waited a while and then preached several sermons on various passages on eternal life in which he tried to disabuse people of the idea that eternal life would be best understood as a place without bills and other worries. In the end, he concludes that we cannot say much about the nature of eternal life except that, "if we live we are the Lord's, if we die we are the Lord's; therefore living or dying we are the Lord's." Therein is our identity; not what we are or aspire to be in earthly terms. And that, said Sittler, was the only sermon he felt he needed to preach on that subject.[9] Many if not most people of faith find comfort in earthbound imaginings about loved ones who have entered the church triumphant. It is natural to do so. However, Sittler reminds us that the preacher as theologian is responsible to proclaim the gracious promise of the Word, the crucified and risen Christ, that we may give ourselves over to trust in that promise as our all sufficient hope.

A Matter of Style

A notion of which Sittler was quite fond was the idea of "style." When it comes to preaching this was not, as one might suppose, a dissertation on preaching style, rhetoric, delivery, or the like. Rather, style for Sittler was an orientation to life that good leaders have, a gracious way of being in the face of life's demands, a matter of character. In this regard Sittler was much impressed by a paragraph on style written by the nuclear physicist Robert Oppenheimer in a 1948 speech entitled "The Open Mind." Several quotes from that text help us understand what Sittler appreciated about this conception of style and what he would have us appreciate as well. Oppenheimer wrote, "It is style which complements affirmation and limitation with humility. . . . It is style which makes it possible for us to act effectively but not absolutely." To be in ministry as a leader who must face uncertain tests of resolve requires that one act with responsible courage while yet recognizing fully that we do not possess divine omniscience and even have the ability to laugh at ourselves. That is "style." The thought

---

9. Joseph Sittler, *Running with the Hounds*. (Valparaiso, IN: Center for the Study of Campus Ministry, 1977) 111–20.

is then completed by Oppenheimer's next sentence: "It is above all style through which power defers to reason." "Reason" here is the ability to take the larger view and temper one's power in deference to the greater good.[10]

Perhaps style for Luther would have come down to his advice to Melanchthon, in the latter's struggle with a decision, that he should "sin boldly yet more boldly still believe." Recognizing the ambiguities and uncertainties Christian conscience faces in many of life's significant decisions, we nonetheless have been set free to decide, not with arrogant certitude but with the assurance of God's favor. In any case, this character of "style" in Sittler's thought also fits well with his orientation to the Christian life marked by the demand of the law and the abiding assurance of grace,

> To have to live under the absolute demand is the only way, given man's power of dissimulation and self-deception, to keep life taut with need, open to God's power, under judgment by his justice, indeterminately dependent upon his love, forgiveness, and grace.[11]

Style not only grounds the ethos of the preacher and orients her to her task; it begets a spirituality that prepares one for theological engagement with two deep-seated and presumptuous cultural impulses that Sittler discussed and that are clearly inimical to the character of style.

The first of these cultural impulses Sittler called the "tyranny of the self." Though he associated this problem with the existentialism that was at that time in full flower, his description of this trait takes it beyond the bounds of that philosophical referent into the realm of a fundamental and perduring human characteristic. This sort of self-centeredness finds expression in people's tendency to filter all data of faith and life through self-preoccupations. The result is a first-rate problem for theology and preaching. People in a state of self-absorption are closed to voices of that "cloud of witnesses" that is the church of all ages.[12] Thus, Sittler laments:

> Preaching becomes primarily personal; the history of the church becomes an anecdotal arsenal useful for its supply of supportive items. The "mighty deeds of God" are transformed into such interior "patterns of sensibility" as are readily marketable, and

---

10. Ibid., 102–7.

11. Joseph Sittler, *The Structure of Christian Ethics* (Louisville: Westminster John Knox, 1998) 55.

12. *The Ecology of Faith*, 12–14.

> the mighty TE DEUM of the people of God becomes trivialized into a "worship experience."[13]

Elsewhere in his writings, Sittler offers this acerbic companion thought:

> We are tempted to regard God primarily as a God for solitude and privacy and only secondarily as a God for society. We have a God for my personal ache and hurt, but no God for the problems of human life in the great world.[14]

The second "tyranny" is that of "boundlessness." Here Sittler traces the American spirit of the ever-expanding frontier. For Americans historically there is little sense of limits; there is always more. Though it does not come up in this particular discussion, it is worth noting along the way that this belief in the boundlessness of resources, opportunities, and economic growth, which still pulses in our societal bloodstream, is directly contradicted by the ecological realities that Sittler brought to the center of the theological stage. In this particular lecture, however, Sittler's sharp point is that the outlook of boundlessness is one that does not correlate well with the realities of biblical eschatology that reveal humanity's true limits. Moreover, he maintained, the realities of limit and boundary toward which eschatology points us ". . . have not deeply entered into the American national consciousness."[15] Nonetheless, Sittler evinced a cautious hope that the emergent scholarship of interpreting the meaning of history in terms of biblical and theological categories might heighten awareness of the eschatological that he sensed might be entering the American mind. It is the preacher's task to take the fruits of this scholarship and bring them into dialogue with the culture.[16] I dare say that this charge remains as vital for preachers today as it did nearly five decades ago when Sittler first gave it. This is especially so at a time like this, when the realities of our limits are being tested by lingering wars, economic woes, and a threatened environment. Once again, Sittler's insights prove durable.[17]

---

13. Ibid., 14.

14. Joseph Sittler, *Gravity and Grace: Reflections and Provocations*, ed. Linda-Marie Delloff (Minneapolis: Augsburg, 1986) 35.

15. *The Ecology of Faith*, 24.

16. Ibid., 25.

17. As I researched this article and came upon Sittler's tyrannies of self and boundlessness, I was struck by the close correlation between these and the key observation I made in my book *Greed: Ethics and Economics in Conflict* (Minneapolis: Fortress, 2000). There I argued that two deep-seated traits of our culture, the priority given

Introduction

Spirituality for the Preacher's Calling

"Spirituality" is certainly a word to be conjured with. It can mean many things and be used to many purposes among people of faith. For some it refers quite simply to prayer life and devotional disciplines that form the substance and practice of their spirituality. For others it is a piety of faith deep in emotional experience and/or devotion to the moral life that sometimes challenges the intellectual pursuits of theology as too much of a "head trip," inimical to true spirituality. Readers can fill in other possibilities from their own reflections on the subject.

If I interpret Sittler correctly from the bits and pieces of various sources, I believe that "spirituality" refers primarily to the way in which the habits of the Christian faith, nurtured in gospel by the Spirit, are continually engaged with all facets of life and the world. It is a keen sense that the entire world is God's world and its ultimate meaning and destiny is revealed in the Christ for our contemplation, service, and joy. In an interview entitled "Spirituality Explored,"[18] Sittler spoke, implicitly to pastors, of the need to keep growing. This involves intersecting with "real people" as they reveal the many truths of human existence, both through their knowledge and their needs. But it also means that preachers should stay alive in literature about Scripture, church history, and the general culture. Literature, the arts, and poetry, which Sittler continually called upon and encouraged others to do likewise, provide aesthetic windows to both the noble and ignoble in human nature and the wonders of nature itself.

Clearly for Sittler intellectual pursuits were not in conflict with spirituality but, rather, an integral part of the spiritual journey of the faithful. He would have the preacher captivated by the astounding intricacy of our world and with requisite curiosity about what things mean. He continually admonished pastors to stay abreast and gave himself as an example, as one who goes to his "betters" so that he can "walk better." So, for example, in biblical study they should take a page from him by going to the serious scholars and not be content with simplistic "Bible helps." Scripture is never an open book but "an ever opening book."[19]

---

individual freedom and belief in limitlessness, in combination foster the phenomenon of greed and its acceptance.

18. "Spirituality Explored."
19. Ibid.

Part 2: Preaching the Word

The Golden Thread

The golden thread that ties together all the aspects of context, content, ethos, and spirituality that we have explored in Sittler on the vocation of the preacher is his ever present theology of the cross and the spirituality that goes with it.

The theologian of the cross is always deeply and intentionally contextual, planted in the same earthly ground as was the cross itself. As we have seen, Sittler was keen to see preaching that would take people out of their inner world of self-concern into the wider world. Theology and preaching must confront the realities of that wider world with the pain of want and injustice and indeed the pain of the very earth itself. This is the arena of God's grace revealed in Jesus Christ, the place where we are and the place where God is. Sittler sought intimate contact with reality through profound reflection on the experiences of life and the pulses of nature. He sought it in the burgeoning products of the sciences. He sought it in the arts, literature, and poetry as pathways to the truth of what is.

Notwithstanding his gift for profound thought and his insatiable love of learning, Sittler also taught that the theologian of the cross approaches the vocation of theology and preaching with the humility of one who knows and feels the deep need of the very gospel she is called to proclaim. This orientation of the faith permeates Sittler's whole approach to his own sense of call. It is a spirituality implicit in everything we have sampled so far concerning theology and preaching. It finds an echo in Sittler's reflections on ethics:

> Only the absolute demand [of God] can sensitize man to occasions for ethical work, and energize him toward even relative achievements. And only such a demand can deliver man, in these achievements, from complacency and pride; prevent him from making an identification of the justice of man and the justice of God.[20]

The absolute character of divine demand liberates us from the grip of prideful pretense and turns us to the grace of God in Christ, wherein lies our hope and strength for the Christian life and ethic. Sittler's understanding of the Christian life and ethic, as revealed in the preceding quote, was a clear development of Luther's theology of the cross with which he identified early in his career. In his 1948 Knubel-Miller Lectures, Sittler

20. Sittler, *Structure of Christian Ethics*, 56.

had the following to say concerning Luther's contrast of the *theologia crucis* with Rome's *theologia gloriae*:

> [Luther] meant by this distinction that his theology is a serving theology; it never claims fully to explicate, much less to deliver its holy content. It is a theology of the cross and it shares in the ignominy of the cross.[21]

The preacher who is a true theologian of the cross cannot help but rightly divide law and gospel and, what is more important, cannot fail to preach the gospel in every sermon. Few of us can aspire to Joe Sittler's well-remembered eloquence of speech, but we can all embrace his theological legacy for our preaching and be renewed by it as we discover in him what is best in us.

James M. Childs Jr.

---

21. Joseph Sittler, *The Doctrine of the Word in the Structure of Lutheran Theology* (Philadelphia: Board of Publication of the United Lutheran Church in America, 1948) 64–65.

six

The Word of God

Bible and External Authority

1983

The occasion for this address was the onset of the Lutheran Church in America's Search Bible Study *curriculum for congregational use. For Sittler entering upon a major Bible study initiative in our time inevitably raised the question of biblical authority. In our era preachers cannot count on the Bible being received as the unquestioned inspired and inerrant authority. Rather, the preacher needs to let the innate power of the biblical language and message, with its capacity to intersect with the deepest of human needs, establish the Bible's authority in the minds and hearts of the hearers. To do so is to respect Scripture's self-authenticating power.*

THERE WAS A TIME when I enjoyed the kind of success and clarity when I talked and I prided myself on moving from one to two to three with clear and certain steps. Inasmuch as I can't write any more, I have to depend on thinking and these thoughts are not always as organized in my mind as for your sake I should like them to be. The way I must now operate is like a barnyard chicken picking up pieces here and there as it cackles around the yard. So I will try to pick up certain notions which were sparked in my mind by those who spoke yesterday.

First of all, I've been reflecting about the kind of barriers, swamps, bogs, walls which stand in the way of a successful advancement of this Bible study program. I think that unless we take the measure of the difficulties that stand before us, as we try to invite people to engage the words of the Bible in the midst of our present culture, we are liable to be disenchanted, disappointed, and finally discouraged. Therefore I think it's right that we should openly uncover the problems that all biblical communication has in our present culture and, having looked them in the eye, make a clear resolution that we intend to confront them and also reflect upon the best way to do it.

So I want to put together a cluster of things which I think are important to have in mind and take the measure of as we engage in this thing. First of all is the problem of authority. Let me first admit with you that the Bible no longer has an automatic, revered, venerated authority simply because it is the Bible. There was a time when the biblical counsels, episodes, stories, and admonitions had a kind of instantaneous and autonomous force because they were in a venerated, traditional book. That time, for millions of people—I would suggest for almost the whole of our culture—has disappeared. If the authority of the biblical word is no longer traditionally and generally accepted, or if the authority of the biblical word is not any longer enthralled in commanding institutions like the church, but is rather free-wheeling, then the kind of authority we have to appeal to is intrinsically different. The authority of the passages, words, books that we're going to read and study with our people is internal not external and automatic. The authority of the language of the Bible has to depend upon its internal congruity with human pathos; the pathos of the human condition, the reality of what it means to be human beings in this appalling time. This kind of pathos, confusion, ambiguity, and scatteredness of life is the situation to which we must address the biblical word. And that word will be invested with authority by virtue of its liberating, enlightening, and promising congruity, not by virtue of what we hear in the Sunday morning evangelist's sermons—"the Bible says." "The Bible says," for most people, is no more internally authoritative than what the *Washington Post* says or the *Milwaukee Journal* or my neighbor. The Bible's authority must be uncovered as intrinsic.

There's a beautiful phrase in one of the Old Testament passages from Isaiah in which the Lord says to the prophet, "Lay it to the heart of

Jerusalem." The figure is so beautiful. It is a phrase that in its tenderness effectively appeals to the innermost being of the people. The Word gains its authority and its force because it has an intrinsic power.

Now, I would like to illustrate this "intrinsic" authority of the Bible in another way. Some years ago I was at a conference in New Orleans and the place we met was a convent, which, by virtue of shrinking membership, had been turned in large part over to a conference center. On our way from our rooms to the place where we met each day we passed a little chapel where about ten or twelve sisters were meeting at all the appointed hours of the day for prayers. As I looked into that chapel on my way up from breakfast at 9:00, I saw them in there, the twelve sisters with bowed heads, rapt in complete contemplation, looking up against the bare-wall back of the altar on which was a great, gaunt figure of the cross. And the thought struck me then: Has any particular form, any arithmetical or geometric shape, for so long, so profoundly, invoked the emotion and the reflections of so many people? In all the history of the world, has there ever been a shape like that, which, without words or without even a figure upon it, has somehow been the primal symbol of the human condition? Why has it been looked upon, beheld, [has] invoked prayer, inspired reflection, aroused guilt, promised hope, given comfort? Why that particular shape? At that time and ever since that time, that has been the kind of question for which I have no absolute answer, but suggest this: The ultimate word of God in the cross of our Lord has the power it has because the very shape of it is a formal re-enactment of the shape of my own existence. My own existence and yours has that shape. We are born, we unfold the capacities, the endowments, the promises, the hopes of life, and these enjoy a greater or lesser fulfillment, even approaching a consummation. The richness and plentitude of the world is open for our inquiry and discovery and our curiosity and our delight. This unfolding and burgeoning life does not unfold forever; there comes a time when the unfolding closes in on itself and we know death. Is it not true that the shape of our interior life is one of ambiguity? To every straight, vertical yes, life also crosses the negativity of no. To every promise without limitation, life carries intrinsically a limitation, a boundedness, a term. To every position there is a negation. Even in the most positive and beautiful endowments of life, the possibilities of human love, is it not true that even love is fractured by ambiguity? I shall never forget the wonderful statement of Gilbert Chesterton when he talked about the love which he bears for his wife. He said, "When I say I love my wife I really mean it, but

I also know upon reflection that a main reason for my love of my wife is her uncanny ability to reflect me back to myself at six times my normal size. So that what I love in my love, even my love, is an ambiguous love because under the figure of the love of another, I actualize my self-love. My egocentricity is also part of my fellowship."

There is a great hymn in the old common service book, which is the last one I could read: "O God I love thee not that my poor love would win me entrance to the heaven above; were there no heaven to seek nor hell to flee, for what thou art alone I must love thee." You see our love never comes that far. Even our love, even our generosity, even our self-giving to another, is also characterized by a kind of horizontal negation across the position, the positive, of love. This comes to a kind of terrifying clarity when we think about our own piety and devotion. In response to the Lord's command I say my prayers. And when I pray, I am happy that I am doing it. Then I reflect upon the happiness I feel, the purity and goodness I feel in being in an act of prayer, and I immediately begin to congratulate myself because I am doing it. And then I think, "That's not right." And then I think next, "That isn't right, but if I know it isn't right, then I am relieved in part from the guilt because I know it isn't right." The whole interior life goes round and round and round, with deepening ambiguities which are the burden of being human. Now this perception of the internal life in its limitations, in its ambiguity, in its drenchedness in egocentricity, this is the human situation. Therefore, that great sign of God, that condensation of the reality of God which is the Suffering One on the cross, has to come to me that way if he's going to be a God who really takes the measure of my heart. If God is going to be what we are in order that we might be reconciled with what God is, God has got to become nothing less than both the promise and the awesome ambiguity of our human life. Therefore, no wonder that for centuries ordinary people have sat in rapt attention and have known in the great figure of the cross that they have there beheld a kind of symbolic concentration and condensation of the reality to which we must speak when we aim to teach them the Scriptures.

So that's one thing we must be aware of. The second thing that occurs to me is that we live in a time of a diminished and a flattened-out language. The language of the Bible is so capacious, so opulent, so many-dimensioned, so rich in imagination that we've got somehow to almost create ears to hear it, because the ears of modernity have been flattened by what is happening to speech. Let me elaborate on that as well as I can.

The linguistic community, people who study the science and art of language, have pointed out over and over again that there are two main ways in which speech is used. Speech is used for information, for pointing out the actuality of this and that. That is designative speech. The other kind is evocative speech. Now let's make the distinction.

Designative language is language that articulates the actuality of measure, time, dimension, position—sheer information. If I say, "Shut the door," there is no ambiguity in that statement. It is a clear statement of something that is palpable and visible: that I want closed. That is the kind of speech which an age needs when its main concern is with the structure and the process of the natural world. That goes all the way from physics and chemistry to mathematics to engineering to research. The whole material world, in its structure and the process, looks to that wonderful day when it shall be mathematized or digitized. The digitalization of reality is engaged in finding a mathematical formula which shall reenact in abstract formulas the nature and the structure of steel or iron or hemoglobin or protein. That is the aim of scientific work: to try to bring the interior of things into such clear statement in mathematical terms that we have a shorthand for reality. I have an illustration for what this kind of speech is and why one is uncomfortable with it as the only kind of speech.

The first time I saw a digital watch I was annoyed. Why does an innocent thing like a digital watch make me feel uncomfortable? Why do I admire a thing? If I say, "It's beautiful," that's interesting, but I only learn something when I say, "How is that thing constituted in such a way that I say it is beautiful rather than ugly? Proper rather than inappropriate? Good rather than bad?" So I kept thinking, "Why do I not like that damn watch?" It didn't take much reflection to know why. Time is a very mysterious thing; we all lie drenched in passingness in time. The watch that has a hand that goes slowly around and marks the minutes of the hours and the hours of the day, and the smaller hand that follows it obediently in smaller segments—this is a kind of physical representation of the nature of time. But a watch that jumps from one second to another is a misrepresentation of the continuity. "Time like an ever-rolling stream," the old hymn says. The ever-rolling stream has flowage, continuity. A watch calls my attention to or celebrates that character of time. A digital watch is a misrepresentation of the deep and primitive wonder before the mystery of time. That's but another way of saying, or that's one sharp way of saying, that we must talk, speak about the language of the Scripture to an age whose style of language is deeply characterized by designative speech.

Part 2: Preaching the Word

For instance, when I have some problem and the doctor writes me a prescription, and I take this prescription to the pharmacist, I don't want him to be a poet. The script says that the doctor has said so many milligrams of this, so many milligrams of that. The pharmacist is to do exactly what the man says. He can measure it out. He is to use designative speech; he is to obey precisely precise instructions which point to material in measurable reality. That's designative speech. Computer courses, mathematics, physics, and chemistry—they move with heightened precision toward the achievement of that kind of symbolic or mathematical or quantitative speech; and we, living in a technical and scientific world, live in a world which is dominated by that kind of speech.

Now, there is another kind of speech that I would call "evocative speech," which uses a language that does not have the mathematized precision of designative speech but which has the strange power to cause us to remember, to cast our minds back to visions which we have shared with the speaker. It causes us in our imagination to come alive and, with a kind of pathos, join ourselves to that object to which the speech addresses itself. Let me give you a wonderful illustration of what I would call this kind of evocative speech.

I have a family of six children. Two of them are girls. When one of my children, a very golden-haired little girl, was small, I saw her one day before an open window in the summertime having her afternoon nap. As the breeze came through the window, the hair of the sleeping child was lifted a bit from her head—the breeze moved it. Now there's a kind of an image of a sleeping child that's compacted of many realities: innocence, affection, a kind of instantaneous candor that marks children, plus the beauty of little children. And I saw all that unconsciously; it didn't register in my conscious mind but I can still see that picture. There's a line in a poem by one of the masters of evocative speech, John Keats, in his "Ode to Autumn." Some of you remember from your high school or college days the lovely opening lines of it: "Season of mists and mellow fruitfulness, / Close friend of the conspiring sun."[1] On down in the poem the poet looks for an image of the earth in late October, when the tired fields are resting, when the green has turned an autumnal brown and all the earth is exhausted but beautiful and waiting for the long sleep of winter. The furrows on the brown fields are turned; the poet makes an image of that and talks about that time of year as a little child asleep upon a half-turned

---

1. The second line is, exactly, "Close bosom-friend of the maturing sun."

furrow. Then he has the haunting and magnificent line, "[Thy] hair soft-lifted by the winnowing wind." The very sound of the words, "[Thy] hair soft-lifted by the winnowing wind," is simply magical. It's no secret; the magic is not something heavenly. It's something born out of the poet's sure instinct for the language. "Lifted," "winnowing," "wind." The succession of the "i" sounds has almost the verbal equivalent of a physical movement. "[Thy] hair soft-lifted by the winnowing wind." The old image of my child sleeping by the open window is brought back, made alive, transmitted in memory by the magic of the neurons into present reality and reawakened affection.

Now that's the kind of language for which our generation, I sometimes fear, has almost lost an ear. Yet, without the recovery of that language, and our own appreciation as teachers of the power of that language, I think we are going to have a very difficult time transmitting the Scripture in its episodes, stories, and images. I also fear that we have to fight against something else that's happened in our time. I know I am an old duffer whose life was early and deeply impressed by the sounding sonorities of the old Bible. Hearing the Bible read in the public service of the church by my father as he read the lessons, I did not know then that I was hearing the language of the Bible translated from Hebrew and Greek as the very apex of the magnificence of our English language. That translation came from 1611 to 1615, and that was the day of the prime of Shakespeare and the full opulence of Elizabethan English. How fortunate we were to have the Bible translated at the very top of our linguistic magnificence!

Since that time many things have happened, and I am not mounting a campaign against translations of Scripture in ever more accurate speech. But I cannot but lament something that's happened whereby we have gained exactitude at the price of opulence. We have won in precision often at the cost of internal rhetorical beauty. The point of this is that, when you do teach, I think it would be good to have several translations before you so to bring the capaciousness of one tradition into connection with the higher exactitude of another. Then we get as full as language can get it; the fullness of the biblical reference.

Let me use several illustrations that bother me. I don't intend to change anything. I'm not foolish. I'm convinced that you cannot roll time back nor roll language back. But we can retain some things. On Christmas morning in my parish, or on Christmas Eve, I heard the traditional lesson from the second chapter of Luke and I felt annoyed by two things. The old collect for Christmas Eve, which comes from the Latin of about the fifth century, somehow has not been proper in the new book, and... has been changed. The old one said: "O God who has caused this most holy night to shine with the brightness of the true light." What makes that beautiful, mystical, evocative? "Bright," "light," "brightness of the true light"—all the "i" sounds. Now they're gone, with their crisp and evocative sound. We don't put it that way any longer. Then I heard the lesson begin. As I heard my father read it, it was, "And when the days were accomplished that she should be delivered..." But the pastor in my church was reading from a very modern translation, "And when the time came for Mary to have a baby..." That's not the same statement. Biologically it points to the same event; religiously it's not the same. And what's the difference? Can we specify? *Whether* I like it or not is not the point. *Why* don't I like the one and why do I love the other?—that's objective.

I love the one because it says that what is happening in this event is something that God is bringing about. God accomplishes it. "The days were accomplished" talks about an internal period of waiting for an event; the other is a flat gynecological statement. "The time came for Mary to have a baby." Well, she had a baby. But every father or mother—principally mother—knows you can't rush babies. It takes just so long: more or less nine lunar months. The baby makes up its mind when it intends to be born; we don't. You can push it one way or another, but not very much, and at your peril. "When the days were accomplished that she should be delivered..." has a quasi-mystical sense that God is accomplishing something, not just, "Mary had a baby."

We can go on with this to another illustration from the same section of the Bible which illustrates my point that we must attend to the power of evocative speech. In the Magnificat, is it the same statement when we say, "My soul magnifies the Lord," or when we say, "My soul doth magnify the Lord"? Now, I tried this on my students not long ago. They said, "No Difference, same statement"—objectively, the same statement. It reports that Mary's soul, in relationship to the Lord, stood in a magnifying relationship, to put it logically. But what's the difference between "My soul magnifies the Lord" and "My soul doth magnify the Lord?" The second is rich in intentionality: a focused, intended will. I could say my soul magnifies the Lord or my soul, according to Aristotle and Augustine, does many things. It imagines, it fancies, it thinks, it reflects; my soul magnifies the Lord among other things my soul does. But when the Old English said, "My soul doth magnify the Lord," it made the magnification of the Lord the central intentionality of this woman's life. It has a kind

The Word of God

of focused intentionality, will, and direction, which is very delicate stuff in language but carries an enormous weight. Well, I will go on with this recital with but one more illustration.

Last night when we did the old hymn—beloved of both Catholics and Protestants (it is a catholic hymn)—"Holy God, We Praise Thy Name," look at the march of images that mark that hymn: the adoration of God in eternity by the cherubim and the seraphim, the white-robed martyrs. What difference does it make to say "you" instead of "thou?" We somehow feel that we didn't lose anything. I suppose we feel that way; at least we did it. We act as if we did not lose anything when we use the same kind of language for God we use with one another. It is fundamental to our understanding of God that God is not one of us. God became one of us, but in God's self God is God and not human. The awesome, mystical, stunning difference between God and the creatures, the Creator of all things and we creaturely people, was once acknowledged and celebrated by the use of the formal address: "thee" and "thou" and "thine." I find it very difficult to pass into this "you" business because that's what I use about my wife, my children, myself, and my students. Why have we found it necessary to use informal language about God when before the Cubs play Montreal they sing, "O Canada we stand on guard for thee" and "My country, 'tis of thee"? Whenever we want to raise a thing to a certain level formal speech is an outward and visible sign of that elevation. When we put everything down to the plain level we do not destroy God—the reality of God—but I think we shoot ourselves in the linguistic foot, and make things more difficult for ourselves.

I want to pass on from that now. What I'm really trying to do is take the measure of certain problems that we face in this formidable project. The first, then, is the problem of authority. We must acknowledge that the authority of the Bible lies within its intrinsic interception, its abrupt meeting of life with a no or with a yes. I have another illustration for that. What is the difference between power and authority? Let that one cook a bit, and reflect upon it. There are exercises of power which are undoubtedly powerful. They do work; they secure results. But they have no authority. And there are exercises of authority which do their work without power. Let me be specific. Richard Nixon had the power of the presidency up to the moment he resigned. He had no authority following the disclosures of his role in the Watergate business. He had the power of the presidency but he had no authority. Abraham Lincoln never used, except in a few instances, the full power of the presidency, but he had

123

authority. He didn't have to use sheer power. Pius XII, the pope who preceded John XXIII, had and used the full power of the papacy, in papal encyclicals and in orders from the papacy, and they were obediently acceded to, but they were not inwardly honored. John XXIII never used the outer power of the papacy, but he had enormous authority.

What's the secret here, the difference between authority and power? It's an internal matter. One who speaks with authority is commonly one who, what he says or she says is continuous with the whole nature and performance of the person who says it. My grandmother had authority; my grandfather had power. I remember what my grandmother said, and I have no remembrance of anything my grandfather said except that I had to do it. But I wanted to do what my grandmother said. There is a secret here which must be honored. The Bible has authority, not just power. It has power too, and that's a great word in biblical speech, the power of God. But in a sense, would the power of God be an honored and not simply a malignant or stupid power were it not for the power with authority whereby he [the Christ] became the problems he had to confront? If he had not become our cross-life by taking upon himself a cross, he would not have the authority of the Holy One.

The next thing I want to get at: the teenage mafia, or a little older, the twenty-to-thirty-year-old young people who still clutter up my house. I often listen in to their speech. We have an apartment which is one of those long Chicago jobs with the kitchen clear in the back. When they are all back there gabbling away, I can be in my room and overhear them if I choose. I'm fascinated by certain phrases which this younger generation is using. It's really great to attend to how the chance phrases of this generation are disclosive of the interior character of their culture: their state of mind, their value system, the way they live, their lifestyle. The phrase I hear over and again I overheard the other night. My son was saying to another person, "What's happened to old Lisa? I don't hear anything about Lisa; she sorta disappeared." And another person sitting around the table eating up my groceries said, "O, Lisa, well, she was into ceramics for a while. Now she's into textiles and I think she's fussing around maybe going into something else." They're into this and into that, and into that. This rapid movement by which so many of the young move from this to this to this is a kind of pathetic probing for something to get into them. They had to get into this and that because nothing that is totally admirable has centrally grabbed them.

The Word of God

Let me go a little further with this. I've been thinking about this on those occasions when I've been asked to speak to college faculties particularly humanities faculty and I think it was at St. Olaf when I had a day and a half with the humanities people. I took a long shot partly to evoke their annoyance, and said the purpose of the college is to excite admiration. And I think that's pretty good. I think that if properly unfolded that has a good deal of sense in it. The purpose of a humanistic education is to supply and evoke admiration; to parade before young minds in history, sociology, the sciences, literature, art, that which stands before them as admirable. Dante, Shakespeare, Clark Maxwell, Albert Einstein, all the artists and scientists who have had vision, who organized a mysterious thing into an order, or seen beneath the surface of what looked to be disordered and random a law, a process, a theorem. To evoke admiration. That's very difficult to do because we live in a young world in which a typical phrase is, "well big deal." "Big deal." Let me go a little further with this. I've been thinking about this on those occasions when I've been asked to speak to college faculties, particularly humanities faculty, and I think it was at St. Olaf when I had a day and a half with the humanities people. I took a long shot, partly to evoke their annoyance, and said the purpose of the college is to excite admiration. And I think that's pretty good. I think that, if properly unfolded, that has a good deal of sense in it. The purpose of a humanistic education is to supply and evoke admiration; to parade before young minds—in history, sociology, the sciences, literature, art— that which stands before them as admirable: Dante, Shakespeare, Clark Maxwell, Albert Einstein, all the artists and scientists who have had vision, who organized a mysterious thing into an order, or seen beneath the surface of what looked to be disordered and random a law, a process, a theorem. To evoke admiration—that's very difficult to do because we live in a young world in which a typical phrase is, "Well, big deal." *Big deal.*

I find in my grandchildren nothing unqualifiedly admirable, absolutely good, pure admirable, to be completely admired. How poor my own life would be had I not, in the process of my own education, formal and otherwise, learned to admire beauty, goodness, greatness, perfection, accomplishment. But I find in my own children a kind of overlay. There's something not right. What's the catch? "Big deal." This overlay of irony, cynicism, has been mightily helped by the exercise of the office of the presidency in our lifetime. Those in high office have not honored the majesty of the task of government, so that Mr. Nixon did more to relativize my children's admirations than any communist in the world ever did.

The kind of worm within all the apples, as these are disclosed, does a great deal to create what I call the "spattered life": you're into this, you're into this, you're into this, because nothing is holy, elevated, admirable, and good. And it seems to me one of the great humane values of having religious faith is that it is an organizing center for the living of life. You don't have to be into this or into that or into that, because something has gotten so deeply into you that you are interiorly called toward the admiration of the absolute; a life which orders itself according to something wholly right, wholly good. I thought of this last fall when I was asked to preach on the festival of Christ the King. I preached a very simple kind of sermon, simply saying, "Reflect today upon that kingly man. Think of all the other people who have been great but purely creaturely—malleable, flawed, egocentric—although maybe admirable in their accomplishment. But here is the absolute one, the man who said, 'Not my will but Thine be done,' even to the point of, 'My God why hast thou forsaken me'—but still 'My God.' This is kingliness in its absolute sense."

There is a general religious bias toward a galloping subjectivity. We must not give a hoot about what we feel about a text at the beginning! You are to go into the realm of feeling and response and emotion, to be sure, but your first obligation to the text is to let it hang there in celestial objectivity. This is what the text says. And not begin with everybody making a kind of vegetable soup about their internal feelings and then dressing the text out as a kind of epigram to celebrate this objective. We must attend to the given statement of the text. And a good sermon, a good teaching job, must begin with this angelic objectivity.

There's something in the whole mood of our culture that hates that. We want to hurry up and get to, "What does it mean to you? How do you feel about this?" Well, there's not much danger that I am going to under-honor my subjectivity. I live with it, love it dearly, and I think it's great. I think it is so great that I tend to dip everything in it. This morning the leader of our worship read that passage of the encounter at Caesarea Philippi, and the thing that caused me to smile was when he said, "Peter gave the right answer and flunked the course." Peter answered the question properly: "You are the Christ, the son of the living God." Jesus then went on and said, "This one who you say that I am must suffer many things, and be crucified, be denied, and abandoned." And Peter said, "Oh no, hold it." Jesus' response to him is an almost ferocious response: "Get back of me, Satan." The man who had answered the question aright ends up the by being called of the devil. Well that gives us to think. What was it about Peter's answer that was right? What was right about it was what he said, but the text goes on to show that he wanted God to be God in Peter's way, not God's way. He wanted God to do the cross job without the cross. And that had to be put aside; that is of the devil.

The Word of God and Scripture

1979

Sittler addressed his comments on the relation of the Word of God and Scripture to an audience of pastors. Their context was the controversial discussion occurring among Lutherans with regard to the authority of the Bible. If some of his assertions seem familiar to us, it is because the conversation is a perennial one among Lutheran pastors and theologians. Sittler is at great pains to demonstrate the dynamic qualities of the Word of God; for before it was enshrined in a book the Word was a living act of proclamation. He deftly equates the biblicism of his opponents with the logical positivism of British philosophy, both of which leave little room for the Bible's generative view of language. For Sittler, who maintained a high view of the Bible's integrity, the larger issue was the preservation of the gospel and its freedom to transform the lives of those who hear it.

THE TOPIC "THE WORD of God and Scripture" is not meant to be a talk about two separate things, but about the relationship of two that are often conflated into one. I choose to talk about it for a reason which I want to say at the beginning because it is a very old subject in Lutheran theology, and this might need some explanation as to why a beat-up old theologian brings it forward after four hundred and some years of controversy and talks again about the relation of the doctrine of the Word of God and the doctrine of Scripture. I do it for practical reasons.

The Word of God

The reasons can be put dramatically this way: when a Christian body hangs the whole weight of its theological understanding of the church catholic on a single doctrine, then it had better be very sure that one is well screwed in and able to support the weight! We are a church, the Lutheran body, whose fundamental authority in every confession and in every doctrinal statement since the Confessions has begun with the authority of the Word of God. We are also a church that, in virtue of the strange theological method which has often dominated our thinking, has been invited to conflate these two magnitudes, the Word of God and Scripture, so that we are really saying the same thing in two phrases. To put it another way, a dogmatic theology has, in this country at least, has commonly conflated the two magnitudes so as to read, "the Word of God, that is, the Holy Scripture." Now I want to suggest to you—and this may be one of the reasons why Dr. [Franklin Clark] Fry thought I was truly for "export"—I want to suggest that this is a fundamental blunder. No matter what popularity it enjoys or how firmly we ourselves might have held it, I want to insist tonight that a right Lutheran theology of the Word will make a distinction, without a separation, between the concept of the Word of God and the concept and understanding of Holy Scripture. The second reason I want to do that now is not only that it important in itself but because, in our general Lutheran conversation, and indeed in the whole theological conversation everywhere, coming events indicate that we ought to be precise, exact, and clear about how we understand these two terms and their relationship to one another.

First of all, the anguish within the Lutheran Church—Missouri Synod has caused them to articulate with almost painful exactness the absolute identity between these two. They have not only articulated that, but they have suggested that that is normative for true Lutheranism. But unless you absolutely and without remainder can conflate the doctrine of Word and the doctrine of Scripture, you are dubiously Lutheran. I want *vehemently* to deny that and to insist that a more appropriate and comprehensive Lutheran understanding would make a distinction between the two, without a separation.

The second reason why I want to talk about this tonight, as if that were not enough, is that there is also a growing discussion between the American Lutheran Church, the Lutheran Church in America, and the AELC exploring, as it were, the possibilities of such doctrinal and polity agreements as might lead us to an eventual and—I fervently hope—not too distant consolidation of these church bodies. In order that things should be done rightly, I think it essential that all three of the partners to that discussion come to some clear understanding of how we understand the Word of God. In fact, it is constitutionally imperative that we do so because the present constitutions of the ALC and the LCA both refer to the Word of God and the Holy Scriptures in such a way as to leave the issue open to interpretations which are not those of an absolute identity. I know that they have it that way—that our document says to regard the Scriptures as the norm and so forth—but they never use the word "identity."

Now let's begin then with the understanding of the phrase "the Word of God." As you know, the phrase is a very ordinary one in the Old Testament. Certain illustrations are recollections in how the word is used: "the Word of the Lord came to . . ." By no stretch of the imagination can you identify the meaning of that phrase with a written word or a text or a word magically dropped from heaven. How you are to understand it is not specifically said, except that it has the quality of an absolute and undeniable imperative, under the action of which the prophets spoke as they did. So "the Word of the Lord" there is used to mean "it was made known" with imperative clarity; "This is the will of the Lord." All we read is this astonishing phrase, "by the Word of the Lord were the heavens made." This is a remarkable statement because this means that the Word of the Lord is not a phrase that begins in historical time. The Word of the Lord does not begin with the record of Genesis, with the record of these figures who are representative of humankind, Adam and Eve (in Hebrew, the mother of all the living). Therefore, the Word of the Lord is a pre-creation, as it were, a pre-creation-identification with the power of God by which all things have come into existence. When the phrase "by the Word of the Lord were the heavens made" occurs, "the heavens" in that context mean not just the sky, but it means everything that is under the heavens, in Hebrew. It is a total generic phrase, so that "the Word of the Lord" or "the Word of God" (the Hebrew word is *dabar YHWH*) is not a written or even a spoken statement, though it may eventuate in that. Fundamentally, this means the creative energy of God, whereby God goes out of himself to make his will, power, and work visible—radically known. So that the notion of the Word of God as the primally, basically, fundamentally something that the Lord speaks and a human hears, in such a way that it might be taken down if there were an audio system around—this is obviously not what the Old Testament teaches.

Interestingly, when you move from the Old Testament into the New Testament, particularly in the Fourth Gospel, when we read, "In the beginning was the Word," it seems to say the same as, "By the Word of the Lord were the heavens made." "The Word was with God," "Without this Word was nothing made that was made," and then, "The Word became flesh"—that which becomes something obviously postulates something prior to its having become! Therefore, when the Word becomes flesh, the Word which became flesh predates, pre-exists, that which proceeds from it. "The Word became flesh and dwelt among us, and we beheld His glory"—that word is interesting too. It throws light upon the New Testament understanding of the Word as the incarnate Word—or Jesus, the Lord, according to the first Christian confession.

The light it throws is something like this—something that Luther catches in his hymn "A Mighty Fortress" when he says, "The Word they still shall let remain, nor any thanks have for it." He does not say, "*It is* by our side upon the plain," but, "*He's* by our side," so that the Word of God by which all things are made, which is the dynamism of the creative power of God himself, becomes transparent, present, and reaches a focal point in Jesus. Therefore, the writer of the Fourth Gospel can say, "and we beheld his glory." Now, to see the dimensions that are there, one has again to look to the Hebrew to the word that is translated *doxa*, or "glory," in Greek. And the word in Hebrew is *kabod YHWH*, "the glory of God."

It's unhappy that so powerful a word, and a word full of such opulence in its variety of meanings, should become a current word in our American vocabulary, so that we use the word "glory" or "glorious" for so many things that it fails to designate anything. The kids say that they had a "glorious banana split" or they have a "glorious time" or the "glorious Fourth of July." "Glorious" is a word which points to the indubitable presence of the Holy One—"The glory of the Lord shall be revealed, and all flesh shall see the salvation of our God," or "Glory to God in the highest, and on earth peace, good will," and "The glory of the Lord shown upon them."

Let's look into the way that word "glory" doesn't mean just a general extravaganza (even of a holy or religious kind) but has a very specific meaning. The best way I can get past that in terms of Old Testament language is not by pushing into the language further but by an illustration. Some of you who have been in the Oriental Museum at the University of Chicago (or other museums where there are Oriental materials) have noticed the representations of the great kings of the Eastern Empire—Sumer, Babylon, Assyria. The old kings were often represented, apparently accurately, as always having a very full beard—often in a stylized curl, all the

Part 2: Preaching the Word

way down—a very full and formally formed beard. Also, we know from the recovered images found at Hierapolis, Persepolis, and other places that their faces are often covered with carmine and mascara—cosmetics. The kings apparently were heavily "cosmeticized." The reason for this, in the Oriental notion of kingship, is that the king's word was taken as absolute. The king ruled, according to a document from Sumer, "in virtue of his having been grasped by the glory." Now "the glory" there means an effulgence that goes out from God himself and lays hold of a particular person in whom the great God himself is re-presented. It was also part of the legend of the great king that the effulgence of God, when it came presented to the image of the visage of a man, was so brilliant that no person could look upon it and live. This notion comes out in the Old Testament too. Therefore the king had to mask the power of the glory with which his kingship was invested behind a full beard and with cosmetics smeared on his face. So this rather naive and childlike idea of the insulation of the ordinary people from the glory of the great king gets to the very root of this notion of glory. Glory means, "the shining out of, the glow that the holy imparts or gives off." "Therefore, we beheld His glory, full of grace and truth" (John 1:14).

Now we begin to see that the doctrine of the Word is fundamentally a statement made about God. It is about God in the sense that "the Word of God" means that power, dynamism, that full creative "force" (to use the Star Wars word), that lies in the creation itself, which comes to it via its Creator. That is the fundamental and primary meaning of "the Word of God."

Now when this Word of God has manifested itself through the episodes of a people's career, and they record these episodes, write this history, or tell of the prophets' words, we have a secondary meaning of "the Word of God," one that witnesses to the power, creative force, and imperative that comes forth from the Word. These witnesses to, or chronicles about, or records of the dynamism of the primal Word are also called "the Word of God"—and that is *Scripture*. So that when the Bible is called "the Word of God" we are using the term "Word of God" in a secondary but not illegitimate way. The Bible is the Word of God in that it bears witness to, is a record of, is an incomparable testimony of an irreplaceable generation that said, "We have seen, we have known, our hands have touched, and this we report."

When the primary notion of the Word of God controls our language about "the Word of God" in Scripture, we have the two notions

The Word of God

in the proper theological as well as temporal and chronological order. When we understand things that way, we are very close to that understanding of the Word which enabled Luther to say, "The Word they still shall let remain." His appeal to the Word as an absolute court gave him the courage, insight, and the exact argument with which he was able to speak of Christ's church in such a way as to free it from absolute control by the bureaucratized, sacramentalized, sacerdotalized church of the medieval period.

Another interesting sidelight on Luther and the Word of God: those of you who have read Jaroslav Pelikan's volume in *Luther's Works* on Luther as the expositor of Scripture know how remarkably contradictory Luther seems to have been; but it is only a seeming contradiction. When Luther is operating with Scripture as a scriptural scholar (and remember that his chair at Wittenberg was as Doctor of Sacred Scripture), he throws the written Word back into the teeth of his accusers. "The church called me to be a Doctor of Scripture, to tell the truth about Holy Scripture."

But Luther is teaching as an expositor of Holy Scripture; it is this primary understanding of the doctrine of the Word which controls his speech throughout. He talks about this *lebendige Wort*, the Living Word, to distinguish it from the secondary Word which is a perfectly legitimate, important, incomparable, and indispensable Word of God—that is, the Word as Scripture. But Luther's primary understanding is always that which comes forth from God in deed and act, in law and gospel, and command and, particularly, promise, whereby we dare to stand absolutely in trust under its control.

In his lectures on the Gospel of Matthew given in Wittenberg, Luther speaks of the discrepancies in the chronology of the Passion Week events in the Gospel. Luther says (apparently without a bit of self-consciousness), "Matthew is confused here." He believed that the Markan account was original (and critical studies indicate that he was probably quite right on this, because he had a fantastic sense of what we would call "redaction criticism"). Luther was never a literalist or a biblicist, but we sometimes are led to suppose that he was because (and here is the other part of Luther), when he got into a polemical controversy, or when he was confronted by one of his opponents who insisted "for how many hundreds of years has the church taught . . ." and quoted church fathers and papal decrees and piled up the evidence against Luther, he was perfectly capable of picking up the whole Bible and slamming it on the table, and saying, "It says here . . . !"

I come down on this with considerable force for several reasons. First of all, not only the Lutheran church, but all bodies in Christendom which take the task of teaching and preaching primarily from the Scripture, consider the interpretation of the Word to be a central task of our ordination. I suppose none of us has escaped attack by certain fundamentalist sects that with a highly uncritical and selective operation with the Bible accuse us of not being "rightly" under the understanding of the Word of God. I think the only way for us to create an offense on this point (using the word "offense" not in terms of manners, but in football talk) is not by trading prooftexts with fundamentalists; we have got to teach slowly and patiently the Word of God as I have described it and as our confessions understand it.

The second reason that I think this is important for our day will take a bit of time to unfold, but let me take the time. It's common to say that "the toothpaste cannot be squeezed back into the tube." The "toothpaste" of historical-critical studies, whatever damnations and lamentations are uttered over them, cannot be pushed backwards. As Ernst Troeltsch once said, "History must be overcome by history." You cannot erase it, you cannot annihilate it, and you cannot undo what has been done. For hundreds of years, since the Reformation in the era the Germans called *Aufklarung*, the historical-critical, linguistic, and archeological evidence has piled up with such a mountainous accumulation that there is no retreat from the use of historical-critical studies with every text that has been written.

This business of critical studies is not simply a biblical matter, but for 250 years German scholarship has been working on the Greek classics to try to get an ever-truer text of the great epics of Homer and the plays of Sophocles, Euripides, and others. So it isn't just the field of the Bible in which historical critical studies go on, but particularly since the Illumination these studies have grown in number, in the refinement of their methods, and in the gathering of historical contextual material—all of which throw an enormous illuminating light upon the Bible. The result has been that we now read the Bible not only as an incomparable witness, testimony, and record of the dealings of God the Creator, Redeemer, and Sanctifier with his community, but we also know the Bible to be a human document embedded in historical circumstances and determined by certain linguistic rules. This increase in knowledge serves to bring clarity to that which is received.

To understand historical-critical methods that way is a faithful response to Scripture. The word is now being used in some quarters as if it were a dirty word, used by dirty minds to defame God. That is very strange. Lutherans ought to be the last to accept that cavil because the greatest cadre of historical-critical studies of the Bible have come from our own community. After all, Bultmann, Käsemann, Conzelmann, Fuchs—these are not Irishmen, you know. The word "critical," as it is used in the scholarly world, does not designate an attack upon the truth of the text, but a responsible, detached effort to find out what the text is actually saying. It is to get at the truth—not to annihilate the truth—in order to bring forward the facts of the matter.

To illustrate: Not long ago a very good New Testament scholar pointed out that the chapter divisions in Paul's Corinthian correspondence have been arranged topically. . . . For example, chapter 7 begins, "It is good for a man not to touch a woman," and then he goes on to talk about family life and children and the special grace that pertains to the married state. It is a little hard to bring that off if you obey the first sentence! So what is going on here? First Corinthians is a long letter written in response to questions arising in the Christian community. "Now as to meat offered to idols," he begins in one section, as you recall, "it is my judgment that . . ." Again, he begins, "It is not good for a man to touch a woman." There are no quotation marks in the Greek language. It is very likely that among the questions submitted to him by the Corinthians—and remember, the Gnostics were a very active sect in Corinth—many had to do with sexual asceticism. They might have said to Paul, "Among us it is said it is good that a man not touch a woman . . ." Paul probably quotes the phrase and then continues his own line of thought, for the rest of the chapter, as I say, is utterly inconsistent with that phrase.

I think it is important for me to use that illustration because poor old Paul is having pretty bad press among the women, who tend to pick up certain things in his pastoral counsel which, in the social situation of first-century Rome, Corinth, or Ephesus, are quite understandable. Women may pick up those things and make them representative of a male chauvinist pig, which he was certainly not. Remember, before Paul no one in antiquity (not Plato, Anaximander, Homer, or Solon) had ever said, "As before God there is neither male nor female." Yet this same man is criticized for his comments about women. For example, he said that women are to keep their head covered. And why not? The advertisement of a prostitute in the cities of the empire was to go around with your head uncovered with your hair flying loose. "Let the women keep silent in church," he said—certainly not the everlasting dogma for the church through all generations, but an understandable pastoral word to closely watched communities in which no decent woman spoke in public. Paul is not laying down church dogma; he is laying down understandable pastoral counsel, after most of which he adds, "Now this is my opinion. I have no Word from God on this, but if you ask my judgment, it would seem good to me that . . ."

On that issue I want to say a final word and then open for discussion. (I need to sit down for two reasons: first, I am pooped, and the second reason is that you are more in the mood for discussion if you are not being lectured to from a podium.) The last point I want to make is that all along the intellectual and cultural front quite a new thing is happening: we are learning more and more of the subtlety of language. The disciplines of linguistics, rhetoric, and philology are burgeoning disciplines in our colleges and universities. A whole new generation is being trained *exactly away* from the position that twenty or thirty years ago was controlling the field. Then, the whole business of language was tilting radically in the direction of pure positivism, that is, the notion that any use of language which is not capable of empirical verification is nonsense. A. J. Ayer in his book *Logic Truth and Language* claimed that the phrase "God is love" is an emotive, subjective statement incapable of conveying meaning. It cannot have any empirically verifiable meaning because nothing could either prove that it is true or prove that it is not true. It is a purely affective statement—emotional in quality, made by a group already convinced that God is love. That was the point some time ago; that unless a sentence was completely denotative, it could not be said to have any meaning.

By "denotative" the logical positivist meant to say that the only sentences conveying meaning are those from which you can derive a verifiable action or by which you can predict action whose truth is certifiable. Here is an illustration of a purely denotative language: sulphadiazine is a compound constituted by this many parts of this, and many of that, and so on. That is an undeniably denotative statement because anyone who has the skills can do a chemical analysis and come up with the same compound whether he or she is in Bombay or Peoria. "It is thirty miles from this camp to Bucyrus" is another example of a verifiable statement. That can be verified by anyone who knows what a mile is and will measure the distance . . . Let me offer an illustration of the difference between a denotative and connotative statement. In Shakespeare's play *Richard the Second*, you remember, Richard is returning from Ireland, where he has been in exile in order to assume control over his divided kingdom. He finds that all the dukes, barons, and lords whom he had counted upon to come to his defense and help have been seduced from him by his rival Bolingbroke. When the full extent of the tragedy—the end of his kingship—becomes clear to him, he says, "For God's sake, let us sit upon the ground and tell sad stories of the death of kings." Now, what meaning is there in that? Logical positivists ask, "What is the point in sitting on the ground?" Anyone who knows the history of how depositions occur, by putting ashes and or dirt upon the head and body, knows this is an old ritual—even the prophets speak of it. Anyone who understands how throwing oneself onto the land symbolically represents the annihilation of power knows exactly what Shakespeare is getting at. He reaches back with marvelous poetic power and takes hold of the subliminal meaning of, "For God's sake, let us sit upon the ground and tell sad stories of the death of kings." Even a high school kid understands the pathos of that statement.

This is an illustration of the point that I am making. Let us not as Lutherans be tempted to climb back into the vault of verbal inspirationalism, literalism, or biblicism just at the time when the richness of biblical speech, with its non-denotative, trans-empirical power, is being rediscovered by the literary, poetic world.

To wind up my part of this hour, let me say that I have been a biblical-critical guy all my life, not in the sense that I have the skills to do it—which entail an unrighteous number of linguistic requirements—but I have been a child of my betters. In all my ministry I have tried to read the best biblical criticism, commentaries, and the best possible texts. I have found that their effect on me has not been that predicted by the fundamentalists, namely, that my faith has been ruined or that I no longer trust the Bible. To the contrary, my biblical understanding has been deepened regularly. My astonishments at the Bible's inexhaustible depth has grown every year of my life. My debt to Scripture is so great that I get fairly heated up when somebody says, "You cannot be both scholarly and faithful." That is a proposition to which the church must respond.

The Problems of New Testament Interpretation and the Task of the Preacher

1966

Here is encouragement for preachers vexed by the competing claims of scholarship. Here too is a salutary reminder that the anguish preachers may feel at the daunting task of faithful proclamation is a good sign of the true importance of the call. The complacent need not apply.

THIS SECOND ESSAY WILL be an effort to extend to a concrete problem the proposition stated in the first: that preaching is not an isolated act within the complex of duties that constitute the role of the pastor but rather arises out of the preacher's involvement with the entire existence of the Christian community in history. That community came into existence speaking, confessing, praising, reporting. The New Testament is a product of this activity. That community continues; it continues doing those same things. The preacher is an appointed voice of that community, an annunciatory spokesman of the events that created it. He speaks, to be sure, within and conditioned by the unrepeatable events of his generation, but these occasions are set in the longer story of this witnessing people through the centuries.

Disciplines correlative to preaching can be taught, but preaching as an act of witness cannot be taught. Biblical introduction, training in languages, methods of exegesis, cultural and other historical data that illuminate the texts of the Scriptures—these matters can be refined and transmitted in teaching. But preaching itself, the creative symbiosis

The Word of God

within which intersects numberless facts, experiences, insights, felt duties of pastoral obligation toward a specific congregation, the interior existence of the preacher himself, this particular man as he seeks for right utterance of an incommunicable and non-shareable quality of being and thought—this cannot be taught. It is, nevertheless, commanded—and not only by custom of the church.

In matters of the Christian faith everything bears upon everything. Separate disciplines are artificial although necessary designations of areas of special study. Because they require a competence that is exacting and long a-getting, such operational separations will have to be maintained. But let not the particularity of the operations blind us to the fusion of the data. For if we are so blinded we shall surely continue along the way already alluded to: a way characterized by the man whose multiple hands—exegetical, doctrinal, ethical—operate as if unaware of what other hands were clutching at and grappling with.

The progression of the present chapter is as follows: first, some reflection upon how to stand and listen and enrich thought in the midst of a veritable critical tornado which involves the very materials of proclamation, the biblical record itself; then second, such theological and humanistic counsel as I have found possible in the context of the present storm, in the hope that a taut serenity learned in one phase of incessant theological change may be tutorial to our minds and spirits in other phases that are sure to follow.

In his *Essay on Man* Ernst Cassirer speaks of the long effort in the course of Western culture whereby men have sought for an Ariadne's thread to bind all perspectives of world-reflection and world-engagement together.[1] One of the gifts that comes to us as we gain in knowledge of the history of Christian doctrine is a kind of smiling sophistication, rich in fascination but unscarred by cynicism, as we learn to regard the mighty themes rocking down the centuries. Beaten and buffeted, now recessive and now in freshly aggressive forms, these themes pass through, quietly take on or brusquely slough off the accretions, the modes of thought, and the frantic but passing preoccupations of the passing decades.

Luther, for an instance, was not a disengaged angel from heaven. He was a man, and a German man, in the sixteenth century. He was also a monk in a specifiable strand of late medieval theology and mode of devotion. He was also a German man for whom the papacy was not only, as he

---

1. Ernst Cassirer, *Essay on Man* (New Haven, CT: Yale University Press, 1944).

came to affirm, an institution that had put a stopper in the effervescent jug of the creative and life-giving grace of God, but also a political institution that lugged melancholy amounts of sweat-earned German gold off to Italy for the glorification of enterprises whose declared devotional intention but slightly masked less elevated purposes.

As we seek perspective in our tumultuous time let us remember not only the earthly complexity that enters into all judgments, but also the rising ides of massive cultural movements that have made problematical all efforts to state and transmit historical facts and interpretations to the new mentality so deeply changed in its very *hearing-possibility* by such movements.

The particular issue which I have designated as a "veritable critical tornado" is the task of finding an adequate hermeneutical stance where by to do fullest justice to the intention of the New Testament itself. But we move into a consideration of that issue most usefully if we ask a preliminary question.

Many years ago a famous philosopher of history admonished his readers that just interpretation of facts could only be achieved—and added that even that achievement is always an approximate one—if the question of what events *mean* was preceded by a kind of elemental wonder that they occurred *at all when they occurred!* Obedience to that admonition suggests to us that our best entrance into the hermeneutical question is through the doorway where we stand to ask why, in the midst of so many biblical-historical-theological problems pulsing for fresh attention, there has occurred in this decade an intense and virtually unanimous concentration upon the hermeneutical problem.

Any effort to answer that problem in detail would require nothing less than a history of thought from Galileo to the mid-twentieth century, but a single general statement would be as follows: when, along the entire front of the life of the West, internal pressure builds up, generated by deepening dubiety about the appropriateness of received forms of thought, the structure and process of things, and the adequacy of old forms to address the fresh needs of men—*then a richer, more complex, and more ample interpretive* perspective is demanded. The only term large enough to designate that demand is *hermeneutic*, and the demand and the responding effort characterizes intellectual effort in all realms of experience in our time. The effort appeared earliest and achieved methodological refinement in historical and literary inquiries, but the nature of the effort is the same no matter what the name or the data. In

The Word of God

natural science, social science, and philosophy we stand at a point where freshly forged conceptual tools are called for. And it must be added that if the theological sciences seek to avoid this demand, they can do so—at a price. The price is resignation from history, a "stop the world, I want to get off" withering isolation from all living speech of significance.

In the history of biblical interpretation there has been played out on a particular stage the same action which has been enacted on the big stage of Western culture. The action might be called, "Button, Button, Who's Got the Button?" Recall for a moment the candidates for the office of ultimate interpreter in the centuries since medieval times, and see the button of total effort in world-understanding pass from hand to hand. From Dante, with his massive and concretely peopled spirals from a Beatrician heaven to a polluted, Medician Florence—given precision in judgment by a God-bestowed "love that means the Sun in Heaven and all the other stars"—to Bacon, who charged his time to ". . . relinquish the puerile speculations of the philosophers" in order to "dwell steadfastly among things," and, so swelling, hopefully to descry the origin and governing intention and process of all that is. And Goethe, who, as the vision of total pattern lured him on, sang:

> In the Endless, self-repeating
> Flows for evermore the Same,
> Myriad arches, springing, meeting,
> Hold at rest the mighty frame.
> Streams from all things love of living,
> Grandest star and humblest clod.
> All the straining, all the striving
> Is eternal peace in God.[2]

Here sheer life-force bursts forth and eternally unfolds from nature; and then, exhausted in its multiple forms, sinks down in the peace of an eternal return.

That Goethe's God has little to do with the God of the Bible is nothing to the point here. Closer to us, and to our own place, an American man, Henry Adams, urged on by the impressive apparatus of German nineteenth-century historiography, quested for the button of a historical hermeneutics all through the nine volumes of his *History of the United States from 1801 to 1817* (the administration of Jefferson and Madison),

---

2. J. W. Goethe, *Sprüche*, quoted in Oswald Spengler, *The Decline of the West*, trans. C. F. Atkinson (New York: Knopf, 1926) 1:140.

and at the end, in despair at the impossibility of the task, went back to the thirteenth century, where what he looked for in vain in his own time he could celebrate in its victory in another. At that juncture he wrote *Mont-Saint-Michel and Chartres*, his great story of the Virgin of Chartres and of her power to unify life in all of its aspects and passions.

The current holders of the button are the physical scientists. And while, to be sure, the popular mind entertains the hope that the ambulatory button will stop here and that a final methodology contains infinite power for the bestowal of clear and certain knowledge, the most able custodians of the button give slight comfort to such hopes. We shall cite but two illustrations.

In the April 22, 1965, issue of the *New York Review of Books* there appeared a long review article on books by three physicists: Niels Bohr, Erwin Schrödinger, Carl von Weizsäcker. The last paragraph of the review, written by an announced agnostic, has a fascinating turn. At the conclusion of his discussion of the third of these men and his option for Christianity as a "way of life having radical political consequences" the reviewer writes as follows:

> What distinguishes Christianity, so interpreted, from a non-theistic humanism is very hard to say. Perhaps, to Weizsäcker, even the attempt to *say* this would be a needless concession to out-dated forms of theology. The Christian has a standpoint from which he views the development of man's intellectual and moral life in his own way; and how the resulting spectacle differs from a humanist view (he would reply) is more easily seen than stated. This conclusion is too elusive to be wholly satisfying; attempting to grasp it, I feel like a man who, after a period of fervid atheism, read philosophy at Oxford and found that he no longer understood that which he had formerly *dis*believed. Weizsäcker certainly presents the historical evolution of scientific ideas in a . . . proposition which is illuminating, quite apart from all theological issues. But is there, then, *nothing* in Christianity for us to doubt?[3]

What fascinates in that last phrase is the ironical disclosure that the agnostic lives by doubt—that his doubt is a kind of negative tribute to the necessity for that which shall not be doubted—and his feeling that he has

---

3. Stephen Toulmin, "The Physicist as Philosopher," *The New York Review of Books* 4/6 (April 22, 1965) 12–15.

The Word of God

been betrayed when a faith he continues to doubt self-eviscerates itself of everything that ever made it worth either believing or doubting!

As I come now to the second illustration, let us keep in mind the thesis I am arguing: that as we look (as we shall presently) at the hermeneutical problem in theology we are not dealing with an isolated intramural hassle among idiosyncratic German theologians. The problem is both symptomatic of and continuous with the crucial intellectual task of our time. At the Center for the Study of Democratic Institutions in Santa Barbara there was recently a conversation about utopias and their significance. At one point Mr. Michael Harrington said,

> One important aspect of utopia is to understand its limits.... Some socialist writer—it may have been Trotsky—said that the function of socialism is to raise men from the level of a fate to that of a tragedy.... That is to say, utopia is not going to solve everything by any means. As a matter of fact I have thought for a long time about Marx's prediction that in a society where men are no longer murdered or starved by nature, but where nature is under man's control, there would be no need of God because God is essentially man's projection of his own fears and hopes— a curious image. In contrast to that, I wonder whether, at precisely the moment all economic problems disappear, that there could not be a great *growth* in religion rather than a decline. It is a possibility, because we would have a society in which men would die not from ... idiocies about the economy. They would die from death. And at that point the historical shell around the fact of death would be broken. For the first time society would face up to death itself.[4]

What intrigues one about that statement is identical with the fascination of the first one: the protest of men of the world that no message that is constituted only of human possibilities can have redemptive force—a *no* to salvation claim that does not demand a radical break, a clear decision, a *no* to the claim that the mere continuity of some good is identical with the humanly necessary. Such salvation promises are not adequate to the facts of man's confession about himself—and at this moment not even interesting to the very modern minds that so recently cherished them.

These reflections serve to lead us on to an effort to specify the current issue in biblical hermeneutics. The entire section of this chapter that

---

4. Michael Harrington, in W. H. Ferry, *Cacotopias and Utopias* (Santa Barbara, CA: Center for the Study of Democratic Institutions, 1965) 20–21. Copyright © 1965 by The Fund for the Republic, Inc.

has introduced this step is a kind of appeal to keep our heads, to maintain so just a perspective of the cultural influences that shape the careers of doctrines that we become not blinded partisans in a battle, or so move into the practice of ministry that our preaching be less ample than the many-dimensional modes of the word of God.

"What kind of language best represents and communicates the event of Jesus of Nazareth, the Christ, and does most justice to the affirmation common to the New Testament that God has disclosed Himself in a human life?"[5] That is the current question.

The effort to make a reply to that question is the meaning of the hermeneutical battle. Two possibilities, both firmly attested and demonstrated within the New Testament itself, are being cogently argued. That there are these two, and no more, is a result of the fact that the definition and practice of *apostleship* in the New Testament is a double one. The one is *kerygmatic*, the other *narrative*.

Apostleship, as functioning in kerygmatic declaration, commonly appeals to St. Paul and to the handling of historical material in the Fourth Gospel. Paul based his apostleship upon his having seen the risen Christ. His preachment is kerygmatic; the substance of it is not Christ after the flesh but an act of God who raised up the slain an, disclosed in him the glory of the Father, and grants a new being to everyone who, participating in that man's life, re-enacts within himself this death and resurrection.

The power of this centering upon the kerygma is that it disengages the power, presence, and possibility of the salvation wrought and available in Jesus from the confusion, uncertainties, and historical relativities that are structural to the New Testament if it is interpreted solely as a narrative of history. This kerygmatic proclamation of Jesus as eschatological salvation event makes all past present; it translates all that cannot be established into a word of God that discloses, judges, challenges, and liberates anew by forgiveness—forward to an opening new obedience. Faith is thus restored to its true function: the acceptance of God's acceptance of me as the ground of a new being in authentic existence.

The other way rests upon that New Testament material and mode which sees apostleship function as narrative preaching and commonly appeals to the Synoptic Gospels and to the Acts of the Apostles. Apostleship is in those documents a term applied to those who have been witnesses to the historical Jesus and witnesses to his resurrection. This

---

5. Dan O. Via Jr., "The Necessary Complement to the Kerygma," *The Journal of Religion* 45/1 (January 1965) 33.

The Word of God

position maintains that any attempt to grasp the New Testament's reality must deal with Jesus' whole story and date, not shake itself loose from incessant torment with the mercurial staff of history.

The power of this approach is in its insistence upon the historical as the central category for any effort to bear witness to the central biblical scandal—that God has disclosed himself in a human life. Earthliness, the corporeal, the drama of human historical successiveness, the pathos of temporality and duration—all of this argues for the necessity as well as the force of the redemptive reality as narrative.

But now, to the third step: What does this issue, and all the many violent sides of it, mean for the preacher? I have three suggestions:

Let the preacher keep his feet. He will be helped to do this if he really has such an understanding of the history of Christian doctrine as I was reflecting at the beginning. If he does have that he will not be plunged into despair by extreme claims from either side, but will have learned that extremity is the normal process of theological clarification. He will know that this debate is not likely to be settled in such a way that narrative nexus is demolished by kerygmatic proclamation, or that the first will obliterate the second. He will know, with confidence gained by reflection upon other struggled, that what seems to be a deadlock will turn out to have provided clarifying light upon the New Testament and to have restored vivifying fresh relations to all elements of the biblical literature.

Let the preacher open his head. By that I mean that the preacher must use the fact of his struggle for a proper principle of interpretation as an occasion to ask questions that transcend it, as indeed, such questions have caused it. The real battle, I would venture to suggest, is not whether kerygma or narrative taken separately furnish adequate perspectives from which to understand the New Testament: the real function of the debate is to point to the *consequences* of making a decision exclusively for one as against the other. For if one settles for a de-historicized pronouncement, he had made a decision that will ultimately trickle down to the bottom of all his thought; he shall have made the Christian reality dependent upon some philosophical alliance, or upon some institutional solidity and persistence, or upon some given piety in world view upon which he really reckons to certify his message. If, on the other hand, he settles for a narrative recital, he had made a decision that will ultimately for want of a clear proposal having total significance for total understanding, trickle off into a recitation of far-off events unrescued into presence by any present godly power of judgment and mercy whereby men today are called to decision and to commanding and uncomfortably specific commitments.

Let the preacher make a counterpoint out of an opposition. Counterpoint is a musical term: it means a melody added to a given melody as accompaniment; the art of composite melody, i.e., of melody not simple but moving attended by one or more related but independent melodies. The metaphor is perfect for the point I want to make. For the force of the reality of the Christian faith does not hang upon a single hook. In this regard it differs absolutely from a philosophical doctrine. The Christian reality *because it is historical* is not malleable to a single proposition, even if the single proposition be a true one. In the context of the present issue between narrative and kerygmatic language, let me steal some critical sentences from the essay alluded to earlier.

> The kerygma does require faith if the salvation which it offers is to be entered into, but narrative also requires decision, response, and involvement if the possibilities which it offers are to be appropriated. There is simply no self-evident reason, moreover, why the proclamation of the death and resurrection of Jesus has more power to evoke faith than a narrative containing, say, his eating with publicans and sinners; his conflicts with regard to the law; his disregard of ritual; parables like the Prodigal Son, the Laborers in the Vineyard, and the Talents; and some of the antitheses of the Sermon on the Mount. In fact, for some people the latter may be more evocative of faith . . . Is then the kerygma superfluous? Why did it arise? It cannot be because kerygma alone can make the salvation event present and evoke faith. The reason for the kerygma's rise is not that narrative cannot do anything that kerygma cannot do but that narrative cannot do everything. If the narrative approach were the only possible one, if it were used alone, the event could never be re-presented in its completeness, for full representation would depend upon the recovery of all the details and that would be impossible. . . . The great service of the kerygma is that it grasps the meaning of the whole event in its fullness and presents it in a part—the death and resurrection of Jesus. . . . The meaning of the whole then is made apprehensible apart from a recovery of all the parts. . . . The narrative contains the "yes" of concreteness but the "no" of incompleteness, while the kerygma contains the "yes" of completeness but the "no" of abstraction.[6]

6. Ibid., 34–36.

Let us make another effort from a different angle to see the present hermeneutical problem in perspective. The Western philosophical tradition has achieved enormous sophistication. A leading theme from the beginnings has in our generation tightened to an excruciating point. It is the epistemological problem: how do we know? And does not the clarification of the ways of knowing absolutely define the kind of objects, process, truth that can be known and set the limits of such knowledge? The exchange between Professors Keating and Hefner in a recent *Dialog* is an instance of this effort to clarify ways of knowing.[7]

It was inevitable that the energies of this quest for a certain way of knowing should ultimately attack the problem of history, ask what can be known in history, by what ways. Is there a difference between the world-as-nature and the world-as-history? And can this difference be so clearly specified as to suggest that ways of knowing appropriate to the one are inappropriate to the other?

Indeed, this suspicion of a difference is already nascent in the Greeks' descriptions of their own past and is made clear in the historical writing of Herodotus and Thucydides. The persistent energy of this effort has produced what might be called prime models for envisioning the life of man as historical fact: a cyclical and repetitive model; an organic model after the mode of plant and animals life—birth, youth, full maturity, senility, decay, death, a model of some eternal dialectic visible in the vast play of thesis, antithesis, synthesis (and this process sometimes invested with ultimate significance of a divine order); or a moral model in which history is understood as the working out and disclosure on a massive scale of the powers of virtue and strength. *Weltgeschichte ist Weltgericht.* One has only to study Augustine's *City of God* to see how early and how powerfully evangelical facts and images expanded into intellectual models whereby to articulate a theology of world history.

At this moment in the life of the West this entire development, newly equipped and methodologically refined by a century and a half of what is called "scientific historiography," intersects a second long effort, itself matured by a century and a half of biblical and primitive Christian historical study, namely, the recovery with new clarity and fullness of the early years of the New Testament community.

---

7. William T. Keaton, "A Scientist's Question: Is Theology Based on Education?," and Philip Hefner, "In Reply to Mr. Keeton: Theology and the Question of Truth," *Dialog* 4/2 (Spring 1965) 98–102, 104–11.

Part 2: Preaching the Word

The documents, freshly interpreted in the light of a vastly enriched and hugely complicated context, became ever more strange and fascinating. Seemingly naïve record is disclosed to be a rather well-developed theological document. The Gospels are disclosed as fusing documentation and witness with a fluid, complex, community of faith. They are primarily witnesses to faith and by faith and for the evocation of faith—and all operate with patterns that are sunk backward into the Israel that preceded them; and all, with varying degrees, are contextual with the world that surrounded them.

The problem of New Testament interpretation today is the product of the intersection of these two intellectual traditions, both possessed of an energy freshly alive because of the sardonic historical meaninglessness that haunts our time. With a kind of frantic determination both seek to pierce into the secret of historical meaning.

It is natural that the serious preacher who cannot wait until the titans have slugged out basic lines of interpretation should, like some in the first century, cry out—"I am of Ebeling! I am of Bultmann! I am of Käsemann!" But is it not possible that the very violence of the conflict should suggest a way to stand in it? That the very dust of battle should suggest an intellectual posture appropriate and viable? For the conflict itself attests how many-dimensioned, how fused into polychromatic richness is the massive phenomenology of the Christian community. And that face gives birth to a question: is it likely that a way that is either solely *record* or solely *kerygmatic* shall be certified with such precision as shall solve this problem?

A further question. Is it not possible that the nutcracker of twentieth-century historical method is only modestly effective for the exposure of first-century fact? Is empathy, actual feeling for fact, patterns of relation between fact and fact, so smoothly transferable from age to age?

Indeed, there is something humorous about the solemn intensity with which we suppose that the twentieth-century sense of the pathos of history, equipped with theological (and largely Teutonic) confidence, can pull a single magic lever and open a jangling jackpot of certainty! And particularly when we remember that the position we want to be supported may be a product of our century and *its* human and historical questions that were raised not at all, or in other terms, by the documents. All of this suggests the following: the Christian fact is a symbiotic fact; witnesses to Christian reality are fused and symbiotic witnesses; and a method of interpretation must be informed by a symbiosis appropriate to that circumstance. The ways of knowing must be as supple and contrapuntal and various as history is—not as clear and clean and simple as philosophy hungers for.

Preaching is in trouble everywhere. But let me, for the consolation of us all, point to the virtue in that necessity, speak of the promise inherent in that predicament. The trouble is at the right place and at the right level. The form of the church is under fire. Good! It was fastly moving faster and faster to a bland bourgeois irrelevance. The role of the preacher is problematic. Good! That problematic has been hidden too long under a lying layer of popular acceptance devoid of any substance of authority. The intention of Jesus, and the language form of its New Testament witness, is confused. Good! For the vigor of the debate is evidence that our former preachment of that intention was not adequate to the predicaments of men, and present efforts may find a better preachment not characterized by the soggy obviousness that had come to expression in recent American religiousness. When students ask, "What is God doing in the world?" they are troubled because they do not certainly know. But the question puts the possible Presence in the right place and marks a manly advance from the uncritical and untroubled assumption that God was but an inexhaustible resource for the supply of a temperamentally religious coterie, or a kind of holy balance in an ecclesiastical checking account.

Of course preaching is in trouble. Whence did we ever manufacture the assumption that it was ever to be in anything but trouble?

The Scope of I / Preparation for Preaching

1964

The Word of God addresses the preacher even as the preacher prepares to address the people. The Word, if unfettered by pious moral and theological conventions, strikes out at the preacher in unpredictable and truly revelatory ways. As Sittler illustrates in the interpretation of select parables, this unfettered Word reveals that the scope of our existence is defined by neither our obedience nor our failure but by the will and grace of God.

I BEGIN BY RECALLING to you a verse of Scripture which affirms that "it is a fearful thing to fall into the hands of the living God." We usually think of falling into the hands of the living God as something that occurs to us when, in a dubious adventure, we become aware of the judgment of God. Therefore, that God is present and living surrounds us with the fearfulness of that event. But it is also not commonly understood that when persons set themselves before the Word of God and dispose themselves to prepare for the task of preaching, this is a fearful thing too, because it is to fall into the hands of the living God. And that is why to prepare sermons is a most disorganizing experience. It is, of course, not a disorganizing experience if a person is able to professionalize this encounter; that is, to separate one's activity with Scripture as a paid-for career from our failed, frail humanity.

We long for order and we shrink from all sheer non-orderable energy that always swirls within and leaps out of the Word of God. For the

The Word of God

Scripture, so inert then, so silent there on the page of the Bible, is like a coiled, heavenly snake, and it strikes without warning. There are ways, of course, to deal with this peril, and we are appallingly ingenuous and ingenious in finding such ways. One can, for instance, in dealing with the Word of God don the thick gloves of confessional formulation, and order, expose, cage, and generally handle this sinister thing in safety. Or one can deal with the encounter as they do in the zoo, with appropriately long instruments. We come to the Scripture with a predisposed program. Or we seduce the coiled life of the Word with sweet music from an ethical flute, so that its potential is half asleep. So, as we deal with Scripture, it weaves and bobs to our orders, the way some of us in India saw the cobras weave and bob to the Indian flutist. But if one listens to Scripture—that bottomless, unpredictable, inexhaustible, always dangerous discourse about God and humanity, always out there at the border of the usual—if one really listens, then the usual questions fall away. Such as, for instance, the question, "What is here that I can use?" Or, "What specific chopping job do I have to do in parish or general church to which this particular word provides a sturdy, sharp edge?" Or even the question, "Is it true?" is not a first question proper to ask of Scripture, for canons of truth, as we fashion these, are manifestly not applicable to the Word of God, for all people are liars and God alone is true. How can God's Word, if we listen, possibly second our motions, if we are really and always both searchers after truth and partly and always liars? Our experiences in the grave business of listening to the Word and writing the sermon, however, lead us occasionally into something quite different. As one gets into the Word and listens, one experiences a growing, painful displacement and a growing and painful excitement as that strange, coiled energy of the Word itself begins to take over, despite what I have brought to it, and begins to do with my own thoughts and my own words what I neither anticipated nor desired. We grow up to ordination [in seminary] really attending to Scripture, and a part of the appalling banality and the dullness of our preaching, and the habits we fall into (all of us), is due to the fact that we do not continue this lifelong discipline of listening. We suffer a kind of shrinkage due to an antiseptic habit of listening to the Word.

Now the Fourth Gospel we have been taught is, humanly speaking, a literary document. It has a peculiarity which can be designated, a particularity that can be specified. It has its own interior style. This material is managed according to a purpose, not always clearly apparent, but there is a purpose there. And last night as I listened, as this pericope from the

Fourth Gospel was carefully unfolded—word for word, line upon line—as I listened to that story of the pool of Bethesda, I was hearing things and seeing things that in all the years of my own ordination I had not heard in the same way before. The Johannine speech about God and the way God's effectual power and presence is exercised in this world—in the Fourth Gospel this speech runs on two parallel tracks, and these tracks never come together. The tracks are equally significant, equally clear, equally powerful, but there is no switching apparatus from which one can get from one Johannine theme over to the other. And it seems to be the calculated intention of the writer of the Fourth Gospel that these two themes should be kept contrapuntal, caught in a constant dissonance, so that perhaps depths could be revealed by the tautness that would be dissipated by a forcible harmony. These two tracks along which the discourse of the Fourth Gospel moves can be indicated in two brief paragraphs.

First, the Fourth Gospel clearly speaks of a light that has no name, a "light that lighteth every man that cometh into the world." It speaks of a light that is the luminousness of God the Creator, which is the gifted character of all that is, *ta panta*. There is a light in all things by virtue of being the creation of God who is holy. There is a grace, so the Fourth Gospel teaches, given in and with this creation, and to some extent all humanity participates in it. It enfolds, like an ambience, all life. It stirs as a kind of nameless potency. In all human existence, this light and this potency, says the Fourth Gospel, is of the Father. It has no name. It is a generalized giftedness in all things. Isaiah calls it, you will recall when he confronts it, not by a name, but exclaims, "Holy, holy, holy." And the Fourth Gospel simply calls it "the light." That's the first track.

The second track is equally clear, and not harmonizeable with the first. In the second track, the light is named. It is *enpersonalized* out from the generalized luminousness that characterizes the first theme. This light, according to this other way in the Fourth Gospel, this light which is the light the holy gives off, constitutes in its concrete, named presence the person and the presence and the power of the man Jesus. Its general power and presence all gathers to a point, and the point becomes the center of the circle of every decision and every crucial encounter in our relationship with God.

Now when we learn to listen and understand the interior structure of a document, we listen with a new sophistication, and we are open to all these strange new suggestions out of the Word of God. But now turn to the Gospel of Luke, from which I want to take the exposition tonight.

The Word of God

In the Gospel of Luke you have another clear document which is just as clearly structured. The handling of the material in Luke's Gospel is calculatedly built up to a kind of momentum. This momentum becomes obvious in the twelfth and fourteenth chapter, in which the preaching of Jesus, or pericopes *from* the teachings of Jesus, is managed in such a way that a single theme is built out and filled out in many keys. The theme may be designated: Jesus' affirmation of the love and the freedom of God; the freedom of God whose substance is love, and the love of God whose intention is freedom. This is what he is talking about for these three chapters.

You recall that on one Sabbath, teaching in the synagogue, there came a woman possessed by a spirit that crippled her for eighteen years. Luke characteristically is always almost clinically precise about the nature of the disease, and the time the patient had it. She was bent double, quite unable to stand up. Jesus said, "You are rid of your trouble." And the president of the synagogue, indignant for healing on the Sabbath, intervened and said, "There are six days to do this kind of thing. Propriety would indicate it ought not to be done on the Sabbath." Then you recall Jesus talked to him about the one who has an ox or a donkey—"Does he take it out to water it on the Sabbath day? Here is this woman, a daughter of Abraham—is it wrong to free her or serve her need on the Sabbath day?" What's going on here? What's going on here in its first encounter? Is it the effort of the love of God to escape out of the protocol in which piety always enshrines love—meaning to serve it, but sometimes encasing it? What is going on here is that the freedom of God is fighting to free itself from channels which were created by devout people in order to extend freedom, but suffered a kind of rigidity in the course of religious institutional life whereby it captured what it meant to free.

The next story that Luke tells us in his Gospel also is one that is dealing with the Sabbath. On Sabbath, he went to a meal in the house of a leading Pharisee, and there, we read, they were watching him closely. Now one of the advantages of having sufficient training in the Greek text is that one gets an eye for this kind of thing. "Where they watched him closely" is a Greek phrase that does not mean casually to see that a man was there, or just to have it entered in one's consciousness that Jesus was there. The mood is hostility; the watching is malicious. The mood is anticipation that he'll make a bad move and they will have something on him. This is carefully written into the language. And there was a man you recall, who had the dropsy, and Jesus this time does not first address

Part 2: Preaching the Word

the man, but apparently out of the previous experience with the arthritic woman, he first addresses them, in a sense to "pull the punch" before it is delivered and asks the quite appropriate question, "Is it permitted to cure people on the Sabbath or not?" And recall, they had learned something at least: they said nothing. So he took the man and cured him and sent him away. Then Jesus added again, "If one of you has a donkey or an ox and it falls into a well, will he hesitate to haul it out on the Sabbath day?" To this they could find no reply.

When Jesus noticed how the guests were shuffling around to secure places of honor, he told the little parable that comes just before and constitutes the vestibular preparation, as it were, for the one which Luke then puts next. You recall the little compressed parable about when you're asked to a celebrity feast. Who do you invite? Well, he said, "Do you invite your neighbors, and when you give a dinner, do you invite the rich and your relatives and so forth?" Yes, you probably do this. This is the custom. It still is the custom. Our social custom is that a dinner, which has as one of the elements of it to supply nourishment, has lost this character and most of us invite people to our house who need another dinner about as much as they need a hole in the head. We use the dinner occasion for social intercourse, and for paying off one another's kindness. And Jesus was aware of that situation. And notice how he turns it all upside down in a really shocking way. "When you give a party, invite the poor, the crippled, the lame, the blind, and so find happiness." Here is the evangelical upside-downness of all things, according to Jesus. Here is that coiled snake of heavenly teaching which strikes out with a certain quickness to touch us, you see, at the most sensitive point. For he says—and notice the peculiar, lovely twist at the end of the sentence—"Because they cannot pay, you will be repaid." Because they cannot, you can. Because they have nothing, you have more than you can ask or think. Now right after that there comes the almost amusing sentence, an amusing little vignette: "One of the company [recall that this took place in the house of a leading Pharisee], upon hearing all this," and listening with a kind of understandable shock to this topsy-turvy teaching of the gospel in which all things are new—one of them, hearing this, repeats the old bromide and releases one of those verbal, gaseous bubbles that characterize piety in the presence of great teaching sometimes. And he said, "Ah, happy is the man who someday will sit at the feast of the kingdom of God." And the Greek text says "*But* Jesus said to him"—not, "*And* Jesus said to him," which is a kind of addendum, but, "*But* Jesus said to him," which grammatically is a corrective. It is not showing the man a chair and saying, "Talk on," but really pulling the rug out from under the man. "But Jesus said"—and now let me read in the New English Bible the very familiar parable:

> A man was giving a big dinner party and had sent out many invitations. At dinnertime, he sent his servant with a message for the guests, please come now. Everything is ready. They began one and all to excuse themselves. The first said, "I have bought a piece of land, I must go and look after it. Please accept my apologies." The second, "I have bought five yoke of oxen, and I am on my way to try them out, please accept *my* apologies." And the next said, "I have just got married, and for that reason, I cannot come." When the servant came back and reported this to his master, the master of the house was angry and said to him, "Go out quickly into the streets and valleys of the town, and bring me the poor, the crippled, the maimed, and the blind, and the servant said "Sir, your orders have been carried out. There is still room." The master cried, "Go out into the highways and along the hedgerows, and make them come in. I want my house to be full."

Now let us reenact the various movements from the inside of that little story. And to do that, to remove preliminary problems, recall that this was a Middle Eastern dinner party. The customary celebrity party dinner would most likely be a whole roast lamb, and one doesn't know exactly when a whole roast lamb will be done, hence the second invitation. In the Middle East to this day, as I saw it in Beirut, one invites you to dinner, and sends a servant to tell you on a certain day, "You're asked to come to dinner at my house." And then, when he is informed from the kitchen that the dinner is now about ready, he sends the servant to say, "Come, for all things are now ready." You see, this is pre-TV dinner, which someone has recently defined as "the inedible prepared for the incredible." But in the Middle Eastern situation, this is the custom and explains how in the New Testament the second messenger was sent out. And the servants came back, you see, with the message which you've heard, with the kind of pathetic and discouraging excuses of those who had been invited.

Now everything is alive in our situation to bring us to the point of saying, "This is it. This is the paradigm. This is the model of what ought to be said out of the Word of God." Therefore we preach a sermon; as well we might, because there *is* a sermon to be preached. There *is* a situation, always, to which it can be edifyingly and judgmentally addressed, because is there any one of us who has not, under the kind and incessant graciousness of God, who has not sent in our "cards of excuse"? Have we not voted ourselves out? Every one of us can make a sermon, and rightly hear a sermon, out of that point; each one, each from his own heart, can fill up the formal vacuum with his own behavior, which is the equivalent of any one, or all three, of these excusing invitees. This is what we commonly do. But may I suggest that if we do that, and that is the only sermon we make of the parable, we have committed two errors.

First, we have not stayed with the parable. This is an error because a parable is not a series of chance epigrams strung together like a string of pearls—real pearls on a real string, to be sure, but a string, not a series of isolated pearls. The parable, as securely as a Shakespeare sonnet, has got an interior structure that moves toward a point. It has an interior momentum that moves toward a *denouement*. As securely and surely as a finely wrought work of art, the parable has an interior movement that invites us to ride it through to the end. Now there are, to be sure, sermons along the way, but our listening will never let us stop there, as the only or the most ample preaching of the parable, if we attend and listen to the Word of God.

The second error is not the formal one, but the second error is a theological one. Because if we really put the center of the movement of this parable at the point of the excusing men, the center of the parable is put upon the action of human beings, whereas the right center of every parabolic teaching is always in the action of God. A corollary to the parable is this—and it occurs in our churches: if we preach an ever so edifying and clear sermon about God's grace and shameless, sullen human refusal, we are liable to end up with a homiletical correlative of a theological blunder, because the people will leave the church doing two things. They're liable to leave our preaching clucking over-piously over their own piety, which is at least sensitive enough to see the point and to have identified them with the excusing rascals. They have a way out by the very virtue by which they have been sensitive enough to have got the point.

That's one error that may easily happen. The other error is much worse. They will leave the church with their pity at the wrong place: "Poor old God, there with his burned roast." Poor old God; God is the victim of the parable instead of the hero of the story. Because observe, the parable moves up to, but it moves *through,* this excuse making. This excuse making, if I may use a rather banal image, is but the tee upon which the ball is set for the stroke of the driver. This but sets up the parable for its large point. For see that the momentum and dynamic of the parable drives right on through.

The Word of God

The master is not finished. The lord of the dinner remains the lord of the situation. The excuses may sadden him, but they do not stop him. The excuses may momentarily divert the story, but they do not end the story. Notice what happens: And when the servant came back and told his master these things, the master said, without a moment's hesitation, "Keep right on going, keep right on inviting, because I want my table to be filled with guests, and I want my house to be full." What's this saying to us? This is saying to us that the lordly action of the eternal in history goes through all the barriers and the difficulties and the betrayals and the stupidities, for even the churchly ossifications, which we place in its way. But the lordly action retains its lordly character. Our sadness is not God's program, though it affects God's heart. Our rejections are not the program of the eternal, because observe the way the story ends: "You go out wherever they are"—and here God becomes unbecomingly reckless. You see, the same freedom and love that characterizes the parables that led up to this continue to dominate this one. "Go out into the byways and hedges"—which is still in the English countryside an understandable word, but in the American scene we would have to find equivalence—"Go out into just any old kind of place that is, and find about any kind of person there is, and bring them up, bring them in."

And you observe how the parable ends: "I will that my house shall be full." First, "I will." Our will is expressed in the excuses. God's will is expressed at the end of the parable. It is my will that controls: "I will!" Second, "my house." This is not your house, this is my house. The whole abounding creation. The gift of the world. The gift of the Son of God. The embodiment of the Son of God in the body of the faithful—this too is God's house. The church is always tempted to make it *her* house, *her* church, exercise *her* protocol, define her judgments. Clamp up on the invitation and the proprieties of the church, her solidified mores, even if she can find historical reasons for these. But this parable in its lordly ending, "I will that my house—not your house—shall be full." He doesn't say full of what, or from whence, or according to what kind of response evokes the response, but simply, "I will that my house shall be full." The Godly will, the Godly house, the Godly opulence in which all things are at home with him—this is the magnificent, kingly, lordly end of the parable.

Now what finally does this parable say that relates it to my theme, "The Scope of I"? This parable, in a kind of oblique way, teaches that the scope of the biblical language always escapes categorization. The outward reach of, and the interior unfolding, uncoiling energies of the gospel are everlastingly going out and down and around. The "I," the scope of my existence, is not defined by my obedience or my excuse making. The scope of my real existence of God is drawn forward to the largeness of the will of God; to the largeness of God's house, and to the fullness of God's intended life for me, which is openness of my life, not only to God, but to my life among the sisters and brothers. The reality of my selfhood is never exuded from my private selfhood, even a selfhood sanctified in God, because I am sanctified in God in order that the proper ambiance and amplitude of my selfhood should be in the house of God's will among the receivers and respondents to God's invitation. How shall I be obedient to that? We cannot stop our reflections short of the great full statement, "I will that my house shall be full."

seven

Preaching and the Biblical Imagination

The Search for Theological Method and Its Requirement of Preaching

1961

Preaching is a serious theological event that engages the listener and the cultural milieu. This Sittler trademark, observable throughout this book, is clearly laid out in this essay. The task, Sittler always insists, requires staying current with theological developments. Here Sittler practices what he preaches as he moves through key contributions from the leading theologians of his time.

IT IS OBVIOUSLY POSSIBLE for many ministers to keep separate their theological reading and reflection, and their preaching. Given the leaky structure of the human mind whereby contents of one area are regularly sloshing over unto others, this consistently maintained separation is an unusual feat. In trying to account for it I propose to say some things in the last lecture about practical facts in modern American church life which operate to encourage, if not to demand this deadening and guilt-begetting circumstance.

In this lecture I am proceeding on the assumption that the minister really knows that theology and preaching belong together, wants help in keeping the marriage alive and, while aware of the strain on the brain involved, is willing to endure it. The help proposed is to affirm that there is significance for preaching in the contemporary search for theological method, designate and describe an aspect of that search by reference to an impressive discussion of it, and finally delineate what its findings suggest for the public declaration of the Word.

The task of theology, as I understand it, is to make statements which clearly, intelligibly, and in just relationship set forth the content of the Christian faith as that faith is known and celebrated in the church. This definition requires that we understand theology both as a content and a task. It is a content because there is a sameness in the issues, divine and human, which it talks about, and a continuity in the substance of what it affirms about them. But it is the purpose of such statements to be intelligible; i.e., to say what is said in such a way as to communicate clearly to another mind precisely what the claim is. And because this activity goes on within a world where canons of clarity, requirements of intelligibility, and the nature of immediate human needs are in constant flux, the task of theology is a never-ending one.

In his *Seventeenth Century Background* Basil Willey asks why it was that "explanations of things which were satisfactory to one century were not satisfactory to another." To explain means to "make clear," to "render intelligible." But clarity and intelligibility is not a static quality of a statement; it is rather a quality of acceptability in a statement which quality is determined by the entire culture. "An explanation commands our assent with immediate authority when it presupposes the 'reality,' the 'truth' of what seems most real, most true. One cannot, therefore, define 'explanation' absolutely; one can only say that it is a statement which satisfies the demands of a particular time and place."[1]

The current search for a proper theological method is surely due to the fact that our generation finds older "explanations" simply not clear, intelligible, or in just proportion. There is a "disharmony between traditional explanations and current needs." Statements of one period are "felt as fact" in virtue of their congruity with the spirit, practice, and basic assumptions of a time; they are not "felt as fact" by another period because, in the unstoppable running of water over the dam, the spirit, practice, and basic assumption of a time became altered. The degree to which the common life is aware of this alteration has nothing to do with

---

1. Basil Willey, *The Seventeenth Century Background* (New York: Columbia University Press, 1942) 13.

Preaching and the Biblical Imagination

the case. That is why, to stay within our immediate field of preaching, justly celebrated sermons of thirty years ago, while admirable in terms of craftsmanship and witnessing vivacity, cannot be heard now as they were then. They make statements that are no longer "felt as fact"!

A proper theological method will be one that meets these conditions:

1. It must operate open-eyed in the midst of the problem of hermeneutics, or principles of interpretation, as these are propounded by the biblical record. I am assuming, of course, that the earliest record of what men affirmed the Christian faith to be is admitted as having central status.

2. It must operate with a kind of epistemology which is appropriate to the kind of events and claims which have been clearly generative, formative, and sustaining of the Christian faith and community. I choose a specific example of the contemporary search for a proper theological method not only because of its intrinsic responsibility and impressive force but because, having come to life in this school, its right to be heard will not be lightly questioned.

In 1957 Richard R. Niebuhr published his *Resurrection and Historical Reason*.[2] The argument of this book constitutes, I believe, the opening of a fresh and exciting period in American theological discussion. It does this because it is profoundly and accurately aware that the kind of thinking which declared Jesus Lord and Christ by his resurrection from the dead is a kind of thinking which is a function of the historical consciousness of the community within which that claim was made. It affirms, further, what fifty years of critical biblical and historical and theological studies have made completely clear: ". . . that Christ and resurrection are inseparable, and the old dichotomy of Jesus of History—Christ of Faith does not solve this problem; it only dissolves Christ and the Church."

The theological method for which Niebuhr makes a solid and persuasive plea is so clearly set forth in certain of his own summary sentences that by putting several of them in sequence the scope and rationale of his proposal is plain. Says Niebuhr:

> Certainly one of the indisputable offices of theology is to open the mind of the present community to the way in which the primitive Church apprehended the event that became the

---

2. Richard R. Niebuhr, *Resurrection and Historical Reason* (New York: Scribner's, 1957) 49.

focus of its self-understanding. Any attempt to relate ourselves to the historical Jesus in a manner fundamentally alien to the experience of the New Testament church is based on a sophistical idea of history, and ultimately leads us away from the object of the quest.

In several chapters following this stated program the writer describes and analyzes nineteenth-century and current ways of relating ourselves to the historical Jesus, and gives particular attention to the options elaborated in the work of Karl Barth, Rudolph Bultmann, and John Knox. He finds none of them to be adequate, and all inadequate for varieties of the same reason: they do not take seriously the kind of knowledge of Jesus the Lord which the resurrection record assumes. Barth, because he makes an attempt ". . . to answer the methodological and historical problems raised by the nineteenth century by foreclosing all discussion of epistemological questions and insisting that the subjectivity of Jesus Christ, the God-man, is the only important reality confronting the mind of man." Bultmann's program of demythologization is assessed as inadequate because "Faith is oriented not on the picture of Jesus, but on the instantly proclaimed Word; it arises not in memory of the past, but in the eschatological moment without past or future." And further, ". . . the real purpose of historical investigation is the discovery of new dimensions, not in the past, but in the historian himself." New Testament theology is thus disqualified from playing a constructive role in the forming of a theological method which shall take seriously the problem of faith and history, and particularly this faith, rooted as no other religious faith is, in the very concreteness of history, and becomes nothing more than ". . . the first permanent expression of the distinctively Christian consciousness, and begs the question of the external history of that consciousness,"[3] "thus leaving . . . theology with nothing to discussion except the human need for self-understanding in general."

The work of John Knox is given detailed attention. Its basic thesis is that ". . . the data with which biblical theologians have to deal . . . will become luminous only if they are approached not as simple facts but as events." Event is, to Knox's mind, the basic category for an analysis of history and the way in which it is known. A historical occurrence is simply an occurrence that was perceived and remembered. In other words, it evoked the response of a historical subject. . . . There can be no

---

3. Ibid., 57, 58.

Preaching and the Biblical Imagination

ahistorical knowledge of a historically revealed Lord, no relationship to Jesus Christ apart from the power of memory or from the community in which that memory is lodged.[4] This method of interpreting the relation of faith and history, operating with the triad—Jesus Christ–church–New Testament—drives the argument, by the power of its internal relations, to declare: "The Resurrection is a part of the concrete empirical meaning of Jesus, not the result of mere reflection upon that meaning. . . . It was something given. It was a reality grasped in faith."[5] When, however, one investigates where and when and what this "resurrection-event" really is, what he ends up with is the community's experience of the Christ-Spirit within it. And so adequate a transcript of the event itself is this "remembering" community that the resurrection of Jesus is not a datum of faith but a postulate of the community's experience, and the apostolic narratives of resurrection are superfluous, from the point of men of faith.[6]

Niebuhr introduces his own constructive discussion with several statements which are not only a correct report of the biblical-theological situation in our time, but also provide material for our effort to say something useful about the theme of this lecture: what are the requirements for preaching which are suggested by this search for a proper theological method? He writes, "The impasse into which Protestant theology has come through its efforts to give significance to the resurrection tradition shows that the dogma of pure reason does not have sufficient resources to give Protestantism that kind of knowledge of Christian origins that its life and doctrine require." What is necessary, Niebuhr declares, is ". . . a critique of historical reason, a reason that will not seek the possibility of biblical history in the conditions of natural science or idealistic metaphysics, but rather in the answer to the distinctive question, how do we know historical events."[7]

How do we know historical events? That question, standing between the biblical narrative of the mighty acts of God and the existing individuals who look up at us at the moment when, having read, we close the book and begin to preach, is the question. And if the preacher does not ponder it and wrestle with it, exciting and informing his pondering and wrestling with the best resources of biblical and theological labors, then

---

4. Ibid., 62–63.
5. John Knox, *Christ the Lord* (New York: Harper) 60.
6. Ibid., 69.
7. Niebuhr, *Resurrection and Historical Reason*, 89.

nothing really useful can be done for him. For what does it mean that the declared redemptive power of human life comes to us in a narrative? This: that time is the category of the historical; that because the redemptive power of God has become time, faith-engendering witness cannot be borne to that power save in a kind of preaching which is a rhetorical address to men in their time-determined and time-imprisoned existence.

There is a noetic potency in temporality. Preaching must be such an activity as invites the hearer to suspect a congruity between what is declared to have been done by God in time, and his own self-consciousness as a creature of time. By the term "creature of time" I do not refer only to the fact of duration, clock time, the observable but scarcely exciting fact that there is a before-and-after pattern in human experience. I refer, rather, to a fact that has been observed by every critic of Immanuel Kant, that time and space are not comparable categories. Space is a conception. Time is a feeling. It is a word to indicate something inconceivable—a "sound-symbol"—and to use it as a notion, scientifically, is utterly to misconceive its nature. In the entire company of older philosophy I know but one profound and reverent presentation of time: it is in the fourteenth chapter of the eleventh book of St. Augustine's *Confessions*. "*Quid est ergo Tempus? Si nemo ex me quaerat scio; si quaerenti explicare velim, nescio!*" (Translation: "What is time then? If nobody asks me, I know; but if I were desirous to explain it to one that should ask me, I know not" [Loeb Classical Library edition]). It is possible to illustrate this statement about time in many particulars. The most quick and living way is simply to muster, for the evocative and response-begetting power they have, a miscellany from man's general confessional.

From John Milton's "Nymphs and shepherds dance no more" to our present century is a long time. And this time has seen a magnificent multiplication of devices, institutions, analgesics, and therapeutics designed to make man, the "time-creature," more content, prosperous, and secure in his "brief and mutable traject," or designed to obscure the fact of death by narcotizing the living as we cosmetize the dead. But the intervening centuries have done nothing to diminish the passion with which men regard mutability and passingness. The passion has become rather less restrained—for life can become so air-conditioned as to make its contingency seem a huge and somewhat rotten joke.

That distortion of the New Testament witness to the resurrection of Jesus Christ (which carries its distinctiveness clearly stamped upon it) whereby its character has been translated out of particularity to the generality of immortality, makes it increasingly difficult even to declare the hope of the resurrection. For resurrection deals bluntly with man in his temporality—and claims to overcome it. Immortality deals with man in his ideal non-temporality and essays to persuade him that his actuality is not his reality.

> But men at whiles are sober,
> And think by fits and starts.
> And when they think, they fasten
> Their hands upon their hearts.[8]

So it is that the facts break through, and in so doing draw out from men reflections immediate and forceful. As, for instance, the lovely "Epitaph" by Walter de la Mare:

> Here lies a most beautiful lady,
>   Light of step and heart was she;
> I think she was the most beautiful lady
>   That ever was in the West Country.
> But beauty vanishes; beauty passes;
>   However rare—rare it be;
> And when I crumble, who will remember
>   This lady of the West Country?[9]

The interpretation of resurrection as merely the persistence of human or divine memories in "minds made better by their presence" can hardly persist beyond the crumbling of the rememberers.

The noetic power resident within the self's understanding of passingness must, in preaching, be conjoined to the revelationary power resident within a story of redemptive deeds accomplished in sequential, dramatic form, within time and passingness. The congruity of the two magnitudes—man's pathos and God's passion—both unfolding their power in time and history, is the most general theme of biblical preaching: it is the homiletical counterpart to the "interpretation according to historical reason" for which Niebuhr appeals. If, as he affirms, ". . . one of the indisputable offices of theology is to open the mind of the present community to the way in which the primitive church apprehended the

---

8. A. E. Housman, "Could Man Be Drunk?," in *The Complete Poems of A. E. Housman* (New York: Holt, Rinehart, and Winston, 1959). Copyright 1940, 1959, by Holt, Rinehart and Winston, Inc. Reprinted by permission.

9. Walter de la Mare, "An Epitaph," in *Collected Poems, 1901-1918* (New York: Henry Holt, 1920) 1:160.

event that became the focus of its self-understanding," so it is an indisputable office of preaching to do the same thing.[10]

But not in the same way, for theology and preaching are distinct offices of the church. It is the task of theology to keep categories clean, to explicate the faith of the church in categories which are inwardly fashioned by the particularity of the events and affirmations which are constitutive of the community of the people of God. It is the task of preaching to enflesh these categories with the living, episodic, and anecdotal concreteness of historical and present eventfulness. This concreteness does not deliver its force in a simple melody; it requires, rather, a kind of counterpoint—voices in such contrapuntal relevancy as shall fuse together the passion from above incarnately become present in order to redeem the pathos from below.

What is required in order to move toward the accomplishment of this? As I now attempt to elaborate several requirements which that task imposes upon the preacher, it will be evident that we are still absorbed in the large figure of speech with which we began: the ecology that determines the fertility of the fields of faith. The single stone of a declaration of a specific grace, or of a promise of power, or of an all-obliterating forgiveness, or of a judgment—such single stones are set in a ring of remembered mercies. They are what they are; but what they are in their separate brightness gathers a glow and achieves a large circle of meaning, a certain steadiness of godly fact, when set in the ring of the great story.

Two propositions indicate specifically what, in my judgment, is necessary. First, a reformation of worship whereby the noetic power of time may support the content of biblical preaching. For worship is that activity of the household of God in which the content of the moment is ensconced in the events and the remembered career of the great story.[11] Worship is personal; but it is never individual. Just as it breaks personal life open to the sweep of the arc of grace in such a way as to gather the person in all the immaculate selfhood of his particularity into the fold

---

10. It is not necessary for the sake of the present argument to share this chapter's high evaluation of Niebuhr's book, nor to consent to Niebuhr's analysis and judgment upon the ideas of others who are presently busy with biblical hermeneutics. The preoccupation of the entire theological world with this issue is a significant point.

11. I have tried to make this clear in another essay during the North American Conference on Faith and Order in Oberlin in 1957. The essay is printed as an appendix to this book. The proceedings were published as *The Nature of the Unity We Seek* (St. Louis: Bethany, 1958).

Preaching and the Biblical Imagination

of the relentless Shepherd, so, with no loss of existential immediacy, it breaks open the trap of the moment to the power of the possible.

If this prospect means fresh attention to the content and role of liturgy, let us not blanch in free church horror or smilingly relax in liturgical satisfaction. We dare not blanch, for our choice is not, as one of my colleagues is wont to say, between liturgy and no liturgy; the actual choice is between liturgy which may accomplish ecological deepening and liturgy which does not, i.e., between good liturgy and bad liturgy. If the church really is, among other things, the community that remembers Jesus, then liturgy is but the obedience of the practice of the church to the reality of its mind! And we who have grown up within the liturgical tradition dare not relax as if we, by our deeds of preservation, were automatically obedient. For a liturgical tradition, shaped for recollective vitality, may be so disengaged from the glowing stone of the instant Word as not only to fail to enshrine it but actually constitute a devout irrelevancy. Repetition of the mellifluous can become torpor concealed by piety. And often does.

Recall now the evidence, illustrated previously by Niebuhr's discussion of the current theological concern with the resurrection narrative in the New Testament: that teaching and preaching have not done with this matter. Efforts to contain the meaning of the church's testimony to the resurrection within various categories of interpretation have, rather, thrust its character as intransigently belonging to the realm of historical reason sharply into the center of the church's present mind. And suppose now a preacher to this moment who has followed the biblical, philosophical, and historical battles of the past 150 years. Suppose him, further, to be a man who is compelled so to preach the gospel of the resurrection to the common life as not to betray in his pulpit what he learns in his study. Is it actually possible to declare the dimension of the meaning of the resurrection if that declaration is unsurrounded by, unsupported by, and, in the trans-momentary reality of worship, uninvested with the non-propositional noetic force of historical time? It is possible, yes. It is also possible to speak tenderly to a man who suddenly finds that he has but a few months to live, as if "He were the first to ever burst Into that silent sea"—but we commonly do not do so.

All things are more bearable if we make a story of them. And ultimate desolations are made both bearable and significant when the story is the Ultimate Story. That is why man's time, in the Order for the Burial of the Dead, is inserted not only into its own pattern of passingness, but into God's time. That is why, whether we honor liturgical continuities or not, we enfold the broken rhythms of existence within a mightier rhythm in the words of Psalm 90:

> Lord, thou hast been our dwelling place in all generations. Before the mountains were brought forth, or ever thou hadst formed the earth and the world, even from everlasting, thou *art* God. Thou turnest man to destruction; and sayest, Return, ye children of men.[12]

How the powers of the Christian past are to be related to the living moment so as to help such a central affirmation as the resurrection of Jesus Christ to bloom in the mind to its indeterminate dimension, I do not clearly know. But I do know that shallowly devised, mood-engendering stimulants to unstructured piety are not helpful. A structure appropriate to this substance, because recollective both of what this substantial affirmation gathers up into itself and of what affirmation and counsels flow out of it, serves to make available to the action of the Spirit the noetic powers resident in historical reason. Hundreds of years of Christian preaching have taken place in such a context; and while it is properly asserted that the erosion from the mind even of the church of the rich referents traditionally clustered about the Easter narratives makes dependence upon them questionable, it must nevertheless be pointed out that a process can be reversed.

There is heartening evidence that a biblical soil-conservation program is presently at work. The following facts support this belief: the participation of the churches in the theological conversations of the ecumenical movement, which perforce have had to find their common starting point and common vocabulary in biblical literature and theology; the growing body of specifically biblical theology, produced by the very vitality of fragmentary and monographic studies. These studies, extracting the differentiation of the parts, and astounded nevertheless by the historical fact that there has been discernible unity transcending them in the mind and life of the church, have thrust into the foreground a fresh interest in the unity of the biblical tradition, and in the doctrine of the church. To these forces from within the churches must be added another from without. An increasing body of contemporary literature has laid hold of old biblical themes, episodes, central terms and symbols because it finds there, presumably, stuff elemental and big enough to contain and furnish forth its message. We remark the curious fact that just

---

12. Holy Bible, Authorized Version.

Preaching and the Biblical Imagination

as, thirty years ago, the churches had about succeeded in excising Bach and Palestrina from the ken of the new generation at the moment college and high school choirs were finding them—and church schools, afraid of the recondite reaches of the doctrine of the Lord's Supper, beheld their children at school signing "O Magnum Mysterium" and "Ave, Corpus Verum"—so too the preaching fashion, having become in large part the holy branch office of the local psychiatric clinic, is now confronted with "J.B.," "The Fall," "Christmas Oratoria," and the considerable theological imagery in "Four Quartets."

Easter is not an episode; it is both a culmination and a new beginning. Resurrection is an assertion about God before it is a puzzling reported fact about Jesus. And the persistent heart of the puzzle is due to the fact that the first shines through the second, and has never been understood in the historical mind of the church in any other way. And worship in the church must set that stone in that setting—as, for instance, in the old propers of the missal for *Quasi Modo Geniti*, the first Sunday after Easter. By an ordered round of readings—Old Testament, Gospel, and Epistle—plus the fragments in Introit and Gradual, the church once secured the people against the poverty of the preacher; extended the orbit of this season's declaration beyond the fugitive inspiration of the moment. The Introit for that day, as indeed for the entire post-Easter season up to Ascension Day, makes clear that the One "with whom we have to do" in the resurrection is God. Here are selections from these Introits:

> The Earth is full of the goodness of the Lord:
> By the Word of the Lord were the heavens made.
> Say unto God, how terrible art thou in Thy works:
> Through the greatness of Thy power shall
> Thine enemies submit themselves unto Thee.
> O Sing unto the Lord a new song,
>   for He hath done marvelous things.
> His right hand, and His holy arms, hath
>   gotten Him the victory.
> Make a joyful noise unto God, all ye
>   lands, sing forth the honor of His name
> Make His praise glorious.

The Collect for the Day, by the very amplitude of the gift prayed for, makes clear that the deed of God's power in the resurrection of Jesus Christ is in a continuum of grace whose endless field of operations is nothing less than the restoration of human life to its Godly intention.

Part 2: Preaching the Word

Profoundest theological assertions in these simple prayers are made a part of the worshipers' consciousness.

> Grant we beseech Thee, Almighty God, that we who have celebrated the solemnities of the Lord's Resurrection, may by the help of Thy grace, bring forth the fruits thereof in our life and conversations: through the same Jesus Christ . . .

In the Introit the source of resurrection action is stated, in the Collect the scope of resurrection action is acknowledged, and in the Epistle and Gospel lessons which follow what is required of the hearers is set forth. This requirement in the Gospel lesson (John 20:19–31) is stated not propositionally but in a narrative: the story of the appearance of Jesus, the disbelief of Thomas, and the response of the Lord.

Simply to have these elements in this sequence in the single hour of worship does not, to be sure, guarantee anything at all. What is suggested, however, is that these words of the remembering-church-in-time provide a pattern within which the nature and size of the resurrection faith and promise is secured against reduction and trivialization. Reformation of worship cannot convey faith; it can go on a considerable distance toward making clear what the Christian object and substance of faith is.

The second proposition in which I suggest what the quest for theological method requires of preaching is this: the pace of historical reason, whereby ultimate meanings are disclosed, is not the pace at which problems of faith arise; and preaching must be a leading activity of that nurture of the church whereby this is acknowledged and dealt with. That is to say that what the gospel has by way of reply to a man's problem cannot be proclaimed, disclosed in its salvatory depth, or enfold his problem in its strange reconstitutive power with the same instant clarity and immediacy as marks the problem. What I need is clear, immediate, and pressing; what has been accomplished and is available for my need cannot be packaged and instantaneously delivered as from a holy pharmacy. Problems arise in the lives of individuals, and the terms in which the problems of faith become articulate are a function of the total life of the generation. But the replying instruction into the faith which is the church's true treasure is not commonly available to human need in the clinking and separate coins of declaration, diagnosis, judgment, and grace. The need and the reply must, in the complex ecology of faith, find their congruity. This seeking and finding have been many times described, and G. K. Chesterton's account is a particularly moving one:

Preaching and the Biblical Imagination

And then followed an experience impossible to describe. It was as if I had been blundering around since my birth with two huge and unmanageable machines, of different shapes without apparent connection—the world and the Christian tradition. I had found this hole in the world: the fact that one must somehow find a way of loving the world without trusting it; somehow one must love the world without being worldly. I found this projecting feature in the Christian theology, like a sort of hard spike, the dogmatic insistence that God was personal, and had made a world separate from Himself. The spike of dogma fitted exactly into the hole in the world—it had evidently been meant to go there—and then the strange thing began to happen. When once these two parts of the two machines had come together, one after another, all the other parts fitted and fell in with an eerie exactitude. I could hear bolt after bolt all over the machinery falling into place with a kind of click of relief. Having got one part right, all the other parts were repeating that rectitude, as clock after clock strikes noon. Instinct after instinct was answered by doctrine after doctrine. Or, to vary the metaphor, I was like one who had advanced into a hostile country to take one high fortress. And when that fort had fallen the whole country surrendered and turned solid behind me. The whole land was lit up, as it were, back to the first fields of my childhood.[13]

This process, which is the inner history of every man whose life in the whole weight of its problematic character and its ambiguous self-consciousness has been lived within the sound of the voice of the Christian tradition, has a pace that is slower than the urgent haste of individual perplexities. And in every generation it is the peculiar task of preaching to lay the shape of the healing to the peculiar contours of the hurt. This ministerial task requires a double sophistication and a double pace: the preacher must constantly repossess with the deliberate steadiness of history's pace the accumulated resources of the fields of faith, and he must at the same time race along with his time in instant knowledge of its lusts and loves, its longing and its lostness. Only thus can he sink the moment's problems into the accumulated humus of the long history of the people of God.

---

13. G. K. Chesterton, *Orthodoxy* (New York: John Lane, 1908) 144–45. Reprinted by permission.

The Role of the Imagination in Preaching

1961

This is the first of two lectures on the role of imagination in his 1955 Beecher Lectures. For Sittler the imagination is more than clever twist of the text or an apt turn of phrase. One of its functions is to fuse the theological what *and the rhetorical* how *of each text; indeed to show the inevitability of the* how. *Here we find a succinct definition of imagination: ". . . the process by which there is reenacted in the reader the salvatory immediacy of the word of God as this word is witnessed to by the speaker."*

AS WE NOW, IN this chapter and the next, inquire into the role of the imagination in preaching, we may seem to have shifted from any further concern with the ideas thus far submitted and to have entered a fresh area of reflection. To do that has not been the intention; it is rather proposed in these two sections to ask and make an effort to describe and illustrate how the notion of faith as maturing in the ecology of the history of the people of God required of preaching a vigorous and controlled use of the imagination. We have indicated under the figure of ecology in the world of nature the complex and intimate relationships operative in that process whereby Christian affirmations are made in terms integral with their status in the witnessing and remembering community, and also heard in terms which prevent their distortion into rationalistic, moralistic, naturalist, or psychological categories. In the course of the argument the noetic force of time in the process of apprehension and the significance of the revival of liturgical worship as the church's pedagogy have been pointed out. The claim has been made that worship which thus fuses the present with the remembered past is the rich and allusive theatre within which Christian affirmations are made with an amplitude proper to their nature, and responses are invited at a level proper to their gravity.

Before we get into the argument at all it is necessary to make clear in what sense the term imagination is here used. This clarification is necessary because the term has been so debased, particularly in discourse about preaching, that it were better not to use the word at all if another were available. But no other word is available. What one must do, then, is strip from the word those connotations which make its popular use perilous for our present purpose and re-present the term in its naked intention.

Imagination is not used here to designate that mere vivacity of the mind whereby unlikely juxtaposition of things or notions imparts startling cleverness to discourse; it is not a quality produced by the accidental endowment of the temperament with whimsicality. Contemporary preaching is full of dramatic and piquant turnings of the text, irresponsible arbitrariness in strained if ever so personable interpretations of biblical figures, events, and statements. That these practices are indulged in does not define imagination; one might be so unkind as to suggest that they define the preacher.

Imagination in its proper meaning is never an addition, it is an evocation. It is perception, not piquancy. Its work is not cosmetic or decorative; it is a function of percipiency. It is exercised not only in the perception of new qualities in things, but also in the discovery of hitherto unseen relationships between things. Richard Kroner, the Gifford lecturer in 1942, concluded a long chapter on the function of the imagination in the life of faith with this paragraph:

> Imagination owes its power to its peculiar nature. It is not, like sensation or intellect, confined to either the realm of sense reality or of intellectual notions and general concepts, but it belongs rather to both realms, and it is, therefore, suited to span the gulf between them. The imagination is at home in the sphere of change as well as in the sphere of changeless ideas; it is rooted as much in the visible as in the invisible world; indeed, its peculiar excellency consists exactly in its capacity of making visible what is invisible and of detecting the invisible element in the visible situation. Imagination binds together what the thinking separates; or, more precisely, it maintains the original unity of the elements separated by abstract thought. Imagination is as realistic

> as it is idealistic; it is as sensuous as it is intellectual; it moves in a medium in which the extremes are still united and undissolved.[14]

We move even closer to the definition of the role of imagination in preaching when we proceed from that judicious statement about general religious discourse to affirm that specifically Christian discourse is intrinsically needful of the same thing. For the central revelation of God in an incarnation of grace in a world of nature inwardly requires that all discourse inclusive of these two magnitudes is of necessity dialectical. And imagination is the name for that category-transcending and fusing vision and speech which is proper to the given character of God's self-disclosure. The problem of proper Christian statement may be put in another way.

The "power and the truth" of the Christian gospel is in the level and the dimensions of its assault upon the hurt God-man relationship. When once it is acknowledged that man is a creature of nature who nevertheless cannot settle for the natural and that he is an object of grace who nevertheless must celebrate grace *in* the natural—it is at the same time settled that any adequate theological explication must forever be two-sided; that is, dialectical. Its statements will always have to walk the knife edge at the frontier or fuse together the magnitudes of nature and grace.

This double character of Christian communication, if lost or blurred by oversimplification, banalization, or moralization, can perhaps achieve a hearing—but usually at the cost of the truth. Every simple term of the faith must be set forth in such a way that the multiple dimensions of its own content are exposed.

Faith, for an instance, is related to man's nature and his need. But if presented as simply engendered by nature and need and not as a faith in the faithfulness of God—that is, as trust in its object—it is distorted into a psychological reassurance, or degraded into some sort of bonding agent which can then he exploited as a necessary adhesive for the wholeness of the personality.

Love is related to man's nature and need. But if presented simply as a free-flowing human resource, itself in no need of the fires of redemption, it becomes a name for the most adored illusion ever to seduce mankind. Christian love is born not simply of love itself as expanded, sensitized, or even cauterized by suffering, but out of the love wherewith we are beloved, wherewith we are made "acceptable in the Beloved." In

---

14. Richard Kroner, *The Primacy of Faith* (New York: Macmillan, 1943) 138.

the understanding of the New Testament the passive form of the verb is always the womb of the active.

Hope, in the Christian understanding, is not simply resolute hopefulness. It is a "living hope" to which men have to be "born again." Its source is not in a religiously informed and optimistic reading of history or in the solitary human career as this may be temperamentally disposed toward the bright side of things. Its source is again its object, the "God of hope" who, we pray, may "grant us joy and peace in believing."

Only this double character of the Christian faith and life can make sense of the strange speech of the New Testament. The world is there called our proper place of obedience, the place where we are to "go and do likewise," the theatre in which Christ is to be obeyed by service to "the least of these, my brethren." And this same world as nature *and* as history is called "no abiding city," a place of pilgrimage. It is given us as our house precisely on the ground that it does not become our home. Every confession of Christendom stressed this double character of the Christian hope. "Not yet . . . yet even now."

These considerations add up to the judgment that while it is possible to make undialectical single statements about general idealism, for instance, it is quite another and a more imaginative task to expose the inner core of faith which looks like and works like idealism but is compounded of utterly different stuff. It is possible to expound simple moralism; it is another matter to communicate that kind of moral gravity which has no faith in morals but, being justified by faith, has a dynamics for moral responsibility that is forever confusing to the moralist! It is possible to make a moving sermon out of "bear ye one another's burdens." It is also possible to make a second equally moving sermon out of "every man must bear his own burdens." The task is considerably complicated however by faith's knowledge that both statements are fused and made concrete in a burden bearer of God's own choosing. "Then Jesus, knowing that He came from God and went to God, took a towel and girded Himself and began to wash the disciples' feet."

Because preaching presses for a God-determined and Christ-realized *ethicality*, and because the gift of grace whereby this possibility is bestowed is ensconced in a holy story, the character of Christian preaching is a unique kind of discourse. Current philosophical preoccupation with language analysis cannot, indeed, say what this discourse should be. It can, however, by its critical scrutiny designate the differences between propositions aimed at logical cognition and propositions aimed at the exposure of specifically the Christian and Christianly-ethical alternative.

Paul Holmer, in his article on "Kierkegaard and Ethical Theory,"[15] analyzes the difference in type of discourse between "... those who claim cognitive significance for ethical claims and those who claim ethical and religious and metaphysical significance for logical discourse." In his exposition of Kierkegaard's writings on ethics, Mr. Holmer speaks as follows:

> Ethicality is not a matter of searching for conceptual truth; it is rather a matter of seeking to become the truth.... The end of the process is not, therefore, understanding as it is in the instance of all prepositional truths but is rather 'becoming' something different than one was. Ethicality does not produce objective truths—it transforms the subject. The aim in ethics and religion is not to know the truth but to become it.... To the ethical and religious man there is no need to weep if the cognitively delineated cannot properly be called reality.... Needless to say this implies no derogation of science or gnosis—it means only that one does not apply intellectual criteria to all things human and that one states in a new way that man is not only a subject for knowledge but is also a subject in the process of making his own existence. Further, Kierkegaard insists that there is a kind of structuralization within the emotional cosmos, the inward life, too. Swenson has very aptly remarked that Kierkegaard has shown "... that the life of feeling has inherent structure and system, that valuations fall into coherent systematic groups, that emotions are not merely a structureless mush ..." He believes there is a kind of logos obtaining within subjectivity.

By an elaboration of two propositions I hope to illustrate the role of the imagination as it has been defined and asserted to have a proper role in preaching. The first proposition is this: that imagination invests the specifically Christian moral intelligence with perceptive sensibility.

There are places in the Scripture where this "logos obtaining within subjectivity" must operate to make the mind permeable to central meaning. When Isaiah protests that "the heart of this people is fat," he is lamenting something that cannot be equated with mere intellectual lethargy, recalcitrance, or even moral perversity. He is reporting a particular instance of what is general enough to have caused the ancient Litany of the church to cry:

15. See *Ethics* 63/3 (April 1953) 63.

Preaching and the Biblical Imagination

> In all times of our tribulation;
> In all time of our prosperity;
> In the hour of death;
> And in the day of judgment:
> > Help us, good Lord.

There are dynamics of damnation resident in prosperity, and they are of so sinuous and powerful a nature as to deserve acknowledgment in a series that includes tribulation, death, and judgment. There is a fat as well as a gaunt way to go to hell. There are stupors that obtain because of the decay, or the sheer blubber-encasement of some natural percipiency. For this situation Isaiah could only say that hearts are fat!

The investigation of the relationship between fat and perception is not a matter, I suppose, that formal epistemology concerns itself with; but in its words about the knowledge of God the biblical account is steeped in it. And if the imagination of the preacher does not pierce through the chinks of formal concepts and inwardly recreate what hides there, the moral heart of the matter will remain inert. Take, for an instance, Moffatt's vigorous rendering of Ephesians 4:17–19. The writer is on the trail of something that shows itself at the level of torpid intelligence, loss of purpose, and the decay of common animals decency. But he knows that these manifestations are symptomatic of some fracture that is below and anterior to them all. He writes, therefore, to ". . . insist and protest in the Lord that you must give up living like pagans, for their purposes are futile, their intelligence is darkened, they are estranged from the life of God by the ignorance which their dullness of heart has produced in them."

There is a difference between a fat heart and a dull heart. The fat-hearted are likely to be dull, but all the dull are not fat. There can be a virtuous kind of dullness of heart; a tight-lipped, efficient, decent, and unimaginative refusal to let facts be facts or, rather, a so contented existence within one's chosen and familiar world of fact that equally obvious but unexpected facts are dismissed with the same brisk impatience as a good mechanic reveals when a bumbling apprentice hands him a wrench when he needs the pliers. It is one among the many values I have for a long time gained from the work of Joseph Conrad that he perceives and pictures this grey kind of damnation with peculiar clarity. Here he is in *Typhoon*, introducing the captain:[16]

---

16. Joseph Conrad, "Typhoon," in *The Portable Conrad* (New York: Doubleday, 1959) 1, 207. Reprinted by permission of J. M. Dent & Sons, Ltd.

Part 2: Preaching the Word

> Captain MacWhirr, of the steamer *Nan-Shan*, had a physiognomy that, in the order of material appearances, was the exact counterpart of his mind: it presented no marked characteristics of firmness or stupidity: it had no pronounced characteristics whatever, it was simply ordinary, irresponsive, unruffled.

The captain's ship was on her way to a port with some cargo and 200 Chinese coolies returning to their village after a few years of work in tropical colonies. When the typhoon struck, these men, trapped in a lower deck amid a catapulting inferno of loose sea chests and other gear, were pounded to a wounded mass of misery. And all the time, as during the crucial hours before, the captain simply stared at the falling barometer in sheer refusal to open his stolid mind to the knowledge of what, even before the storm came, he ought to have done. Conrad has, in the body of the tale, the following paragraph. It speaks of the China Sea and of a captain; it also speaks of the deep and undramatic damnations wrought in the world by the dull and heavy-lidded men of good will who will not look!

> The sea itself had never put itself out to startle the silent man, who seldom looked up and wandered innocently over the water with the only visible purpose of getting food, raiment, and houseroom for three people ashore. Dirty weather he had known, of course. He had been made wet, uncomfortable, tired in the usual way, felt at the time and presently forgotten. So that upon the whole he had been justified in reporting fine weather at home. But he had never been given a glimpse of immeasurable strength and of immoderate wrath, the wrath that passes exhausted but never appeased—the wrath and fury of the passionate sea. He knew it existed, as we know that crime and abominations exist; he had heard of it as a peaceable citizen in a town hears of battles, famines, and floods, and yet knows nothing of what these things mean—though, indeed, he may have been mixed up in a street row, have gone without his dinner once, or been soaked to the skin in a shower. Captain McWhirr had sailed over the surface of the oceans as some men go skimming over the years of existence to sink gently into a placid grave, ignorant of life to the last, without ever having been made to see all it may contain of perfidy, of violence, and of terror. There are on sea and land such men thus fortunate—or thus disdained by destiny or by the sea.

There is a second way in which this proposition—that imagination invests the specifically Christian moral intelligence with perceptive sensibility—authenticates itself. We cannot come at it more bluntly and accurately than Buffon did: "The style is the man himself!" Suppose that the substance of the sermon is a section from one of the Epistles of St. Paul. The substance and the style are here so wedded that the full-blooded personal substance of what the man is saying cannot be apprehended if the imagination has not been quickened and informed by the style of the utterance. There are ways of saying this, but we shall be better instructed if we test Kroner's statement that "Imagination maintains the original unity of elements separated by abstract thought" by testing it against a concrete instance of the Pauline style.

In the whole of Scripture there is perhaps no passage in which is so tightly compressed and interwoven a more various company of massive ideas as in the eighth chapter of Romans. To make a unity out of that complexity, a symphony out of that baffling polyphony of powerful voices, is a task before which the dissecting intelligence feels its incompetence. And yet one has to know little of Paul to know that he, who wrote this, was in no confusion. His mind, though intricate in its matter and process, was no chaotic jumble of high epigrams. The task then is to seek from the inside of that passage its vital motif, its invisible cohesive element. And it is in this task that the imagination, if it has been informed by acquaintanceship with the ways of men as immemorially they have uttered in speech their turgid and passionate hears, may silently and in strange ways come to an apprehension of what otherwise alludes the mind.

With the character of that passage in Romans in your memory, consider this: that there is here exhibited a quality of the mind in its working which is not permeable to the merely analytical intelligence. Here is a quality that inheres as much in the *how* of a man's speech as in the *what* of it. The prose is forward-leaning, eager, exuberant—a manifestation of that end-over-end precipitedness that Deissmann remarked in Paul's writing, and caught in the phrase "his words come as water jets in uneven spurts from a bottle held upside down!" By imaginative association of this peculiarity of Paul's prose with other evidences of this quality in experience we can come close to knowing what it was that made him write so. And when we know that, we shall perceive in this particular instance the value claimed for the imagination in our first proposition—perceptive clarity. For is not this exuberance precisely what nature regularly exhibits at every moment of arriving at something? A horse runs with a new rhythmic vitality when he turns the last curve and straightens out on the home stretch. This vitality is due not only to the drive to win but arises out of something elemental—the combination of joy and release, the sudden realization of a long and burdening task almost done. An intricate piece of music draws its diffuse parts together in its last pages and in a muscular and positive *coda* resolves its far-wandering voices. Mighty Burke, when he "arrives" at the end of his persuasive paragraphs, gathers together his powers of thought and language for coalescence into final words of authoritative eloquence.

To have "gotten through," to have come to the end, to sense the laborious process of "working toward" about to break through into an "end achieved," is a feeling we all know. I once worked in a shop where it was my job to operate an electric drill, boring holes at marked intervals in four-by-four timbers. For the first three and half inches, it goes its way with a steady, dull growl. And then the sound becomes more open, the machine gains speed, small splinters fly as the bit bites through the last solid stuff and spins and whines with singing ease. All "arriving," all completion has this quality, whether it be a four-inch timber, a symphony, a running horse, or a work of the mind. Can you, I wonder, have failed to observe that our minds have this quality in their working?—or can we fail to catch the tempo of "arriving" in these paragraphs of the apostle? For thirty-four verses Paul's powerful mind twists and turns and torments with as mighty a complex of ideas, actions, and heavenly wonders as ever lived together in a sane man's mind. His language, like thought, is muscular, contorted, and tense—but always leaning forward . . . boring . . . boring into the hard deeps of his great subject. And then, at the thirty-fifth verse, "at last he beats his music out" in that amazing march of affirmations: "What shall we say to these things? . . . If God be for us, who shall be against us. . . ." and passes into that one of intolerable joy that ends the chapter.

Here is imagination operating exegetically to do for a passage what studious mastery of its individual parts could never accomplish. For the imagination understands that this chapter is not only argument but adoration, not a series but a sequence, not an order but an organism. Meanings "by the way" are only to be understood from the peak of spiritual song which is the brave conclusion. The ideas here are not unrelated equals pitched into a rhetorical concatenation by enthusiasm; here is, rather, the sovereignty of grace battering its way to victory through all the torments and doubts and opacities of this man's embattled soul.

In a second proposition it is possible to state how the imagination, immersed in the Pauline substance and peculiar style, works to prepare the preacher for more lively and fuller utterance of the writer's intention.

The proposition is this: Imagination is the process by which there is re-enacted in the reader the salvatory immediacy of the Word of God as this Word is witnessed to by the speaker.

The peculiarity of the style mirrors the fierce dialectic set up in the psyche by the invasive Word. The strange jump, the quick, unselfconscious corrections, the contradictions—these, which bring pain to the teacher of composition, bring theological light to the preacher. The natural-religious man can make a clean explication of his case; and the beatified child of grace could, presumably, write untroubled prose descriptive of his life in God. But the epistles of Paul stand at the intersection of nature and grace. They are the utterances of a man drawn taut between the huge repose of "a man in Christ" and the huge realism of a man of flesh and earth. It's the same man at the same time bearing witness to an inseparable movement of faith who can say: "Wretched man that I am. . . . There is therefore now no condemnation." "I don't care what you think of me. . . . I am troubled about what you think of me." "Work out your own salvation in fear and trembling because no man can work out his own salvation and does not have to, for God is at work in you!"

Preaching dare not put into unbroken propositions what the tormented peace of simultaneous existence in nature and grace can utter only in broken sentences. What God has driven asunder let no preacher too suavely join together. When we find, as we regularly do, that Paul stops the forward rush of active-voice statements to crack the integral structure of the affirmation with a joyous and devout regrounding of everything he is saying in the ultimacy of the passive voice, then we are obliged to stop with him. The salvatory power of the Word of God is eloquent precisely at the embarrassed halt. Where grammar cracks, grace erupts.

"I know," says Paul. And then he reflects upon what he knows, how he came to know it, and what kind of a religious confidence it was within which such knowledge occurred. The reflection stops the assertion cold, and he writes, "I mean, rather, that I have been known."

"I love," says Paul. And then he reflects upon how he came to the point where he can say that, by virtue of what startling and reconstitutive convulsion it has been made possible, and he stops the active voice in the remembrance of ". . . this Son of God who loved me, and gave himself . . ."

"I accept," says Paul. And then the reflection! And in the course of it the remembrance of the forgiving madness of the Holy which is the creator of all sanity, the huge and obliterating acceptance by God which empowers all acceptances among men. The passive both destroys and recreates the active in its own image; and the Christian life is spun on the axis of this holy freedom whose one end is sunk in the accepting mercy of God, its other end in the need of man for an ultimate acceptance.

This transformation of the realm of the active by the power of the passive is a key not only to isolated fragments of Paul's witness, but also to an understanding of the man's total bearing within the world of nature and history. A peculiarly illuminating instance of this transformation is the memorable passage near the end of the Philippian Letter. "Finally, brethren, whatever is true, whatever is honorable, whatever is just, whatever is pure, whatever is lovely, whatever is gracious, if there is any excellence, if there is anything worthy of praise, think about these things."

This paragraph, occurring as the summary of the argument of the entire epistle, is strange. It's almost as if Paul had forgotten what he had written, or taken back what he had so passionately affirmed, or suddenly replaces his intense and consecrated gaze by a genial and relaxed smile. For three chapters he has hacked away at the adequacy of all the confidences and solidities of religion, morality, and culture. I count everything as loss . . . even as refuse, he says—and drills through to the "surpassing worth of knowing Christ Jesus my Lord . . . that I may know him and the power of his resurrection, and may share his sufferings, becoming like him in his death, that if possible I may attain the resurrection from the dead."

And then the shift. From the packed and intense inwardness of that statement, which locates the dynamics of the faith-full life of the Christian within the enacted morphology of the incarnation and resurrection, he passes, after sundry personal and admonitory asides, to the blithe and humane: "Finally, brethren, whatever is true, whatever is honorable, whatever is just, whatever is pure, whatever is lovely . . ."

This change in tone is not a shift in center. It is, in fact, not a shift at all. It is simply the language of a man who raises his eyes from the center to the circumference. It is the maturation of centered faith into a kind of evangelical humanism. It is rhetorical celebration of a basic Christian paradox: The way to breadth is by the road of narrow concentration; the road to beauty, graciousness, justice is a road that begins with the beauty of holiness, the graciousness of grace, the justice of judgment. The really humane is a function of the fully human; the fully human is beheld and bestowed in the new man who is the second Adam who, obedient in Gethsemane, restores to God and to himself the first Adam, faithless in Eden.

These too brief samplings of the Pauline style, while sufficient perhaps to make our formal point, suggest further and more subtle things to be learned from the Apostle to the Gentiles. To these we shall give some attention in the next. But these do suffice to bring under question the venerable practice of preaching from isolated texts, or even brief pericopes. This practice, perilous enough when exercised upon the Gospels, is intrinsically disastrous when applied to the epistles of Paul. For to a degree unmatched in the world's literature, anything the man wrote has to be made luminous in the glow of everything he wrote. The apparent unsystematic of his language must be inwardly controlled and ordered by the central systematic of his passion. And he is the first to protest that this passion is a passive; that it is God's before it is his, and that it is his only because God's passion became a historical fact in a locatable garden.

Reflections on Bach

1974

Sittler preached this autobiographical sermon at Carleton College in Northfield, Minnesota. In it he speaks of his lifelong passion for the music of Johann Sebastian Bach, known to some as "the Fifth Evangelist." As he voices his appreciation of Bach, the preacher skillfully recommends the composer's sense of order, clarity, and the divinely revealed pattern for life, so evident in his music, to a college generation in sore need of all three.

THIS MORNING IN A very informal and a quite personal way, I should like to offer some reflections about the music of J. S. Bach and its influence upon my cultural and religious knowledge—and also something about the entrance into love of that music which has characterized my life. This cannot be a conventional sermon on a biblical text because those who wrote the Bible didn't have Bach in mind precisely. Therefore to twist any text to meet the intention of this service would be improper, if not impossible. Nevertheless, I want to begin with certain statements illuminative of my comment that the man and his work have deeply shaped my life.

The first music I ever heard was the music of Bach. It was in the parish church where I grew up. I knew *Bacchanal Luft und die Sturme* and *Ich ruf zu dir* and *Herzlichsten Jesu* as chorales before I ever knew "O Little Town of Bethlehem" or "The Church's One Foundation." In addition to that experience, there came another, quite accidental one that was nonetheless important and I hope interesting to you. In the early years of this century, the great corpus of the organ music of Bach was not held in high repute, largely because it wasn't heard. And it wasn't heard because in those days there were in the United States very few instruments that could realize the strong, boney, structural lines of the inner voice of the music. I lived for ten or fifteen years in Cleveland, Ohio, where there was the little organ shop of the man who built the fine instrument in your concert hall across the way. And for many, many, nights in the years 1932 and 1933 three musicians, a musicologist, and I, a simple parish pastor, sat in that organ shop while Mr. Holtkamp tried to design tonally an organ which would have sufficient clarity to capture the interior structure of the polyphonic organ music of J. S. Bach. I claim no part in that achievement except that, as one who knew of the role of that music in the history of the church catholic and its role in liturgical use in the parishes, I could bring a certain kind of common sense to what was going on. And, happily, in about 1934 a large gift to the Cleveland Museum permitted them to rebuild what up until that time had been the typical Romantic organ. The Romantic organ has its merits, but the realization of the music of J. S. Bach is not one of them, because the Romantic organ aimed for total sonority and the music of Bach requires absolute clarity. We spent a lot of time and effort building what, so far as I know, was the first Baroque organ in the United States.

Now I should like to speak a little bit about the cultural importance of Bach. I would be ill advised, indeed presumptuous, in your presence, in this school with so fine a music department, to try to talk musicologically. I have neither the competence nor, happily for you, the desire to do that. But let me try to distill into a few words what I think to be the principle cultural impact of the life and work and the music of J. S. Bach.

In the music of Bach you have an illustration of the fact that the strength and truth of a generality depends in large part upon the precision of the particular. We sometimes talk as if one could do art in general, or music in general, or undertake to develop the various categories of the life of the mind in general. The music of Bach, I think, illustrates how the road to the highest and most catholic generality commonly lies through a very clear grasp of the particular.

Bach was a church musician. Not in general, but a church musician of a very clear, well-defined tradition. In that tradition, in the eighteenth century in the church of the Reformation to which he was appointed as cantor and organist, Bach knew exactly what was supposed to happen on Sunday morning. In the great round of the church year the lessons for the day were set. The whole structure of the service aimed toward the amplification and the clarification of a certain aspect of the Christian faith. His job as a musician was not to do the work of other musicians competently, though he did much of it, but to write and produce, Sunday after Sunday, cantatas or motets for the worship of the church. It was out of his attention to the concrete particular that he achieved a magnificence which made him available to the most general. It seems to me the artist is in this way exemplary of the most profound works of the mind. One begins with attention to the concrete, the present, the given particular, and by the unfolding potentialities of the given arrives at a voice or symbolization of that which transcends the particular. But which transcendence is hardly achieved if one begins with a gaseous generality. We remember that Palestrina did not write church music in general. He wrote within a well-defined situation in the Roman Catholic tradition. We know very well that Dietrich Buxtehude did not write music for all Germany. It became music for all Germany because out of a very clear tradition of Saint Mary's Church in Lübeck he wrote the music for its celebrated vesper services. The same could be said of the hymnist Isaac Watts, writing out of the rich, folk, passionate tradition of protesting Wesleyanism and the dissenter churches in England at the beginning of the Industrial Revolution. He wrote hymns which, because they grasp the interior passion of the particular, are capable of expansion to the most general.

Ideas of cultural importance expand out of the given. We often look upon the processes of creativity as being somehow hampered by the reigning traditions, the given mores, or the available disciplines in an art, even in the arts of philosophy or scientific thought. I think this ought to be brought under question. For it seems to me that what we, from the outside, look upon as a kind of limit that quenches, may be a discipline that releases. To be forced to work within the limitations of a custom, form, or a given practice may indeed be an act of deliverance to the creative intelligence of that very passion and discipline, whereby within the given form it accomplishes so much. One could use numerous illustrations of that, but I will spare you most of those and say that one of the most admirable things about the work of Bach is the innovation accomplished within the apparent limitations of the musical forms which tradition had delivered to his hand. There is a chorale prelude on the old chorale *O Mensch bewein dein Sunde gross*, "O Man Bewail Your Gravest Sin." That work has always fascinated me because in several complex lines near the end of the prelude, which indeed Charles Marie Widor has called the greatest page in the history of music, it develops a general theme stated by the chorale itself. They move into such a knotted complexity that you wonder how the man will ever get out of the box he has built around himself. And then, at one miraculous moment, this whole tightened tension is marvelously resolved in a beautiful little slide away from a knot which musicologically I cannot express, which is almost parabolic of the kind of life I've led. Most of us do work ourselves or think ourselves into paradoxes or contradictions to which we think there is no possible escape. The memory of that chorale prelude rings in my memory as a kind of a confident hope that at least one man brought it all together.

The second part of what I want to say has to do with the significance of the work of Bach for the religious community, particularly for Western religion in general. Here I want to gather my thoughts under several words. First of all, the magnificent *order* in his music. I began to wonder about how to put this about a week ago, when I had to begin attending to this job, when I asked myself, "Why is it that your generation is astoundingly interested in Bach and you play and listen to so much of his music?" There has never been so much Bach played on the public radio or heard in concert halls or performed in collegiate choirs and orchestras. Why is it that this generation should be particularly grabbed by the music of this man and of other musicians of his period? I think it's the sheer intersection of the difference. Let me try to unwrap that a bit.

What you love is the difference: the music is absolutely orderly and we aren't. In the midst of a messed up, ambiguous, questionable, dubious, suspicious world, there's something of remarkable order here, which I think speaks to us—not of what we are but what we aren't and that maybe, nostalgically, we wish we might become. In fact, more than one philosopher has said that the fundamental operation in all works of the mind is an effort to achieve order. It seems to me that our disordered time hears in Bach a certain promise and does so with deep affection.

The second word is *clarity*, and here again the appeal is due, I think, to the both judging and promising difference, because clarity is mostly what we haven't got. We are unclear. Not only your generation, but I who am now an old duffer, are unclear about our identity. We are constantly shifting in our notion of what ought to have priority in terms of values. All of us, particularly in this nation, are unclear about the ability of the orders which have characterized our public and private life. Do they have the capacity to contain the vitalities of life and to order them toward maturation? We're unclear about this. But old J. S. Bach somehow writes a fugue which, in swift, bright, undeviating velocity, goes from the starting point to the marvelously satisfying coda without looking to right or left. It is this swiftness and lack of ambiguity that I think attract this generation in much of the music of Bach and his contemporaries. We may not like the statement he's making, but there's never a moment's doubt about what the statement is: admirable clarity.

If I might divert just a moment, there's something to be said here too about the importance of Bach's music for our educational processes. In the last five weeks, I have been in eight colleges and universities. And such a fouled-up groping for the possible I have never before beheld. I think it is one of the admirable qualities of this strong and beautiful college that it still seems to know what it's about; that it has not gone gimmicky; that with a kind of steadiness of vision it seems to know that general illumination and maturation, without disciplined attention to certain abiding particularities, ends up in bad education. And therefore, it seems to me that this order, in its ability to achieve clarity, is one of the reasons we listen with appreciation to this music.

And thirdly, in Bach I find a symbol of this: humanity's historical life can be drawn into a pattern by an eternal object, whereby the wavering and diffuseness of our lives are drawn into a figure. Now, this is not a generation that greatly esteems transcendental patterns. But whether we esteem it or not, let us stand with the kind of admiration before a man who *did* know the historical reality of his own existence in his time and his vocation. He did know what it meant to have his whole life drawn into a clear, consistent, and elevated pattern in life, thought, and work by virtue of an eternal object, which acts as a kind of pattern-making allure to all the comings and goings of our human existence.

The fundamental religious lesson that we learn from Bach is that he himself articulated in his music. He also did so in a violent and angry letter to the blockheaded church consistory that ruled over St. Thomas Church in Leipzig, in which he says, "I would have you know, gentlemen, that I cannot worthily offer my work to God if I must please everybody." Here is in his work and his words the religious point, the fundamental declaration of the Christian faith, which he celebrated when he signed his work *Soli Deo Gloria*, "to the greater glory of God." Life can be pulled together. Historical diffusions and phenomena, along with clashing values, can be drawn into a pattern. The historical can be redeemed in both beauty and truth by the allure of the eternal.

Preaching Symphonically

1975

Sittler often reflected on preaching by way of analogy to music or sometimes as a form of music. In this sermon he discusses the contrapuntal of law and gospel and the challenge faced by preachers as they rightly distinguish these two tones of God's Word. He warns against the heavy-handed division or separation of law and gospel. The text does not present a stencil for the preacher to trace; rather, it suggests a symphony of themes found throughout Scripture. While his comments reflect a peculiarly Lutheran problematic, the relation of justification and sanctification, the questions he raises in this sermon confront all Christian preachers.

IF AN ISSUE IS both insoluble and undismissible, it's likely to be important. The lessons today to which I invite you to informal reflection present us with exactly such an issue. Luther once said that the norm by which a theologian must be judged is his ability to distinguish between law and gospel. And the eminent Dr. Walther, some centuries later, went him one better and said that the mark of the theologian is to be able rightly to divide law and gospel. Unhappily, all Lutherans are tempted to suppose the word "divide" means to separate, and not to distinguish between. And a good deal of the problem in which we find ourselves in trying inwardly to comprehend and receive the gospel and then find ways to live it out in this appalling world—a good deal of that problem derives from the understanding of the word "divide," because we understand it in terms of "separate" law and gospel. And there is very little in the tradition of teaching the history of Israel in our schools that would modify that fundamental misunderstanding, whereby, despite what we learn in our schools, most men and women I hear preach keep on talking about the Law as somehow a form of the God-relationship which is absolutely abolished and of no account.

Now, I want to call you to reflect upon that this morning. And want to suggest that whereas we are indeed *saved* by grace, we may also be *seduced* by grace. That's exactly what Dietrich Bonhoeffer meant—he pointed to that temptation in his memorable word about "cheap grace." We all rejoice, I suppose, in the church's provision for us of a new lectionary, a lectionary in which the material from the Old Testament is both more plentiful and more aptly chosen to go with the other lessons. But our rejoicing in that new lectionary might be properly somewhat modified by the acknowledgement that it increases the torment of being a responsible preacher. Because when we *preach symphonically* out of the Bible—not just episodically—when we preach symphonically out of the Bible, trying to penetrate to the meaning of its fundamental themes, and not just picking up juicy bits of homiletical temptation here and there, we find ourselves plunged into a torment from which all one's life there is no release. Therefore this morning I want to call upon you to reflect with me upon the theme, the complex and difficult theme that is presented in these three lessons when they are read together, as in the public worship of the congregation they now regularly are. We had the lesson from Deuteronomy. There is no doubt about what it means: There is a God. This God has a will, a purpose and an intention, and God proposes to carry it out. This God of all things that are, to his people Israel, presented the Torah, the will and the intention, the Law of God as a demand. Now we may understand "demand" in two ways. We often mean by "demand" that, if you chose to take up a certain enterprise, it is demanding. The word "demand" here doesn't mean that. It doesn't mean *what* you have to do if you do it at all; it means *that* you must do it. Therefore the Torah, the Law of God, the requirement intrinsic in the God-relationship based upon his God-initiated covenant, is not an elective demand. It is the demand that goes with the creation of life itself. Now, in Deuteronomy there are strong, graphic, rhetorically memorable ways in which that is put: binding the exterior symbolizations of this demand of God between the eyes, and around the wrist, and on the doorpost of the house, and on the gate of the estate. How powerfully it is said that these are not elective requirements, because the lesson ends with the promise of a blessing, and also the notice of a curse.

And then, immediately, the second lesson that we are called upon to reflect upon this day is the lesson from the Romans in which it is said that the righteousness of God—that is, that right that God establishes and requires—that the righteousness of God, is now "manifested apart from the Law," and grace-drunk Lutherans are inclined to translate that, "against the Law," with no relation to the Law. It is annulled. It is annihilated. Which is not what the text says. And in other places Paul makes it even more clear: when he cries to a man who said, "Let us therefore sin the more that grace may abound. We can work both sides of the street"—to which Paul replies in a Semitic word of horror, "God forbid!" Now, having talked about that which God gives is grace, in relation to what he demands, God's Law, we then move right on to this totally confusing Gospel lesson. In that context our Lord says that whether or not you are in a right God-relationship is not unrelated to the way your faith controls your *life*, not just your interior, devout, reflections. Here it is clearly exposed, that kind of particularly Lutheran temptation that I'm talking about: the Lutheran temptation to suppose that to *be* in grace, to celebrate grace, to know that grace is indeed amazing, may also lead to the most sanctimonious form of fundamental disobedience. Having talked about the Law and then that which comes alongside and fulfills the Law, apart from the Law itself, this Gospel lesson clouts us directly over the head with the statement of Jesus about, "If you do not the things I command, you shall not enter into the kingdom of God."

Now these reflections, taken together, I think illustrate what I mean when I said that to be a responsible preacher of the gospel is a tormenting business, from which in this life there is no release. This is a particularly difficult problem right now. As if we were indulging in a kind of frantic flight from the difficulties of dealing with things that are both insoluble but undismissible, we flee to the bosom of Jesus. To be a Jesus-person is a very devout way of copping out of the God-relationship. "Jesus only" is a fundamentally blasphemous statement. Jesus himself had no interest in "Jesus only." He was not constituted from himself, or by himself, or for himself. "My need is to do the will of him that sent me." To understand grace as a kind of sentimental relationship to Jesus whereby, if one wallows deeply enough in that relationship, a parking lot at the local hospital will always be secured—this is a kind of devotional blasphemy which completely ignores and denies the fundamental thrust of the church's meaning when she puts these three lessons together. When we think about Jesus, let us think about Jesus as an aperture into that fundamental reality which founded all of his own thought. Calvin was quite right: "Our business is with God." And Jesus, in many ways, said the same thing.

As a background to thinking about an authentic relationship through Jesus, with the Father, as a background to that, recall that remarkable episode about which I have never heard a sermon. (I think it may be too hot an issue to handle). That is the episode in which a woman, her bosom heaving with maternal sentiment, said, "Oh, how happy God must be to have a Son like you," and Jesus turned to her with the biting reply, "Yeah, rather, blessed are they that hear the word of God and keep it." May I suggest that the Law is a primal form of grace. There is no Law which is not distinct and pregnant and permeated with the grace of God, who covenants out of grace to lead his people in this life and give them laws and directions. And there is no grace which does not have in the background, as the formal program for its gracious reception, the doing of the Law. Therefore, when an issue which is both insoluble and undismissible constitutes a lifelong torment for the theologian and the preacher, it is just possible that the only way to re-solve what is formerly in-soluble is to thrust it into the mystery of the sacrament of the Lord's Supper, where both the commandment of God meets us and the grace of God invites us to participation in *God's* solution of our insoluble.

PART 3

Sermons

Introduction

The Preacher as Theological Artisan

EVERY SO OFTEN ONE hears a preacher say, "I'm no theologian," as if to confirm the modern division of labor between systematic theology and preaching. The implication of such a comment is that while the theologian engages in fine distinctions and specialized forms of knowledge well behind the lines of battle, the preacher is out there in the trenches attending to the needs of real people. Our contemporary culture of global communication and instant accessibility no longer allows such a neat distinction. In fact, in its formative years the Christian church did not allow it either. Its great theologians like Origen, Augustine, the Cappadocians, and Luther were also its most influential preachers who gave shape and specificity to the Christian message in their daily sermons. What they advanced was not a theological treatise or a perfectly formed homily but the Word of God for the people of God in a particular time and place.

Joseph Sittler belongs to the same tradition. His theology was characterized by awareness of the splendor of God's cosmos as well as the pointed, dialectical struggles that take place at every level of reality, including nature, human nature, and God. Intellectually and spiritually, he was controlled by both sides of that truth. His was a theology made for preaching, for the preacher is subject to the same tension, or "tautness," as he liked to call it, between breadth and specificity and produces a message out of it every Sunday.

Although he understood the tragic conflict implied by the theology of the cross, Joseph Sittler is best remembered for his vision of the whole. He refused to segregate grace from nature, redemption from creation, gospel from law, church from culture, or the particular from the universal in God's theater of operations. In one of his sermons he quotes a seminarian who blurted out in class, "If God is not enough God for everything, he isn't enough God for anything." It might have been Sittler talking. But just when we are about to place him with the visionaries, like one of his heroes, Teilhard de Chardin, he reminds us of the revelatory importance of disjunction in nature and human life: "Where grammar cracks," he said in his Beecher Lectures, "grace erupts." "What God has riven asunder, let no preacher too suavely join together." He moves, sometimes rather abruptly, from the vastness of intellectual traditions to the homely illustration or impolitic opinion. He has no problem alternating between the lyricism of poetry and the bluntest language imaginable.

In one of his sermons on Romans 8, which is perhaps the keenest display of Paul's dialectic in the New Testament, Sittler captures both the grandeur and the spoilage of creation:

> Man's life is deeply imbedded in the root, in the ground of nature, just as the leaves on that plant back of me are embedded in the ground in that pot. Thus the whole creation, in the beautiful figure, the whole creation *and we ourselves* are groaning in travail, waiting. The picture here is not only of an untroubled opening toward God's fulfillment, but a tumultuous and painful opening, so that the episodes that we might regard as being disruptive of the human community may be the groaning of nature and history to bring out a future better, a future justice.

Later in the same sermon, he abandons the Latinate elegance for which he was celebrated and cuts the evildoers down to size with Anglo-Saxon punch: "The practical people of this world know that there is a lot of cheap meat for dogs and cats available if they chase down the last of the remaining 300 sperm whales . . ." And of the oil and gas executives he adds, "[They] say in effect, 'Just give us more money to pump it faster from more places and to get it quicker from where it is to where it ain't, and we will solve our energy crisis. That is one of the stupidest remarks ever made by a sane mind; that we solve the problem of a non-replaceable resource by using it faster." In a couple of paragraphs the reader is treated to a theological lesson in creation and a rhetorical lesson in the languages of preaching.

Although he was a theologian, when Sittler stepped into the pulpit he did not offer mere applications of a higher knowledge gleaned elsewhere, but, in Gerhard Ebeling's description of good preaching, he "executed" the text. That doesn't mean he killed the text with background information or trivial stories, but he *activated* it for continued service to the church. Like Luther, he believed theology was something you do, and, like Luther, he did much of his biblical theology on Sunday morning in the presence of astonished witnesses.

He arrived at his first parish in Cleveland in 1930 at the headwaters of the Great Depression. He worried that he had not experienced a revelatory "call" to ministry, but then he remembered his pastor-father's admonition, "If by disposition and some endowment, you can do what terribly needs doing, how loudly do you want the call to yell at you?" The tiny congregation in Cleveland Heights, Ohio, did have terrible needs—of its 141 members, 60 percent were out of work and many were hungry. Sittler remained there for 13 years. The way he remembers it, "[N]o jazzed-up veneer, 'clap hands for Jesus gospel' would do. It had to be at the level of tragedy, of deprivation, of the ultimate loneliness, of being unable to look your own children in the face, at the level of that kind of *pathos*, one had to say something on Sunday morning or shut up." It might have been in his first parish that he learned how providentially God's passion for the world fits into the passions and deprivations of humankind.

But Sittler being Sittler also meant that even in the humble circumstances of his first parish, his love of great music continued to flourish. For in the same city an organ builder named Holtkamp was building the first Baroque organ in the United States, an instrument, as Sittler puts it, that would be capable of realizing "the strong, boney, structural lines" of Bach's music. Young Pastor Sittler, along with three musicians, a musicologist, and Holtkamp, participated in that building project for two years. Bach was never far from Sittler's theology or homiletic, most notably (in this volume) in his "Reflections on Bach" delivered to students at Carelton College.

Sittler viewed preaching as an extension of the Hebraic power of naming. For him the linguisticality of existence was not a philosophical idea but a theological conviction. By means of language, human beings take part in the divine-like act of creation in which poets, artists, musicians, and—dare we say?—preachers lead the way. In "The Care of the Earth," the preacher speaks almost wistfully of the poet's ability "to say out loud and with resonant clarity what we all would wish to say had we the dark music and the language." The preacher, too, functions as an artisan—a theological artisan—who crafts from the materials of God's Word partial, suggestive, and time-sensitive fragments of a truth so filled with majesty that it is unutterable in its wholeness. He loved to cite Isaiah's inaugural vision of the splendor of the Lord and the lowliness of the prophet whose lips must be cleansed before he can speak. The sonorousness and allusiveness of Sittler's own language can give the impression of preacher who loves the sound of his own voice. He did have the knack of topping off a dense exposition of a theological concept with a memorable aphorism. For example, the partialness of our knowledge leads to mystery, which can only lead to doxology:

> And I've made the discovery—at least a discovery for me—that where Paul sings out most clear and clean and simple is when he's singing doxology. It's very interesting that the church was singing, apparently before she was cerebrating. She made music before she made propositions. The truth of the gospel lies more in the congruity of images than in the verifiability of the propositions. When the church emerges out of the shadows of antiquity, we hear her with a song in her mouth.

He did love words. Which makes it doubly important that his readers understand the source and disposition of that love. It originated in his father's church in the biblical, liturgical, and catechetical language in which he was nurtured. It would be an interesting exercise to note how many Sittler sermons hinge on the meaning of a biblical word and its contemporary nuances. As an old man he reflected on how as a boy he was moved by the words of the communion liturgy, "Therefore with angels and archangels and all the company of heaven, we laud and magnify thy glorious Name evermore praising thee and saying . . ." He admits that he didn't understand it, but he knew, "this is big. This is high."

The value he places on language bears directly on the glory of God's Word. Aristotle said, "A free man should not talk like a slave." Sittler would have paraphrased those sentiments by insisting that those who have been set free by the ministrations of the Word have no business trivializing it. Thus he rarely engages in the great weakness of preachers everywhere, the sermon illustration; he never tells a story or cites an example in order to shore up the Word of God, as if the biblical account is uninteresting or lacks concreteness. He probes the textual revelation until it yields the most concrete result imaginable, which is the hearer's realization of life in the presence of the risen Christ. In its outcome, if not its style, his preaching most resembles that of Dietrich Bonhoeffer.

The effective use of language brings its own kind of clarity and its own brand of authority. Mark Twain said that the difference between the right word and the almost right word is the difference between lightning and the lightning bug. When the preacher-theologian finds the right word, we see things we hadn't seen before. If we were used to thinking of exegesis in terms of historical archeology, Sittler's use of the word "imagination" helps reframe the meaning and scope of exegesis. If one considers preaching to be a matter of individual performance, the single word "ecology" changes all that. "Ecology" creates a new image and evokes a new understanding of an ancient task. The metaphoric effect of "The Ecology of Preaching" is a preacher, text, and tradition that are situated in something larger than themselves. Much larger: "The scope of the covenant of grace is here presented [in the Noah story] as identical with all that is."

Unlike many contemporary preachers, who compulsively dart from point to point and story to story, Sittler patiently explored one insight derived from the text. He did not rifle through the text for usable notions but invariably discovered the one thing needful in it. How many points should a sermon have? He would have agreed: at least one. He did his work so thoroughly that even the contemporary reader continues to be moved by the *necessity* of this particular line of reasoning and these particular formulations.

Augustine wrote in *On Christian Doctrine* that a sermon has the capacity to teach, delight, and move, and sometimes all in the same sermon. Sittler's patient exposition of the Word of God in its historical and cultural settings inevitably cast him in the role of teacher to a church that was rapidly losing touch with its own theological heritage. By the same token, the beauty of his language and the pungency of his aphorisms never failed to delight. The sheer inventiveness of "The Nimbus and the Rainbow," with its insightful comparison of the precision of grace laid on one person, symbolized by the halo, and the wider span of God's blessing on a city or a people, symbolized by the rainbow, is intellectually satisfying. One can *enjoy* a Sittler sermon. But, following Augustine, Sittler was also capable of moving a congregation to a deeper awareness of the majesty of God or the cruciality of the cross. When these moments come in the sermon, they are often associated with Sittler's willingness to convey his own sense of discovery and to make testimony.

In the past sixty years homiletics has entertained and exhausted many fads—encounter, experience, ecstasy, story—but Joseph Sittler never really bit on any of them. To hear him again, he seems comfortable doing it his way and in the process not only teaches, delights, and moves his congregations, but forms them for responsible lives of faith. He never pretended it was easy work. If it was easy, he wouldn't have written a book called *The Anguish of Preaching*, in which he merges his voice with the Apostle's: "I am again in the pain of childbirth until Christ is formed in you" (Gal 4:19).

Richard Lischer

The Care of the Earth

1961

In characteristic fashion, Sittler's prophetic words on behalf of the care of the earth are deeply integrated with worship of God in God's holiness. In this well-known sermon and in his many other writings that sound the call to environmental responsibility the ethical imperative is never detached from faith's living encounter with God.

A SERMON MAY MOVE from idea to fulfillment in various and sometimes strange ways. It may be useful as an introduction to the theme of this sermon to say how that happened in the writing of it.

In April of last year I read a poem in the *New Yorker* magazine; the poet is Mr. Richard Wilbur. What the poet was saying struck and stuck for several obvious reasons. Beneath the quite clear apprehensions that float about just under the surface of our minds there is a root apprehension that churns deep down at the center. It is vague, but it is also relentless and undismissable. And the poet's words interest this inarticulate anxiety, stop it cold, give it a "local habitation and a name." The substance of this anxiety is common to us all, and it is heavy. It is the peculiar function of the poet sometimes to say out loud and with resonant clarity what we all would wish to say had we the dark music and the language.

The substance is this: annihilating power is in nervous and passionate hands. The stuff is really there to incinerate the earth—and the certainty that it will not be used is not there.

Part 3: Sermons

Nor have we anodyne to hush it up or power to run away from it. We can go skiing with it, trot off to Bermuda with it, push it down under accelerated occupation with the daily round, pour bourbon over it, or say our prayers—each according to his tactic and disposition. But it goes along, survives, talks back.

Not in abstract proposition or dramatic warnings but in powerful, earthy images the poet makes his point. The point is single, simple, and absolute: humanity's selfhood hangs upon the persistence of the earth, *her* dear known and remembered factualness is the matrix of the self.

> When you come, as you soon must,
>   to the streets of our city,
> Mad-eyed from stating the obvious,
> Not proclaiming our fall but begging us
> In God's name to have self-pity,
>
> Spare us all word of the weapons, their
>   force and range,
> The long numbers that rocket the mind;
> Our slow, unreckoning hearts will be
>   left behind,
> Unable to fear what is too strange.
>
> Nor shall you scare us with talk of the
>   death of the race.
> How should we dream of this place
>   without us –
> The sun mere fire, the leaves untroubled
>   about us,
> A stone look on the stone's face?
>
> Speak of the world's own change. Though
>   we cannot conceive
> Of an undreamt thing, we know to our cost
> How the dreamt cloud crumbles, the vines
>   are blackened by frost,
> How the view alters. We could believe,
>
> If you told us so, that the white-tailed
>   deer will slip
> Into perfect shade, grown perfectly shy,
> The lark avoid the reaches of our eye,
> The jack-pine loose its knuckled grip

The Care of the Earth

> On the cold ledge, and every torrent burn
> As Xanthus once, its gliding trout
> Stunned in a twinkling. What should we
>   be without
> The dolphin's arc, the dove's return,
>
> These things in which we have seen
>   ourselves and spoken?
> Ask us, prophet, how we shall call
> Our natures forth when that live tongue
>   is all
> Dispelled, that glass obscured or broken,
>
> In which we have said the rose of our love
>   and the clean
> Horse of our courage, in which beheld
> The singing locust of the soul unshelled,
> And all we mean or wish to mean.
>
> Ask us, ask us whether with the
>   wordless rose
> Our hearts shall fail us; come demanding
> Whether there shall be lofty or long
>   standing
> When the bronze annals of the
> oak-tree close.[1]

By sheer force of these lines my mind was pushed back against the wall and forced to ask: is there anything in our Western religious tradition as diagnostically penetrating as that problem, as salvatory as that predicament?

Out of these back-to-wall reflections I therefore ask your attention to several statements that seem to me alone deep and strong enough to make adequate sense. These statements have in common this: they deal with the *enjoyment* of things and the *uses* of things. And together they add up to a proposition: delight is the basis of right use.

The first statement is the celebrated answer to the first question in the Westminster Catechism. No one will question the velocity with which this answer gets to the point or that the point is worth getting at! The

---

1. Richard Wilbur, "Advice to a Prophet." Copyright © 1959 by Richard Wilbur. Reprinted from Wilbur, *Advice to a Prophet and Other Poems* by permission of Harcourt, Brace & World, Inc.

question is: "What is the chief end of man?" The answer: "To glorify God and enjoy him forever!"

The first verb, "to glorify," is not primarily intellectual. It does not concern itself with the establishment of the existence of God, or with a description of God's nature. The verb is not aesthetic either. It is not concerned to declare that God is good or beautiful, or propose that it is a fair thing to worship God. Nor is it hortatory, that is, it does not beat us over the head with admonitions about our duty to God.

The verb "to glorify" is exclusively and utterly religious! The verb comes from the substantive "glory": and that term designates what God is and has and wills within himself; it announces the priority, the ineffable majesty, the sovereign power and freedom of the holy. Glory, that is to say, is what God is and does out of himself; and when we use the term for what we do in response, that response is given and engendered by his glory.

The priority-in-God, and the proper work of this verb may be illustrated by its function in the sixth chapter of the book of Isaiah. The young prophet, rich and eager in his expectations of the new king, Uzziah, is stunned when the king dies. He goes into the temple, and then comes the vision of the glory of whose ineffable power the face of the king is but the reflection.

> In the year that King Uzziah died I saw the Lord sitting upon a throne, high and lifted up; and his train filled the temple. Above him stood the seraphim; each had six wings: with two he covered his face, and with two he covered his feet, and with two he flew. And one called to another and said: "Holy, holy, holy is the Lord of hosts: the whole earth is full of his glory."[2]

The glory is the light the holy gives off. The earth is a theater of the glory; it is rich with the ineffable glory because God, the Holy One, has made it.

The holy is a numinous and absolute word. It is not contained within other categories; it is a category. The holy both evokes and demands thought, but it is a misunderstanding to assume that thoughts can contain the glory and the holy. The holy certainly has the effect that Professor Rudolph Otto in his great work, *The Idea of the Holy*, calls *mysterium tremendum et fascinosum*—but there is an unseizable plus to the term that eludes even the image-making genius of the Jews.

The holy invites prayer, but rejects such an understanding of prayer as would make prayer a tool for working upon the holy, a device for

---

2. Isa 6:1–3.

making the holy disposable by man. The holy demands service, but no service adds up to a responding equivalent just as in our human love one serves the beloved but never affirms his service to be the measure of love.

The chief end of humanity is, then, to glorify God, to let God *be* God, to understand and accept God's life in ways appropriate to the imperial, holy singularity of God. The meaning of this has, to be sure, ethical, psychological, even political implications. But the center is categorically religious.

But this statement about God and humanity, thus elevated, tough, and absolute, is conjoined in the catechism with a concluding phrase, "and enjoy him forever." The juxtaposition of commands to glorify and to enjoy is on several grounds startling to our generation. To enjoy is a strange thing, that is to say, to do about the holy God before whom even the seraphim do hide their faces. This joining of the *holy*, which is what God is, with *joy*, which designates what humanity is to have and do in God—this juxtaposition, in that it is startling to us, says a good deal about modern American understanding of the Christian faith. How it has come about that we are startled by what our fathers joined together without batting an eye is a matter we cannot now go into, but only observe it and ask after its significance. For we may have missed something. If the gravity of the glorification of the holy and the blithe humaneness of "enjoy him forever" seem strange, our churches in the very form of their building may be partly to blame. There is the clean, shadowless, and antiseptic colonial, the monumental melancholy of the Romanesque and Gothic adaptations—bereft of the color and ornament which in other lands are so devoutly joined in these forms. Our traditional churches affirm a heavy kind of solemnity that leaves us indeed with a lugubrious holy, but defenseless and aghast before the joy of, for instance, a Baroque church. Such a church is luxuriant, joy-breathing, positively Mozartean in its vivacity—replete with rosy angels tumbling in unabashed enjoyment among impossibly fleecy clouds against an incredible blue heaven.

We shall not draw conclusions from that—only observe it and let it hang—that the gravity of a life determined by God, lived to the glory of God, is not necessarily incongruent with abounding joy. It is interesting to recall that the most rollicking music old periwig Bach ever wrote is not dedicated to the joy of tobacco (although he did that) or coffee (and he praised that) or the inventiveness among his fellow musicians, nor dedicated to the levity of the Count of Brandenburg, but *In Dir ist Freude* ("In Thee Is Joy")!

Part 3: Sermons

The second statement is ascribed to Thomas Aquinas, surely not the playful or superficial type. Thomas did not affirm Christianity as a consolatory escape hatch, or an unguent to the scratchy personality, or a morale builder to a threatened republic—all contemporary malformations. But he did say, "It is of the heart of sin that men use what they ought to enjoy, and enjoy what they ought to use." Apart from the claim that it is *sin* that people do that, and apart from the seriousness of the situation if that statement should turn out to be true, is the statement reportorially so?

Yes, it is so, for all of us, and in many ways. Thomas is simply condensing here the profound dialectic of use and enjoyment that distorts and impoverishes life when it is not acknowledged and obeyed. To use a thing is to make it instrumental to a purpose, and some things are to be so used. To enjoy a thing is to permit it to be what it is prior to and apart from any instrumental assessment of it, and some things are to be so enjoyed.

I adduce a small example: it may bloom in our minds into bigger ones. Wine is to be *enjoyed*; it is not to be *used*. Wine is old in human history. It is a symbol of nature in her smiling beneficence—"close bosom friend of the maturing sun." That is why it has virtually everywhere and always been the accompaniment of celebrative occasions, the sign of gladness of heart. It is to be enjoyed; it is not to be used to evoke illusions of magnificence, or stiffen timidity with the fleeting certainty that one is indeed a sterling lad. Where it is enjoyed it adds grace to a truth; where it is used it induces and anesthetizes a lie.

Observe in Psalm 104 how the Old Testament man who sought to glorify God and enjoy him forever stood in the midst of nature. "He . . . gives wine to gladden the heart of man, and oil to make his face shine." "This is the day which the Lord has made;" he exults, "let us rejoice and be glad in it." Why? Not primarily for what he can turn the day's hours into, but rather on the primal ground that there are days—unaccountable in their gift-character, just there. And here he is—permeable by all he is sensitive to: texture, light, form, and movement, the cattle on a thousand hills. Thou sendest forth thy Spirit and they are! Let us rejoice and be glad in it!

> i thank You God for this most amazing
> day: for the leaping greenly spirits of trees
> and a blue true dream of sky; and for everything
> which is natural which is infinite which is yes[3]

3. e. e. Cummings, "i thank You God." Copyright © 1950 by e. e. cummings. Reprinted from Cummings, *Poems 1923–1954*, 464, by permission of Harcourt, Brace & World, Inc.

It is the heart of sin that human beings use what they ought to enjoy.

It is also, says Thomas, of the heart of sin that people are content to enjoy what they ought to use. Charity, for instance. Charity is the comprehensive term to designate how God regards humanity. That regard is to be used by persons for persons. That is why our Lord moves always in his speech from the source of joy, that humanity is loved by the holy, to the theater of joy, that persons must serve the need of the neighbor. "Lord, where did we behold thee? I was in prison, hungry, cold, naked"—you enjoyed a charity that God gives for use.

If the creation, including our fellow creatures, is impiously used apart from a gracious primeval joy in it the very richness of the creation becomes a judgment. This has a cleansing and orderly meaning for everything in the world of nature, from the sewage we dump into our streams to the cosmic sewage we dump into the fallout.

Abuse is use without grace; it is always a failure in the counterpoint of use and enjoyment. When things are not used in ways determined by joy in the things themselves, this violated potentiality of joy (timid as all things holy, but relentless and blunt in its reprisals) withdraws and leaves us, not perhaps with immediate positive damnations but with something much worse—the wan, ghastly, negative damnations of use without joy, stuff without grace, a busy, fabricating world with the shine gone off, personal relations for the nature of which we have invented the eloquent term "contacts," staring without beholding, even fornication without finding.

God is useful. But not if sought for use. Ivan, in *The Brothers Karamazov*, saw that, and Dostoevsky meant it as a witness to the holy and joy-begetting God who he saw turned into an ecclesiastical club to frighten impoverished peasants with, when he had his character say, "I deny God for God's sake!"

All of this has, I think, something to say to us as teachers and students to whom this university is ever freshly available for enjoyment and use. For consider this: the basis of discovery is curiosity, and what is curiosity but the peculiar joy of the mind in its own given nature? Sheer curiosity, without immediate anticipation of ends and uses, has done most to envision new ends and fresh uses. But curiosity does this in virtue of a strange counterpoint of use and enjoyment. Bacon declared that "studies are for delight." The secular counterpart of "glorify God and enjoy him forever." The Creator who is the fountain of joy, and the creation which is the material of university study, are here brought together in an ultimate way. It is significant that the university, the institutional solidification of the fact that studies are for delight, is an idea and a creation of a culture that once affirmed that men should glorify God and enjoy him forever.

Use is blessed when enjoyment is honored. Piety is deepest practicality, for it properly relates use and enjoyment. And a world sacramentally received in joy is a world sanely used. There is an economics of use only; it moves toward the destruction of both use and joy. And there is an economics of joy; it moves toward the intelligence of use and the enhancement of joy. That this vision involves a radical new understanding of the clean and fruitful earth is certainly so. But this vision, deeply religious in its genesis, is not so very absurd now that natural damnation is in orbit, and humanity's befouling of their ancient home has spread their death and dirt among the stars.

Remembering and Forgetting

1961

With a brilliant blend of images drawn from an essay by G. K. Chesterton and the acclaimed film of that day Hiroshima mon Amour, *Sittler brings the human experience of remembering and forgetting to bear upon the core of Christian faith: God with us, the Eternal here in the finite, calling on us to remember that we may know our need but under the force of grace to forget that we may move forward and live.*

WHEN THE CHURCH AFFIRMS, as the church does, that the Christic understanding of life is the amplest, the richest, the most penetrating, and the most supple of all possibilities, then the church that affirms that is obliged to take upon herself the burden of saying as clearly and as fully as she can, what she means by this astounding claim. And it is in a particular sense the duty of a pulpit in a university, standing halfway, as it were, between committed faith that put that pulpit here and disinterested inquiry that surrounds that pulpit. It is the particular duty of a pulpit in a university to unfold the content and the dynamics of this claim with a kind of dogged precision. There is a sense in which a preacher in a university can do this, and a sense in which he cannot. The *university preacher* cannot do this in the sense that a university chapel is not a church. Her words and services are always in part disengaged from the organic wholeness of the witnessing and confessing church, the life of a believing congregation. The great cumulative tides of love, of grace, of remembered mercies, and of remembered charities do not intimately

Part 3: Sermons

bare her life along in a university. But there is a sense too in which a pulpit in a university can unfold the content of the Christian claim with a kind of precision required by the very disqualifications that I have mentioned. For the mind of a university engenders a desire for and certain patience under the administrations of clarity, depth, and precision. One does not, in this place, have to be troubled very much about the marketplace mores of popular preaching. Quick and facile solutions are not expected. Shallow and obvious arguments are not required. The claims of the faith will not be pondered or rejected according to their instantaneous and obvious instrumentality to pragmatic and less than ultimate purposes. In the university, it's the truth that counts. (At least that's what we say.) And if the faith cannot be commended as guaranteeing a kind of lubrication for scratchy personalities or to constitute glue to hold the republic together—both contemporary forms of Christian aberration—this is nothing against the truth.

Now I want in a moment to measure against a particular claim of the Christian tradition, a particular fact of our common experience, but as a kind of invitation to that inquiry, I ask you to listen to a paragraph from Mr. Gilbert Chesterton. This essayist, writing this about thirty years ago, is speaking in a large and general way of how it happened that, after years of active hostility to everything in the Christian dogma, he had come gradually to peer into these same dogmas with a deepening fascination, and ended up by becoming one of the most remarkable apologists for that very tradition. I read the paragraph here at the beginning of the sermon because the multiple images which it employs suggest that there is no single thought or truth or fact or feeling or force by which one moves from unfaith to faith. But this paragraph suggests, rather, that that movement is rather the symphonic and the subtle interplay of many thoughts, many facts, many ponderings and surprises. Mr. Chesterton writes as follows:

> And then followed an experience impossible to describe. It was as if I had been blundering around since my birth with two huge and unmanageable machines, of different shapes without apparent connection—the world and the Christian tradition. I had found this hole in the world: the fact that one must somehow find a way of loving the world without trusting it; somehow one must love the world without being worldly. I found this projecting feature in the Christian theology, like a sort of hard spike, the dogmatic insistence that God was personal, and had made a

world separate from Himself. The spike of dogma fitted exactly into the hole in the world—it had evidently been meant to go there—and then the strange thing began to happen. When once these two parts of the two machines had come together, one after another, all the other parts fitted and fell in with an eerie exactitude. I could hear bolt after bolt all over the machinery falling into place with a kind of click of relief. Having got one part right, all the other parts were repeating that rectitude, as clock after clock strikes noon. Instinct after instinct was answered by doctrine after doctrine. Or (he says), to vary the metaphor, I was like one who had advanced into a hostile country to take one high fortress. And when that fort had fallen the whole country surrendered and turned solid behind me. The whole land was lit up, as it were, back to the first fields of my childhood.[4]

This morning I ask you to attend to one "hole" of fact and one "spike" of biblical doctrine. First the fact—and I elaborate it dramatically rather than propositionally. Some weeks ago there was shown in this community a film of which Mr. Gabriel Breton in the last issue of *New University Thought* writes this exaggerated sentence: "This film is the most important film that has been produced in the last twenty years because it is the first successful attempt to depict the human psyche from within." The name of the film is *Hiroshima mon Amour*. The place about which the film tells is the city of Hiroshima, fifteen years after the bomb. The woman in the film—the woman from Nevere, in France—is trying, as the film opens, to live in the universe of love. Live fully physical and fully personal love. But there is that in the world which makes sardonic nonsense out of all the values and the promises of love, that in the world which makes such nonsense lies so massively over and around the small world of her love, so defines the entire human condition and penetrates it that, torn between the two—the tenderness of the universe of love and the brutality of the great world—she enters into madness. She knows too that the only way out is to ensconce the present world of madness into the bigger saner world of her entire life, and the way to do this is to remember. The film depicts the tormented effort to recollect in living actuality the deeds, the scenes, the first love, the happiness, the thought and the emotion of her own past. It is her passionate striving, by remembering, towards sanity.

---

4. G. K. Chesterton, *Orthodoxy* (New York: John Lane, 1908) 144–45.

Part 3: Sermons

According to the argument of the film, she both succeeds and fails. She wins and she loses. The film ends with no way out. It elaborates a contradiction that it cannot solve. The contradiction is clear and single and absolute, and it is this: life is constituted by remembering. Because life is organic, continuous, of a piece, my being is my remembered past. Life is constituted by remembering. That's one part of it. But the other part of it is: life is *lived* by forgetting. The moment's necessities can only be confronted and mastered by forgetting. I cannot be a whole person if I am not constituted by remembering. I cannot be a person at all in any moment if I do not forget. Now this is the human condition. This is the way things are. This is the hole of fact.

Now, it is widely proclaimed among us in our time that religion can do something about that; that religion in general, the kind of wide and windy view of life, can do something about the hole of that fact. I do not believe it. What one hears in the name of religion, so often, as a proposal adequate for the profundity of that contradiction—what one hears as adequate for that, is no hard spike at all. It's a great deal more like a perfumed wad of cotton batting. The usual version that's supposed to be adequate for that runs something like this: Religion is good for you. It helps you live positively. It helps you forget the past. Lean forward hopefully into the future. Refusal to forget does not rob yesterday of its burden, but it robs today of its possibility. Therefore, live forgetting. Live episodically, like a card catalog. If there is that in the past which keeps digging away at you, take it out, toss it away, forget it. This is very thin stuff. It betrays the profundity that the film exploits. Life *is* continuous. It is cumulative. It is constituted by the livingness of the whole of the past in every actual moment. And, as a matter of fact, we know that it's thin stuff. That we do know this is certified by the fact that we really do not trust that version of religion to accomplish anything radically redemptive.

When one hears the reasons that religion is commended for the general health of the personality, and then analyzes these reasons, one makes a surprising discovery. What is really being claimed, generally, is that religion offers a kind of open-ended optimism, which may be a propitious climate for really therapeutic flowers to blossom in. Religion in itself is nothing positive. It's a kind of negative prolegomena to things that might possibly work. It is a kind of conciliatory context, a warm, moist, mental air which keeps the patient quiet while the real powers of redemption go about their proper business.

Remembering and Forgetting

Now the Bible takes the whole dialectic of remembrance and forgetting with considerable more seriousness. The Bible assumes the truth of the film *Hiroshima mon Amour*. It assumes the truth that people are not morons of pasted-together moments, that life is organic, that the whole of the past does constitute the substance of the moment. The Jew, for instance, whose words we heard in the Old Testament lesson this morning, the man who stood by Babylon's waters, where an alien people demanded of him chipper music—this man knew himself to be defending his sanity when he cried out in pathos, "If I forget thee, O, Jerusalem." And this same people knew the other side of the contradiction: that nevertheless, without a forgetting, a blotting out, and a removal from the groaning back of the present of the pressing past, life simply could not be lived. And therefore this same people could cry, "Blot out my transgressions from before thine eyes. Let not my secrets come before the light of thy countenance."

There *is* a hard spike of dogma that fits that hole of fact, when we permit it to be a real hole and a real fact. Its power comes through some such passage as we read for the New Testament lesson, from the letter to the Philippians (3:12–14). "Not," says St. Paul, "that I have already obtained," or not that I am already perfect, "but I press on to make it my own." Now watch the action of the verbs: "I press on to make it my own, because Christ Jesus has made me his own. Therefore, one thing I do: forgetting what lies behind and straining forward to what lies ahead," and so forth. There you see the entire matter of the dialectic of remembering in order to be and forgetting in order effectively to live. This whole matter is put in a strange new context. Paul was no positive thinker. He was rather witnessing that he could be a heroic and realistic man because God is a positive thinker and a positive actor. The active verb, "I forget," because "I remember" and, remembering, I dare to forget. This active verb "I press on," observe, does not stand alone, as a kind of a personal moral effort, pumping itself up into a kind of psychic bravery by judicious selection and moral hypnosis. All the active verbs of life now operate for the apostle in a world of relations between God and humankind, human beings and human beings, a world of relations in which the basic fact is the passive verb of what God has done, which now makes a quite new possibility for all the active verbs of human life.

I do my remembering, as I do my forgetting, within the tough circle of the remembering and the forgiving God. I press on to make it my own because God has made me his own. The pathos of time—which is the theme of *Hiroshima*—the pathos of time cannot be solved by eternity,

213

for I *am* time. I am mutable, successive, chronological, time's creature. Within terrible time I must remember, for I am not a spatter of words, but an unfolding sentence that began a long way back, and will unfold on and on. And within terrible time I must also forget, for the urgent moment, in all its urgency, must spring unfreighted to its appointed task. This contradiction of time cannot be solved by eternity, but by the eternal *in* time. There's the spike of dogma that fits strangely into the tough hole of fact: the eternal *in* time, the all-remembering and the all-forgiving God become my time, my situation, the ultimate reality become the torment, even of Hiroshima. If *that* could happen, that could do it. That hard spike of Christian dogma, that God's passion does become my pathos. That God's deed of participation in Christ becomes my time, my place, my Hiroshima. That the eternal, while remaining eternal, will not do, but this eternal become my temporal place and fact will do. That is the hard spike of dogma, to be sure. Efforts to reduce it to positive thinking have succeeded only in making it a despicable, tepid counsel to people in real torment—a kind of paltry aspirin for actual anguish. It's a hard spike that God has become fact, that the Eternal participates in time. It's hard. But it has the advantage of filling the hole. And filling it, it holds deep things, both torments and delights, together.

How to Hear a Parable

1961

Luke 14:12–24

Another more didactic version of this address has been published. The following sermon, which emphasizes the role of hearing, comes direct from Sittler's pulpit. Its title accurately captures the preacher's purpose. Before he gives an exposition of a particular parable he will comment on the reading of parables, by which he means the hearing *of parables. First, we open our ears and hear, then behold with wonder the extraordinary thing God is doing in our daily lives. In his exposition of the parable of the Great Feast, the preacher warns against focusing on the excuses of the invitees at the expense of God's innovative and expansive mercy. In short, the preacher warns against a false reading that ends in law rather than gospel.*

It is not proper to drag classroom concerns into the pulpit, but today we propose to listen to a parable, so that by listening to this one we may be helped to listen to others. Because the parables of Jesus have been so mauled and misused, it might be profitable today to consider in some detail the previous question—not how to understand a parable, or how to understand God and ourselves as a parable teaches us we ought, but the previous question: simply, how to *hear* a parable. For certainly, if we do not clearly hear we shall not understand correctly or obey justly.

Two propositions, then: First of all, we must hear what the man said. Now that would seem to be easy, but an illustration will, I think, indicate that it is not easy at all to hear what the man said. Suppose that we had no records at all about Abraham Lincoln in his pre-presidential life, but records of his life only after he became the president. And suppose further that he had not written a word and that all we know of him came from writings about him by his friends, his fellow party members, men who were passionately devoted to his name, his person, his memory, and his call. And furthermore, suppose that these purposes and plans, and all of the anecdotes from his early life, were now being disseminated in a huge international program far divorced from the simple setting of New Salem, Springfield, and the Illinois prairie, out of which these anecdotes sprung. All the stories, anecdotes, and epigrams of Lincoln would now come to us in a context not, to be sure, discontinuous with the man and his word but in a completely expanded situation. What then would be the duty of the historian? It would be this man's duty to disengage the story or the anecdote from the expanded and the changed context in which it comes to us. He would have to strip it of uses to which later concerns had put it, interpretations with which other parties had invested it.

Many of the parables of Jesus come to us like that. The embeddedness of these stories that Jesus told in the later life of the church—the predicaments, perils, and promises of that community—this is the interior situation of a parable.

The second proposition points to the exterior situation. We must exercise caution, and one could put it this way: In reading a parable, one must try to get to the central intention, the single point, the kernel. Attend to that! And try not to make something out of every figure, metaphor, or incident that is instrumental to the making of the central point. Everything in our church practice and in the mores of homiletics counsels the opposite, that is, to use everything in the text in service to a central point. We allegorize, we make morals out of metaphors, we try to hang heavy loads on every nail that's driven into every two-by-four of the scaffolding. A parable is often a scaffolding that encloses a construction. But when the construction is done, then the scaffolding is laid aside, and one attends to that for which the scaffolding is erected.

Consider the parable for today. It is aimed at a particular target, a precise situation. The situation was as follows: Jesus always spoke and acted in the name of the love and freedom of God. Always that. And God's freedom is exactly the freedom of his love—a love that wills to call and restore all people to his fellowship, his fullness, and in this restoration to achieve the authenticity of their lives. It is one of the perversions of religion to control what it ought to be controlled by.

So it was in the setting of this parable. We read, "On Sabbath day," that is, on a holy day, "Jesus went to dine in the home of a chief Pharisee," that is, a member of the strictest and most self-conscious watchmen of the religious tradition. We read that while he ate there, they watched him. Now the verb "to watch," in the original language, does not mean to behold with a certain amiability to see what he's like. The verb clearly suggests a tense, narrow, livid watching for an offside move. The mood is clearly one of hostility. So they watched him. They had not long to wait. A man suffering from dropsy was there, and Jesus turned to those about him, the regulators of the faith and freedom of God. He turned to them and said, "Is it lawful to heal on the Sabbath day, or isn't it?" And significantly then, caught in the old box between the obviously right and the ordered correct, they were silent. So Jesus healed the man, sent him on his way, and to those who watched him he said, "Which of you, having an ox or an ass that is fallen into a well will not immediately pull him out on the Sabbath day?" And they could not reply to this.

Then there follows another little parable, preliminary to the one we're moving in on. It makes the same point: that with God, things are not as they are with us. We have our canons of high and low, important and unimportant, the great and the small, the exalted and the humble. But the freedom and the love of God—so Jesus says in this parable—the freedom and the love of God disorganizes and makes a holy shambles out of all of these canons. For God is clear, direct, undeviating in his purpose. He wants his creatures to sit at the table of his love; and if our calculating and protocol-loving table arrangements get in the way, they have to give. The point is made in the story that introduces our parable. It reads this way: "When you give a dinner, do not invite your friends, your brethren, and your rich neighbors, that they also invite you in return, and thus you be repaid. But when you give a feast, try it this way: Invite the poor, the maimed, the blind, and you will be blessed, *because* they cannot repay." This is a strange and a holy logic. Because they cannot, you must; because of nothing, something. Because no gracious reciprocating, a new kind of grace, which doesn't operate with calculating reciprocity. Now this logic of the love and the freedom of God, this peculiar madness of grace, was apparently too fast for one of the observers who sat there. It was, as it were, just catching the outside corner of his understanding. So he did what we all do when we are embarrassed by the crystalline character of the true, or the directness of the pure: he reached back into his store of platitudes, he found one, and he tried to use it as a lid over the bubbling vivacity and the newness of the freedom and the love of God that Jesus was making manifest. "Ah, blessed," he said, going on, then, with the rest of the platitudinous bubble, "Ah, blessed are they who shall sit at the feast of the kingdom." This man crawled back from the burning edge of God's grace into the cozy warmth of religion, and there he was safe. But it is precisely to this man in that situation that Jesus now tells the parable, to which all the rest of this is a kind of windup.

The account reads, "But he said to him," and the verb or the word "but" there clearly indicates he wasn't confirming the man's crawl back into religiosity, but was rather correcting the man. Here are the components of the parable he now tells: A man gave a great dinner and invited many people. Two notices went out, sent out by a servant. The first notice went out to tell people that they were on the list of those whom the Lord of the feast was inviting to his dinner. And then after that, the servant went out again with the second notice. Remember, this is a Near Eastern situation. This is not a kind of a TV dinner that one stuffs in the oven for thirty minutes. In the Middle East this dinner would probably be a whole roast lamb, and the moment when a large roast lamb is done precisely cannot be anticipated to the split second. Therefore when all things were ready, the servant was sent around to knock on the doors of the people who were invited and to say, "Come, now, for all things are ready." But everyone had an excuse. "I have bought a field; I must go see it." "I have bought some oxen; I must go test them." "I have married a wife; therefore, I cannot come." So the servant came and reported to his master all the excuses.

Before the gracious potentialities of our lives which the love and the freedom of God confront us with, this excuse-making is so common that we would naturally be tempted to come down hard at this point and to assume that this sullen unresponsiveness is the point of the story. Each of us *could* do that. Each of us could fill in the formal character of these excuses of field, oxen, and domestic situation. Each of us could fill this with some personal content, and each of us could leave this place this morning, clutching devoutly some penitential remembrance of our recalcitrance before so gracious a God. But if we do that we would only accomplish a highly devout missing of the point. We should then have made a moral house of the instrumental scaffolding of the story. We should then leave this place with our pity at the wrong place! We should

How to Hear a Parable

leave this place pitying God, the Lord of the Dinner. We should then leave this place saying, "Poor old God . . . sitting there at his great table with his burned roast."

But the parable isn't finished. Listen: So the servant came and reported these things to his master. Then the master in anger said to his servant, "Go out quickly into the streets and lanes of the city, and bring in the poor, the maimed, the blind." The servant said, "Sir, what you have commanded has been done, and still there is room." And the master said to the servant, "Go out now into the highways and hedges." Translate that into our situation, it would mean, "Go out where the commonest and the unexpected people are and urgently compel people to come in, that my house may be full." Now suddenly everything has shifted. The center of the parable is jerked away from the invitees and their refusals; the master of the feast remains the master of his feast. He is still Lord of his *largesse*. *His* purpose is the joy, the fulfillment, and the fellowship of those who have been called to his table, and *he* remains the lord and the executor of that purpose. Human refusal and recalcitrance may sadden him, but they do not stop him. What he intends for all people, according to this parable, he accomplishes.

Now let us, in these shifting and revolutionary times, reflect upon that. Around the tables of this world, some changing of places is going on. The guest list of history, having acted in sullen ways, is beholding movement among the blind, the poor, the maimed, the forgotten. God wants all to know the joy and the fullness of life in him, and hence their fullness in themselves and among their fellows. This joy and fullness are not unrelated to food and warmth and health—and not unrelated to justice, either. Before the ancient Greeks conceptualized a philosophy of justice, Israel, a God-bearing people, knew the joy and the burden of the righteousness of God. They knew what God requires. "What doth the Lord require of thee? But to do justice, love mercy, and walk humbly with thy God." If that is so, we also have a theology of history. And if there is a theology of history, the preoccupations of culture—fields, oxen, marrying wives, running universities—can indeed retard or advance God's purposes for all his family, but they can neither divert him nor stop him.

And more: This parable, and the setting of it, suggests that the first children of this knowledge—the beholders and the bearers of this vision, the properly accredited voices of this message—are always the most deeply tempted to make a possession out of its passion, a religious "loaf" out of the yeasty, Godly dough which this parable points to. They are the earliest tempted to suppose that their decisions are ultimate. Poor old God, there at his table; he'll have to wait in Cuba, and in Portugal and Spain, and in Birmingham, and in Chicago until the accredited orders of the proper, and the pace of it, have solemnly determined who shall come to dinner. We have a colorful expression to designate the gathering tension of a good story as it moves toward the final releasing line. We call it the "punch line." It's a sober requirement in these stories that our Lord told, the purpose of which is to tell the truth about how things really are between God and man and therefore between and among all humans and therefore between humankind and the potentialities of nature. It's the requirement of these stories that we get the punch line at the right place. There is simply no doubt about where it is here or what it is. It's right at the end. God wills a lot of things, but not just an undifferentiated heap of things. There is an order to his will. There is a priority in his purpose. In these salubrious days in popular Christianity, it is gauche to speak of the wrath of God. Love is assumed to be irresolute and purpose is assumed to be pasty. But there is a steady anger at the heart of the holy. It comes out in the punch line, "That my house shall be filled." Not our house, *his* house. Not according to our specifications of the good, the beautiful, the just, or the convenient, but according to *his* will.

The Unjust Steward

Date Unknown

Luke 16:1-9

In this sermon, as on so many occasions, Sittler combines teaching about the craft of preaching—in this case how we should interpret parables and the familiar theme of attention to the innate power of language—with his actual proclamation based on the text. What we have in this selection, then, is a number of reflections pertinent to the vocation of preaching along with a surprising and remarkable treatment of one of the most difficult parables in the New Testament. Finally, this is as good an illustration as any of Sittler's keen ability to break open customary interpretations of familiar texts to reveal new insights.

AT THE OUTSET, I want to announce what I propose to do. To speak about the parables at all, I want to have an elongated—but I promise not too elongated—introduction. Whoever would talk about parables in these times of contemporary investigations of parables must talk about language. And however *un*comfortable it may be to do that, I'm going to do it. We use language a great part of everyday for all kinds of important, unimportant, *and* insignificant throwaway uses. The air is shattered everyday and most of the night from radio and television by uses of language. Language is so magnificent an instrument that we have to stop in the middle of the cacophony and think deliberately to realize all over again what a magical thing it is. How by a few words an evanescent thing, a mercurial thing that you can't get a concept wrapped around, that you can't get a clear idea from, that you have only a dim recollection of, by the magic of a few words that may come to life in front of your face.

Let me use several illustrations of what I call the magical combination of condensation and evocation which is the nature of language. I was reading not long ago Moseley's book on the rise of the Dutch Republic. I cannot account for the eloquence, the almost tearful beauty of the last phrase in his chapter on William of Orange. It's so simple; there is a kind of mystery in the beauty of it. He said, "While he lived he was the father of a gallant people and when he died the little children wept in the streets." Wherein lays the emotional, reportorial, factual precision, and passion of the statement? I'll take another. John Keats in the beginning of a mystical poem:

> O what can ail thee, Knight-at-arms,
>   Alone and palely loitering?
> The sedge is withered from the lake
>   And no birds sing.

I thought of that when I heard read in our church last Lenten season the statement from the passion history with four little words—or more than four, six. Judas went immediately out and it was night. I don't think the man's simply telling us what time it was. And I thought of that the other day when I was reading a modern translation of the old epic *The Odyssey*. There's a long, long passage about Odysseus' trip along the tumultuous sea and the gallantry of his long swim until he finds . . . he finds the island and falls exhausted. Homer, or whoever it was, wrote the simple sentence which is so appropriate for the end of a great day: "The sun dropped into the West and all the roads were dark."

There is a magic in both simplicity and in the extravagant use of language. Unless we are aware of this, we cannot even approach the parables with a mind sufficiently humble to appreciate the magnificent concentration and evocative power of the parables of Jesus. Let me use another illustration. It's almost as if the speech of Jesus and the actions of Jesus were intended to gain cognition by amazement. There are several ways to amaze the mind: we can pile up knowledge, we can impress by logic, and we can pile up data that shocks the mind. But insight into something can often be achieved *simply* by amazement, by astonishment, by a kind of word that simply explodes the expected, that articulates the never-to-be-expected, and our Lord seemed to delight in it both in the parables and in the miracle stories.

C. H. Dodd once said, "Parables are spoken miracles, and miracles are acted parables." That is, they have the same effect and it is stunning. Recall the case of the Canaanite woman reported of in two of the Gospels. She is sometimes called the Syro-Phonecian woman. Jesus left his own country and he went into a land of foreigners. The woman didn't know who he was—knew nothing about him except that the people around who had heard of him called him Jesus and added "Son of David." So she gave him the whole treatment and said, "Jesus, Son of David, have mercy on me, my daughter is grievously sick." And you recall that the disciples and others did all they could to abate her enthusiasm and turn her away from confronting Jesus. And he himself, he himself with a type of inexplicable roughness, shoved her off: "I'm not sent but unto the lost sheep of the House of Israel." You don't belong to the club—scram. And an even worse statement: "It is not right to take what God has intended for his own and give it to the dogs." And the word "dogs," east of Beirut, is a nasty word in ancient time. Nevertheless, the woman, you recall, keeps at it. Finally she said to him, I don't know anything about food for the chosen or anything about your mission to the chosen people and I don't know what your disciples are up to, I'm really not sure what you're up to, but there is that in you which is somehow related to the problem of my daughter. And she grasped him around the knees—which is what worship means in Greek—she grasped him around the knees and said, "Lord, help." In other words, skip the sociology and the nationalism and the theology. Help. And Jesus said, "I have not seen such faith, not even among the religious." Now that is an illustration of what occurs so irregularly it cannot simply be an episodic slip of the evangelist.

It happened the same way with the Centurion's Son (Luke 7:1–10). [Sittler notes that the Greek word could refer to a servant or a son. Today's NRSV translates it "slave."] This was the regimental officer in charge of the local occupying force. We read that these Jews spoke of this Roman officer in terms of both respect and affection. "He has liked our people. He's even built us a schoolhouse. Would you please, sir, do what he asks you?" What the man asked of Jesus was, "Sir, my son, he's ill. You don't even have to come under my roof." Now in Hebrew and in Greek this phrase "to come under my roof" is a kind of idiom that means you don't have to identify yourself with me socially. "You don't have to come under my roof. Just say the word and it will be done." And he says, "I am a man under authority"—*exousia*, power. I know something about authority. "I say to one man, 'Go,' and he goes. I say, 'Come,' and he comes." I give an order and it is carried out. I know something about that kind of thing and you have it. "You don't have to come under my roof." Jesus beheld him with astonishment and said, "Go your way; your son lives."

Now, what's going on here? That same kind of situation is the one which we must reenact in our imagination; to stand before the parables to listen carefully. When I accepted the invitation to be here as the preacher during this conference week, I naively said that I would preach on three parables—and I intend to do so, as you will see in a moment.

I was not aware of what I was getting myself in for. There has been an eruption of new studies of the parables that are so fascinating, so disjunctive with former ways of talking about the parables, so illuminating to the preacher that I simply got lost this winter and read and read or had read to me [Sittler alludes here to his failing eyesight] everything I could lay my hands on: Jeremias, Funk, Dan Via, Norman Perrin, Amos Wilder, and some more. So, I'm in the unhappy situation of having my head loaded but no notes. I ask your patience as I try to put together both the rest of this introduction to the parables and then get to the parable of Unjust Steward, which was read in our hearing just a moment ago.

A parable is a form of speech which says more than it says. It's not an allegory in which a simple story causes you to scrounge around for meanings which are somehow roughly equivalent to the story, like Aesop's fables. Parables are not allegories. Parables are not just narratives either, because they are narratives that, right in the middle, turn back upon themselves and do a strange reversal. You start out listening to the story of the Good Samaritan. It sounds like a familiar story of what is liable to happen between Jerusalem and Jericho or in the city of Chicago anytime a poor man gets beat up and is left on the side of the road. A good man comes, and you shall nod your head, yes, that's the way it is or at least the way it ought to be, and suddenly the parable pulls the rug out from under the expected. Because the point of the parable is not, you ought to be charitable to your unfortunate neighbor. There are easier ways to say that. It is not an exemplary story; it's not a bit of piety.

The parable is a fierce, a fierce attack upon the religious, and turns them 180 degrees around. A parable is full of exaggerated language because it says the absurd thing to prepare the mind by bewilderment for the unexpected possible thing. The parable says an exaggerated thing in order to disorient our minds for a new orientation toward the un-dreamed of.

The Unjust Steward

The parable says something crazy in order that that we should be totally annihilated and disorganized in order to hear something new.

What is the new thing to which the parables are addressed? This is clear in the Gospels: the kingdom of God. Almost every one begins with some form of the words "the kingdom of God is like" or "the kingdom of God is as if." It is a funny kind of construction only bad Greek can bring it off, but it is perfect. "The kingdom of God is as if a certain man was planting in his field . . . ," and the parable is off. So there is no doubt about what the parables are about, but in order that that "about" should break through the thick skin of our theological habits and bring us back again to the primeval force of what Jesus was about—the kingdom of God—the parables have got to turn us upside down and sometimes inside out. In order that you should not think that this is just the superheated imagination of a retired theologian, but the truth about the parables, I want to go back where it began: the magic of language.

I have to use the word magic because language deserves it. But I have to say it over and over again because everything in our contemporary life dulls and blinds us to it. If you listen to the television, as I'm sure you all do, you are saturated with words and language—sheer repeated banalities. How can we recover the pure shock of the beauty of language? One more illustration, then to the parable. In 1621, a great English preacher, John Donne, was preaching on Christmas Day in St. Paul's Cathedral, and he has a gorgeous passage on the mercies of God. He uses a series of metaphors. Let me give you a few of them. He wants to make clear the point that there is no way of preparing for the unexpected movements of the mercies of God. You can't calculate it, program it, prearrange it, or even preconceive what kind of preparation might evoke the mercies of God. He says, "God, to whom we pray for our daily bread—God never says you should have come yesterday or you must begin tomorrow, but today if you will hear his voice . . . ," and then watch the metaphors roll. "He can bring thy summer out of winter, though thou have no spring." You know, it would take three pages of good systematic theology to explicate that. He puts it in a simple, beautiful line. "He can bring thy summer out of winter, though thou have no spring." This *is* the way in which the grace of God can short-circuit, run around, in unexpected inexplicable and never comprehended ways, and somehow reach and touch.

"There was a certain man and he had a great estate." The structure of the parable is perfectly clear. The man was rich; he had a big business. He had hired a man to be steward—we would call him "estate manager."

And word came to him with apparently sufficient proof that the man was dishonest—he was stealing. And the master of the estate—remember the parables are always about God, always about God and us—called the man in and said, "You know what they are saying about you, and furthermore you know it's true. I relieve you right now of the stewardship. Bring in your books. You can no longer be steward." The man to whom this was spoken immediately said to himself, "Now what am I going to do?"

Now we get the first sign of the kind of candid, crooked directness of the man—a crook, but direct and clear. He said to himself, "Now what am I going to do? There are clearly two things I can't do: I'm too weak to dig, and I'm too proud to beg." And then immediately he says, "Aha, I know what I will do," and he went to his master's creditors. He called them in—and the story gives us only a couple instances, but the suggestion is that there was quite a list. He said to the first man, "How much oil do you owe my master?" The man told him. He said, "Take your bill and cut it exactly in half." And the man did it. Then the steward said to another man. "How much do you owe?" He said, "Cut it down one fifth." And the man did.

All of us would shake our heads. Yes, this is the way life is. Not everyone is straight; there are crooks. If one is going to lose his job he might as well prepare a place to land, which is exactly what the man did. Jesus, having told this story, then gives us the line which leaves our balanced notion of morality, faith, Jesus' reputation for being devout—it just leaves that in a shambles. *Phronimos* is the Greek word for "prudent" or "shrewd." Our Lord commended this shrewd crook.

Now, watch it! I want to stop right there, but I have to stop you too because in reading the lesson in the New Testament apparently there are some things added on there that are both puzzling and apparently fairly meaningless. Apparently there are parts of New Testament catechetics or preaching or moral theology that slipped into this text. In dealing with a parable, take the story, and if there are little lessons added on to the end—and often these lessons are a terrible let down; they approach banality—just try reading the parable and leave those out. It's not that they're wrong; the early church probably was telling this parable and adding those little moral lessons to it. This one says, "Make friends with a mammon of unrighteousness, because when you get fired, they will receive them in heavenly habitations." What type of heavenly habitations do the unrighteous have? It doesn't make sense even to Judaism—not at all. Judaism in fact would be appalled at such a statement. Something's gone wrong here. One of the beautiful things, the great lessons to be

The Unjust Steward

learned of the application of good, devout, sound biblical criticism is that it helps us recover what our Lord said. He said, "And he commended the unjust steward for his prudence, his shrewdness." Amen!

If I leave you stuck with that, I have done what the parable wants to do. It doesn't want you to take a huge blow and turn it into a popgun about making a friend with a mammon of unrighteousness. We don't need our Lord to tell us that. The parable ends with the blow—asking you a question. The parable is not there to answer a question, but to see that you do not escape the important question: what kind of a kingdom of God is this that's coming in which this manifestly, admittedly, lawfully disestablished crook wins the commendation of Jesus? Our Lord commended the unjust steward for his shrewdness. Let me suggest what may be the case. And I say "may be" because I don't know. It's the beauty of the parable that after 1900 years we still don't know. But when you can't shut a thing up, nor can you certainly solve it, it must be important. If there is a statement in literature, art, or in the New Testament that excites me into insoluble puzzlement, in my case for seventy-six years or so, it must be a statement I'm not sure I've gotten to the bottom of, as with this parable. But I'm beginning to feel it with my toes. I get a tip from Luther.

Luther has a sermon called "The Holy Swindler." And this is what he suggests. I think it is consistent with the thrust of the parable, with the structure of the story, with the way Jesus uses this word about the kingdom of God to break through our encrusted suppositions that we already know what it is and tease us into thought by the puzzlement of the story. Jesus commended the unjust steward not for his morality, but for his canniness, for his shrewdness. What might that mean? Look at it this way: here is a man who, whatever other unpleasant or evil characteristics he had, was direct. It comes out that way in his first sentence: "What shall I do? Quick, I know what I will do," and he went about it. Jesus commended this man for his shrewdness.

Why did he tell this story? Was it perhaps this: that Jesus says this man does an admirable thing because when he knew the nature of his master he didn't try to con him? He didn't try to slip anything over on a very wise master. He didn't try to commend himself by things which had nothing to do with honesty so that he could get a remittance of the punishment. He looked the facts straight in the eye and acted appropriately. I think that's one of the things the parable is saying. The Lord commends that. Now Luther in his sermon said, "We like the unjust steward are dealing with a master who knows what the facts are, who sees straight through us." "As before God," said Luther, "don't try to do anything about grace, except accept it." Don't try to earn it. If you have a master who is gracious, don't try to build yourself up as if God's grace were a kind equivalent payment for your morality. God's grace is always an astonishing thing. This man, this crook, stood with complete clarity before the truth of his situation and he acted appropriately to the situation. That's admirable. It's admirable as before God too. If the God of our devotion and astonishment is really a God of amazing grace, then in the amazement of our clear response, we must deal appropriately with that kind of a God. The way to deal with that God is to hear, to obey, to live out of God's grace—and not vertically, but out of it horizontally in our life in the world. And the Lord commended this crook because of his shrewdness.

The Lost Sheep

Date Unknown

Matthew 18:10–14

This piece is both a workshop and a sermon. Sittler offers reflections on how carefully chosen ordinary language can resonate with the thing it describes; the feelings it evokes are embedded in the words or combination of words themselves. This lesson in language is important to the craft of homiletics in an obvious way, but it also sounds a signature Sittler note: we need to savor and penetrate the language of the text. Thus we discover in Jesus' parabolic act with the little child a deeper meaning of God's relation to all of us and, in the very absurdity of the parable (when looked at closely), the profound experience of faith as risk.

TONIGHT I WANT TO preach very briefly upon the parable which was read in our hearing a moment ago. But as was the case last night, I come at it with a series of reflections which I think by their nature will permit us to be briefer when we do get to the parable. I begin with something that happened on the campus today. A woman who was in this room last night stopped me and said, "You said something from Homer last night and I found it beautiful." I remember the phrase she referred to. After his strenuous day off the island, Odysseus finds comfort and security, and the last line that ends the day is: "The sun dropped into the West and all the woods were dark." And she said, "At the moment, I thought,

'That's a very ordinary statement. What is so moving about it?' And then she continued, "But having dismissed it I saw I couldn't. I kept thinking about it all day." And, indeed, it is a memorable statement.

Now that led me to my first point. It's often the case that we look at things or experience situations and we use exaggerated terms about their force. Particularly among the young, the favorite words are "fabulous," "incredible," "tremendous," "far out"' [today we would probably cite "awesome"]. I asked one of these persons who are paying tribute to some large or moving or important thing exactly what they mean by any of these words. What one commonly gets is a series of gaseous phrases connected by "you know?" And if one says, "No, I really don't know; tell me," then the embarrassment is deepened. The point is it will not do simply to experience beauty, force, tenderness, pathos, and greatness. That knowledge, that experiencing alone is not enough. We grow as individuals in our appreciative life if we keep pushing at the . . . at the mercurial thing that we cannot quite get and say, "Why is it beautiful? What makes it strong? Why is that sentence memorable?" I thought about that after the woman had gone, and I think I know, and it's not a great feat of intellect to specify why that is so. At the end of a tumultuous day when the sun drops to the west, things have come to a kind of serene closing, and the poetry of the line "The sun dropped into the West and all the woods were dark" has a twilight and autumnal serenity to it. That's why it's great. In other words, what the thing is is resonant in the statement by which the thing is remembered.

Let me use another illustration—and this is not aesthetics I'm talking; it is necessary for our preaching from the language of Scripture. There was a poet in the late nineteenth century named Gerard Manley Hopkins, and in his notebooks, which he kept even when he was a child, he put lists of words together. And he marveled at this: that words that sound somewhat the same point in the same direction. For instance, there is a whole list of words whose general sound and intention is violence: "smash, crash, bash, lash, mash." They are all violent words, as if they articulate violence in the word by the violent act it remembers. Now, that's important to know.

And I want to say why it's important by introducing a second theme. Very prominent these days in American public discussion is a general attack upon mainline Christianity—particularly upon the more historically self-conscious churches—that they tend to elevate humanism. "Humanism" has become the nasty word for us, coming from the radical right. What humanism means is a general affirmation that all the possibilities of existence can be exhausted and have to be contained within and unfolded with the potentiality, the promises, the possibilities of the purely human. If that is the case, of course any notion of faith in an objective reality is on logic eliminated. So, humanism is not compatible with faith. But I want to suggest to you that—in preparation for the task of the preaching of the *gospel*—the promises of God, including the kingdom, take on a contour in our statement that somehow fits into the contour of common human existence.

There is such a thing as an evangelical Christian humanism. That is, there is a kind of holy demand that we should live with delight and wonder and all possible joy within the creation. "The earth is, the world is his, for *he* made it." God formed the dry land. The sea is God's. The sky, the air, the water, the cattle on the thousand hills, the oil that makes our face to shine, and the wine that *has* delighted the heart of humankind. To live with wonder, with joy within God's creation is not a quirk of personality having something to do with a happy metabolic system; it is a command. It is a doxological requirement of the God-relationship.

Now, as to this kind of humanism: how does one cultivate it for a vocation for teaching and proclaiming the Word of God or, if not thus ordained, in the common ordination of Christian baptism and lay ministry? How does one move toward that deeper illumination? I think one cannot learn to be a teacher or preacher by pedagogical method. Lord Bacon once said, "Reading maketh the full man, conversation maketh a ready man, and writing maketh an exact man." To become full in the inside of one's person, to become full in the head and the heart and the perception and all the multitudinous interconnections between this perception and that, and this thought and that, is to become a more fully human being. That is not a trick or a quirk; it is not quickly learned.

I have another illustration of that. Why, why is this excruciating attention that I want to pay to the language of Scripture not simply a personality quirk either? It's something that has been the presupposition of forceful, exciting, response-evoking preaching through the centuries. It's in the language—not only in the substance taught or said, but in the exactitude and precision of the language—whereby the kingdom that is declared is, by unfolding the parable of the kingdom, at work in the announcement of it. Jesus not only talked about the kingdom, he himself was the living parable of the kingdom. And out of that he spoke.

Part 3: Sermons

But now the illustration. From our childhood most of us learn verse, some of which we remember. I, by virtue of a very discriminating teacher, learned a lot when I was a child and I simply stashed it away in my head and reread it sometimes. To have these models of exactitude ready to be able to say with precision and brevity what most of us mortals can't bring out—this is a great gift for preaching. The example is this: One summer day years ago when one of my children, a little golden haired girl, was taking her afternoon nap in front of an open window, there was a soft breeze flowing over the sleeping child that lifted her hair up and down as the breeze waxed and waned a bit. The beauty of that picture came immediately to expression in the phrase from John Keats poem, "To Autumn." When he talks about a little girl, who is the metaphor for the golden days of autumn when in the tired fields the furrows had been plowed under again, he images a little child half asleep upon a turned furrow, and then the gorgeous line: "Thy hair soft-lifted by the winnowing wind." "Thy hair soft-lifted by the winnowing wind." The rhythm of the line, the "i" sounds are an exact replication, as it were, of the thing itself. Now let's move on.

There is a danger in the provision of a lectionary system for the preacher and for the life of the church. The benefits I well know. They provide a much richer lection for reading in the public services of the congregation. They also to some degree protect the congregation from the repeated and tiresome idiosyncrasies of the preacher, who may have about three of four different texts he/she loves to jump up and down on regularly. But there is also a danger in the lectionary system. The prescribed readings provide the church publishing house the opportunity to provide little leaflets that tell us what to preach upon that Sunday. They prefabricate like packaged soup. They prefabricate a proclamation. This is the theme for the day. Now to get a theme that covers three disparate texts or even sometimes very closely related texts, that may be all right. There are times when the force and directionality of the theme in each comes to a focal point and intersects so gravely and clearly that it demands that it be treated for the theme. But more often, more often it does not. And to preach out of a general theme is usually to have to be so general that the sermon is a kind of expletive elaboration of the perfectly obvious. Therefore, if one does not preach just from a big theme, he/she honors the particularity of each lesson. Now, as I say, there are times when these lessons conflate, coalesce, and with great imagination and power, but many, many times they do not.

The Lost Sheep

A great deal of hymnody and preaching has been dominated by a single shepherd-sheep text. This domination is both beautiful and powerful. So beautiful and powerful is that theme in the tenth chapter of John that the rich material in the Bible about the sheep, the pasture, the shepherd, God the shepherd, human shepherds, the shepherds of Israel, is completely slapped together under John 10, "I am the Good Shepherd." Now that is to be sure a tremendous, powerful theme. There are good reasons why it has been celebrated in a thousand stained glass windows and a thousand hymns. But, let us lay it aside for tonight for the clear reason that this passage is not about God or Jesus the Good Shepherd. And if we take this passage and flip it into a prefabricated set of sermonic notions about the Good Shepherd, then we will have missed what this particular little parable is talking about. Now let's take a running start at it.

It is sometimes necessary to extract the parable from the context. It is sometimes equally clear that the parable has not been redacted or misplaced or pushed around, but fits the context with such lubricated logicality that it ought to be there, or so it seems to a careful reader. This parable is one of those.

In the chapter in which this parable occurs in the Matthew account, which is very like Luke's account, Jesus is talking or, rather, the disciples are talking about that most unseemly thing: their status and rank within the coming kingdom of God. They got on that every once in a while. As they were talking about that, Jesus did a parabolic act. He didn't tell a story but he did a parabolic act as he called a little child and placed the little child among them and said, "Except ye become little children, you shall by no means enter the kingdom of God." That doesn't mean childlikeness can grasp the kingdom, but it means that what is represented in his taking a child and saying, "become as little children"—not childish, but as little children—the parabolic thrust is there is a kind of holy naïveté—anything can happen. "The sudden puddle happy spring" that e.e. cummings talks about is in imagination of childhood—anything can happen. There is a kind of openness toward infinite possibilities; that's what characterizes the child. "Except ye become as little children."

Then the second step: There follows that really haunting passage which occurs only here. He says, "For I say unto you, do not cause these little ones . . ." Now watch the language. The word for "little ones," meaning "children" in Greek, is *paidion*. He doesn't use that word. He doesn't use a word with chronological age, but with life situation: "do not offend one of the *mikroi*." (From *mikroi* we get our word "micrometer";

it means "small.") It means, do not speak an act in such a way that the little people of the world are offended by your being, by your action, your life. And then he said in another place a rather awful thing: that he who offends one of these little ones—a word which is almost shuddering in its horror—"let him be cast into the depths of the sea and annihilated." It's a frightful judgment. For such a small thing? Then notice the continuation: "for I say unto you that in heaven their angels do always behold the face of my Father which is in heaven."

I have scrounged among my betters in Old Testament—and any good one is my better in that field—and have failed to find an adequate explication of that statement. It has some history in the wisdom literature of Israel and in rabbinical sayings, but back of it is an interesting notion: that "I say to you that in heaven that their angels always do behold the face of my Father," that there is nothing in the human creation, regardless of size, status, importance, or moral relations, nothing that does not have a kind of counterpart in the vision of God and in the mind of God. "Their angels"—that is that replication of their personhood in eternity before the Eternal One himself. It exists there. You dare not crush it. You dare not turn it off. You dare not shut yourself off from it. "Their angels do always behold the face of my Father in heaven." And then immediately comes the parable:

There was a certain man, and he had a hundred sheep and one of the sheep strays away. The next action is that the shepherd leaves the other sheep on the hillside and goes and finds the lost sheep. And then he returns, as in the picture, with the sheep on his shoulder. He calls his neighbors together when he comes back and has a great bash. "I've lost a thing and I've found it. Come and have a celebration with me."

Now, what's going on here? May I suggest that if we try to subsume that picture under the John 10 or the Old Testament pictures of the shepherds of Israel, faithful and unfaithful, we don't advance the point and we may even dull it. We must look just at the picture and ask, why did Jesus, having talked about children and the *microi* and openness to the kingdom, tell of one man having a hundred sheep and losing one? Now, when you tell that story, particularly in a no longer largely agricultural culture, people will sit there and nod, "Well that's sounds like he's a fine man. He lost a sheep and like a good shepherd he went out to find it." But of course it is absurd! Any shepherd knows it's absurd. Anyone who knows the value of a hundred sheep. And leaving ninety-nine unattended to go after a stray one is not very, as we say, "cost effective." It is not smart shepherding that does that. If you've ever taken care of sheep, as I once did as a child, you don't leave them. You don't leave silly sheep. But Jesus uses the absurd shepherd to make the point. It's made in another parable that's very like this one in its thrust. The parable of the woman who lost the coin, remember, a *denarius*, a small piece of silver. And in the vivid language of the parable she literally tore the place apart until she found it. And when she found it she too had a big party, a coffee klatch of some sort, with her neighbors. "I have found my lost coin." You know, if a silver coin—not a collector's item—fell, was lost in my house and I came home to find my wife tearing the place from end to end, I would call the people at the university who make a specialty of dealing with obsessive-compulsive action. The action is absurdly out of relationship to the value of the thing.

Is it possible that the parable is saying to us that we, all of us, not only have a fold, we are a fold? We are a combination, a historical and personal and psychological combination of goods and of evils, of temptations and of resistances, of possibilities of affections and suffused reflections, a whole bag of things which is constitutive of what each of us is. And life in the world tends to make our lives battered; they loose focus. There is no one thing that is so commanding a work and a value that you leave every other thing and like a fool go find that one thing. Jesus talked about it in other ways. It's a foolish way to live. You have to pull your life together not by making a necessarily harmonious balance. Because not everything is an absolute good; not everything is required for the conformation of a life to the God-relationship. You must will one thing. The God-relationship has an apex character. This one thing: is it possible that the absurdity of the story is the point of the story? That the shepherd who left everything, who went to find this one thing, which is precious to him—it's worth taking the chance of the loss for everything else. And he played it that way.

Epiphany, Glory, and 63rd Street

1964

The season of Epiphany is one of revelatory splendor. Central to this time of light that penetrates the darkness of the world is the complex notion of glory. Sittler unpacks this word and in so doing releases for us the gift of God's holiness that, like light, is shed upon our often shabby world. The Isaiah text for this sermon was spoken to the returning exiles faced with the task of rebuilding a devastated Jerusalem. There was little there that was glorious, as one suspects might have been the case on 63rd Street in Chicago.

Isaiah 60:1–6

Arise, shine; for your light has come,
    and the glory of the Lord has risen upon you.
For behold, darkness shall cover the earth,
    and thick darkness the peoples;
but the Lord will arise upon you,
    and his glory will be seen upon you.
And nations shall come to your light,
    and kings to the brightness of your rising.

Lift up your eyes round about, and see;
    they all gather together, they come to you;
your sons shall come from far,
    and your daughters shall be carried in the arms.

Epiphany, Glory, and 63rd Street

> *Then you shall see and be radiant,*
> *your heart shall thrill and rejoice;*
> *because the abundance of the sea shall be*
> *turned to you,*
> *the wealth of the nations shall come to you.*
>
> *A multitude of camels shall cover you,*
> *the young camels of Midian and Ephah;*
> *all those from Sheba shall come.*
> *They shall bring gold and frankincense,*
> *and shall proclaim the praise of the Lord.*

We are still within the church season of the Epiphany of our Lord, and the sermon proposes some reflections upon the single word that dominates all the biblical passages, prayers, and hymns that the community has for hundreds of years remembered and used during this postnativity period.

The word is the *glory*. But with this term, as with some others that carry heavy freight in a cult and a culture, one must walk around and have regard for a number of facts and notions if he is to avoid a too thin and single a meaning.

We begin that complication-in-order-to-clarification by reflecting upon what is intended by two affirmations that are often made in university pulpits. The first one is that the Christian confession of faith is other and more than the mind's acquiescence in propositions. That meant to say that faith is a total act, that propositions have their specifying function, and that the fulfillment of this function does not add up to faith. The second affirmation is that humane studies should be cherished in a university; and that means to say that the humanities are the announcement and record of the depth and amplitude and variety of the wildly human story, and that attention to such studies discourages that oversimplification whose moral end and evil is idolatry.

The concern expressed in both of those affirmations is made specific when we ask after the meaning of the phrase *the glory*, and, in asking that, recall how the church uses language. When the church is not merely relating an episode, reporting, or exhorting, and when she is trying to point to promises and meanings in life, she is always conducting what Mr. T. S. Eliot called a new "... raid on the inarticulate." She of course is not alone in this frantic business. All language in its most grave effort is an attempt to point to what it cannot clutch, to evoke the suspicion of magnitudes it cannot specify, to invite the mind to entertain the possibility that there are realities beyond the operational, and meanings that have no less force because their allure is more steady than precise.

It is indeed possible that we may, at this moment in culture, be more than usually cordial to this truth about language. The nature of things, the way things are in all realms of knowledge, is being disclosed as more and more opaque at the same time that our operational use of things is more successful. This fact sets up a certain disturbance in the mind, and may in fact account for the reentrance into human speech of certain kinds of words which were, not so long ago, regarded as obstructive to thought.

The Oxford English Dictionary has one and a half columns about *glory*; and it is not until usage number six that it comes within gunshot of what might make sense in the first sentence of the lesson read from Isaiah, "Arise, shine; for your light has come, and the glory of the Lord has risen upon you." The obvious matters are cleared up first. Glory, we are told, means "majesty, honor, pride," a state proper to accumulated accomplishments, and such like. We are informed that the term is vulgarly used as a "mere exclamation of delight in the worship of some religious sects." These are not specified, on the ground I suppose that Oxford some centuries ago made up its mind about which is the proper and not vulgar sect. But we are also informed, in a delightful and half-embarrassed aside, that certain low fellows of the baser sort have a household term, "glory-hole"! This is defined as "a box, drawer, receptacle in which things are heaped together without any order or tidiness."

Against such a cautionary background then, let us attend to the way the word glory works in the two Epiphany lessons read in our hearing a few moments ago. When Isaiah speaks of the rising glory of the Lord, he presupposes backward, and he images forward. Back of his statement, and loading it from Israel's fund of experience and richness of language, was this: God is what is originating, creative, absolutely holy. He is the ground, the source of life, the core intention of all that is. And the glory is the signature of his form and presence. The glory is the light the holy gives off; it is the effulgence of that utter nucleus which is in and through all things but captured by none.

The glory partakes of the character of a secret. One's name is a symbol of the unimpartable and unique secret of the self: to tell the name is to disclose the self. Moses was at one and the same time told the *name* of the Lord, and admitted to see his *glory*. Whenever and wherever in Israel's battle with her God she is forced to define her reality in that relationship, the glory appears: in her recalcitrance she is smitten by it; in her quiet

Epiphany, Glory, and 63rd Street

devotion it is the term for the health and glow of rightness with God; in her exile and despair it is the glory, departed but unforgettably luring, that shapes her heartbreaking songs by the rivers of Babylon; and when she is home again in heart and foot and worship it is at Mount Zion, "the place where the glory dwells." All of that is back of the cry of the prophet to a people sunk in apathy, prostrate in despair: "Arise, shine; for your light has come, and the glory of the Lord is risen upon you."

But forward, too: the prophet images forth the glory, and thick material images are drawn dripping like a sponge from the eastern place. Sight, sound, smell, the barbaric color and movement of common life, become the bearers of the promise that all things, though not yet seen, are in motion toward a restoration. Jerusalem stands there on her high ridge. To the east across the wadis are the further flat sands: "A multitude of camels shall cover you, the young camels of Midian and Ephah." And to the west, where falling from the escarpment the land slopes away to the sea, the vision sees the crowding white sails: "all those from Sheba shall come. They shall bring gold and frankincense, and shall proclaim the praise of the Lord."

What's really going on here? Back of and informing the flaming incandescence of these images, what is being affirmed about God and humanity? Except we suspect that the confluence of images can be as meiotic to faith as a procession of propositions, we shall neither hear nor understand. It is here affirmed that there is in nature and history a holy possibility for the fulfillment of all things; that that possibility is, and is holy, because all things exist in the ultimate placenta which is God the creator and sustainer. And the comprehensive term for that perception and that faith is the *glory*.

Christian worship has always understood this. If one seeks for a word common to the entire spectrum of corporate acknowledgment and adoration, and considers all in that enormous range from calculated Gregorian intervals to the spontaneous outbursts of Appalachian shout and song, from the unearthly shimmer of Palestrina to the rocking rhythms of Negro song, it is the force of the glory that is attested.

The image has a rich and steady career in Israel and church; it inwardly controls every episode, and shines like a light beckoning to ever fresh interpretation of every statement. Just as "the heavens declare the glory of God," for they are a transparency symbolic of the ineffable glory "which thou hast set above the heavens," so therefore Israel dared not name the glory in a proper noun. But this glory, uncapturable in category and concept, is nevertheless that which formed and forms this people Israel to the mad faith that neither nature nor history has slipped nor been snatched from holy hands.

Only thus can the full symbolic measure of the meaning of the Christian identification of the Christ and the glory be suspected. When, in the nativity stories, "the glory of the Lord shone round about," and when the child was greeted as the "glory of thy people Israel," the background is given for the claim that in Christ the glory has concretely come fleshly night—"and we beheld his glory, full of grace and truth." And when the darkness of death failed to smother a life luminous with the glory, and the community affirmed him to be alive and creative of nothing less than a new being for men, they put it this way: "Christ was raised from the dead by the *glory* of the Father"!

So too in one of the summary paragraphs in the New Testament that has the sonority of celebration as well as the gravity of a huge faith, it is affirmed that this glory is the life of and irradiates all that is. Four times in the first chapter of Ephesians we are told that apex of life is to *be* "to the praise of his glory." The glory is the reality that fills the space that ontological inquiries mark out; it is the ultimate ambience in which the mystery of our restless lives swing to and fro; it is the persisting allure that draws and drives all things beyond the vainglory of penultimate meanings. It sings in nerve and blood in D. H. Lawrence, in the arching speculations of Plotinus, and it meets us as a gift, an evocation, and a demand in every dirty street, every hurt, upturned face, every failure of fulfillment on the streets of this world.

Very quickly, then, these three: *gift, evocation, demand.*

I. *It is a gift.*

Every man who has ever got stuck in the stickiness of the *possible* as it meets him in the ever so hopeless stasis of the *actual* knows this joyful burden to be a gift! He suddenly, or gradually, has come to *see*; and this creative fusion and vision and form and emerging patterns he knows with immediate and never-diminishing certainty to have been given. There are, to be sure, requirements given with the seeing; and to these he must attend in prosaic labor, thought, experiment, and discipline; but his exercise of these corollary activities never adds up to a kind of justification or deserving. Every vision of fullness and authenticity and justice and of a possible goodness in life has this inextinguishable gift-character.

Epiphany, Glory, and 63rd Street

II. *It is an evocation.*

The vision of the glory, the rising light of the holy that is "the light that lighteth every man that cometh into the world . . ." is God's way of getting heavenly song upon earthly streets, the ecstasy of the cherubim into plain deed of justice among the creatures. The hard-nosed of this world may feel all of this to be nonsense, and see no connection between prayer, praise, and men and women caring for fellow creatures in the glory. But a lifetime of caring is a hard-nosed fact too; and when Saint Francis dealt with a leper in Christ's name, he was not necessarily deluded. All of this is caught in a few lines of verse by Gerard Manley Hopkins. This is manifestly close stuff, and not for the street; but we are, after all, for this hour, in off the street, and this is an arrogantly close university!

> As kingfishers catch fire, dragonflies draw flame;
> As tumbled over rim in roundy wells
> Stone ring; like each tucked string tells, each hung bell's
> Bow swung finds tongue to fling out broad its name;
> Each mortal thing does one thing and the same:
> Deals out that being indoors each one dwells;
> Selves—goes itself; *myself* it speaks and spells,
> Crying *What I do is me: for that I came.*
> I say more: the just man justices;
> Keeps grace: that keeps all his goings graces;
> Acts in God's eye what in God's eye he is—
> Christ—for Christ plays in ten thousand places,
> Lovely in limbs, and lovely in eyes not his
> To the Father through the features of men's faces.[5]

III. *The glory is demand.*

"That we should be to the praise of this glory" sounds like an impossibly abstract hook to hang the conduct of life upon. Everything is against it; everything, that is, except fact, experience, and the interior dynamics of human history. A paragraph from Gilbert Chesterton puts the matter better than I can:

> The eighteenth century theories of the social contract were demonstrably right insofar as they meant that there is at the back of all historic government an idea of content and cooperation.

---

5. An untitled poem in Gerard Manly Hopkins, reprinted from *Selected Poems and Prose* (Baltimore: Penguin, 1953) 51.

But they really were wrong insofar as they suggested that men had ever aimed at order or ethics directly by a conscious exchange of interests. Morality did not begin by one man saying to another, "I will not hit you if you will not hit me"; there is no trace of such a transaction. There is a trace of both men having said "We must not hit each other in the holy place." They gained their morality by guarding their religion. They did not cultivate courage. They fought for the shrine, and found they had become courageous. They purified themselves for the altar, and found that they were clean. The Ten Commandments which have been found substantially common to mankind were merely military commands; a code of regimental orders, issued to protect a certain Ark across a certain desert. Anarchy was evil because it endangered the holy. And only when they made a holy day for God did they find they had made a holiday for men.[6]

---

6. G. K. Chesterton, *Orthodoxy* (London: Bodley Head, 1957) 107.

Effort and Serenity

1964

This sermon marked the opening of the academic year at the University of Chicago in 1964. In it the preacher asserts the centrality of the chapel to the life of the university. The chapel does not offer moral admonitions from the periphery of the intellectual enterprise but, as a "peculiar community," it helps ground the university in those truths sought by all thinking persons. In fact, the substance of its faith is itself a proper field of historical and moral investigation. Upon closer inspection, the chapel proposes a radical alternative to the perennial activities and ambitions of the university, an alternative Sittler identifies by means of the dialectic of "effort and serenity," which is comprehended in the biblical posture of "waiting."

THIS FOUNDATION [ROCKEFELLER CHAPEL of the University of Chicago] exists and is maintained for the worship of God. This chapel and all that takes place in it is not mere ceremonial. Now ceremonial often takes the form of a chapel on a college or university campus. It's a kind of a vague benediction that the university or college waves in the general direction of a tradition which is acknowledged to be dead, but it makes good public relations to act as if it weren't. A ceremonial has been described as an outward sign of a vitality that once had force and meaning, but whose demise is now nostalgically remembered with appropriate actions and noises which continue the sheer momentum of the tradition—like changing the guard at Buckingham Palace. This chapel is not ceremonial.

Second, the university chapel is not understood as a bastion of moral admonition, a sort of religious maiden aunt who flutters around the outer ethical edges of the behavioral sciences. Nor is the chapel to be understood as an adjunct to the office of the dean of students, disengaged, that is, from the life of the university and from its purpose, but retained in order to soften the hard-nosed public image of a tough-minded faculty, and to ameliorate the more dramatic forms of student indiscretion.

These won't do. God is worshiped here because there really is a "peculiar community that exists in history." This peculiar community exists as an affirmation and acknowledgment that there is a God, that something of his nature is knowable and has been disclosed. He has a will and a purpose and exercises redemptive force in history, and something of this purpose can be known and obeyed. This peculiar community is an historical datum of enormous complexity, variety, scope, and creativity. It has shaped entire cultures; it has informed whole waves of beholding and dealing with the world; it has given birth to massive intellectual systems; it has penetrated mind and disposition and human purpose with specifiable and energetic force. Now this activity, this history, and these affirmations are a proper field of inquiry for university attention. This free university includes such within the company of studies which it deems appropriate to a university. I asked that there be read this morning two lessons, one from the Old and one from the New Testament. First, that great Twenty-Fifth Psalm: sung by man to a whole people beset by trouble but willing in trouble to trust, and as a function of that trusting, "to wait on the Lord" and have faith. And second, the great New Testament lesson, its serenity and sobriety: "Be not anxious." Forged not out of a kind of detached and non-actual piety, but forged out of the tears and tares of life.

These lessons were chosen as a kind of a traditional proposal of a possibility. They are like a background of promise, against which I want to ask a question: if each of us were to ask of himself, or one of his fellows, what it is that he most desires in life, he would find the answer hard to come by. For ultimate desire, that is, just plain raw desire—this is steady and volatile stuff, but it continues to bubble unceasingly within every vessel of concrete purpose and intention which we dream up to enclose it. It always continues bubbling when the enclosures for the fulfillment of desire have a seeming adequacy. When a man is able to state what it is that he really desires and begins to make a sentence about it, he knows while the sentences are forming that he is not saying what it is and cannot—and what he most profoundly desires. He knows that concrete purposes are

Effort and Serenity

always penultimate, that the full reality of man's desire is both elusive, steady, relentless, and almost unnamable.

Now a university is a product of this volatile desire in life, and it orders its work along paths always changing and always freshly rich, with the good and the promising and the necessary, that seemed right to do in virtue of the things men desire.

Several illustrations: Human beings desire to know. The university is committed to knowledge, to gain and verify it, to increase the sum of it and to transmit it, to honor it against all unknowing and uncaring, and to have delight in it.

We desire order. Not only outward order, but to learn the way of mind and sensibility, whereby the human mind might comprehend what tends towards order. Not only outward order, but to learn to distinguish the better from the worse, the central and the steady from the peripheral and the passing, and by like, to discern things as they have been and are. Learn, perhaps, to cast some light upon novel things and ever-emerging forms of disorder.

Human beings desire justice. The university serves this desire not by enactments, which are more just than those that presently prevail, but by the excision and the laying bare of the anatomy and etiology of injustice: socially, economically, and in every other way. The university is always an effort to find the meaning of justice, remembering that justice is a vision before it is a matter of law; to understand human needs, desires, and potentiality in privacy and in their multiple relations in the world.

In the Old Testament, righteousness, truth, goodness, and justice are all aspects of a single conception. "Righteous" means right-ness. Justice means something very close to having things right, and in this chapel, throughout the years, is added this Old Testament, as it were, this voice of righteousness—rightness—to the symphony of university studies.

Now all these things are related to what human beings ultimately desire, but none of them alone adds up to, nor all of them together constitute or secure, the sum of what it is that all ultimately desire. We live and work and feel and think relentlessly forward toward desires which transcend all conceptual statements. In the history of our culture there have been efforts to specify by name what it is that men most desire of themselves or of their world.

In ancient Greece the name for that man to whom all look as the one in whom all desires are quieted was the *megala psyche*, that is, the "large-minded man." The person in whom there was no eccentricity or forgotten idiosyncrasy. The man fully proportioned, like the lintel of one of their temples. Every detail wrought out, and in just proportion, each part to the other. The Renaissance created a kind of model of the man who meets this desire. He was the "magnanimous man." One can get the image of him in Castiglione, or in Erasmus' *Education of a Christian Prince*. He was a man who was at home in all worlds: in the world of politics, in the world of civil affairs. The man who was adept at warfare, and in the arts of peace. A man who knew how to constitute all things with justice, right use, and good taste. The magnanimous human being.

Now Israel never stated the problem that way. The tradition out of which this chapel speaks, and which it must speak clearly, adds to what is said in other places in this university. Israel never assumed that the self could realize selfhood or its own desire by a maturation or a reproportioning of the vitalities of the self, from the self, for the self, or for the self among other selves. Israel never put the problem that way. The self as Israel confesses it in this Twenty-Fifth Psalm is always a self in a world whose own selfhood is a creature of a Creator and whose life does not stop short of the vision and obedience in this Creator. This is to realize the self. The Twenty-Fifth Psalm is simply incomprehensible apart from that assumption.

Let me point out two words in the psalm. The psalm says, "To thee, O Lord, I lift up my soul, O my Lord, I trust in Thee." Now it goes immediately from this word about trust to the word that caused me to want to speak about it, and remind you of it, on this particular day. Because in the third verse, "For Thee I wait all the day long, I wait." Now, to wait in the Lord does not seem a very exciting way to live. There seems to be something almost gauche to introduce this word about waiting into what noises that you have heard made at you this week (and you will hear more next week) about what is required . . . the exactness of study and preparation. "Get with it, get going . . ." and "These are the ways to do it."

Then you come to the chapel and a man preaches a sermon about waiting. It seems a very feckless, unattractive image to thrust into the properly carbonated feelings which you bring to this experience this week. But the strange thing about the way the word "wait" works in this psalm is that the word is the most *active* word in the psalm and by no means an invitation to total collapse. The way the word works in the psalm is this: to wait upon that in which one trusts is to be fiercely active in the midst of the life which he holds to be supported and presided over by the one whom he trusts. Waiting is not a collapse; it is a program. It's not an empty stillness, but a kind of resolution in trust at the heart of which there is a stillness, not of my making, not of my destroying, although it is of my betraying. And I submit this word now as a proper word as we enter a new term in this university, on the ground of two final points I want to make, repeating here what I was able to say about a month ago at the time students at the other end of this process were leaving this university. But I think, with some minor changes, what I said then about the nature of this moment in university study, as that is played contrapuntally over against what the psalm says, namely, to wait—this is right to say now.

A university claims to liberate the mind. And when liberal—that is, liberating—studies, are properly done, they achieve that liberation. What is the content of this liberation? We are liberated from loneliness by accepting membership in a larger company, a longer time, a richer conversation in thought and action. We are indeed liberated from stifling egocentricity. For our hot little selfhood *is* questioned, challenged, bewildered, and if we stay with it, supported by what an English teacher in Cambridge once called "residency among all that saddens, gladdens, maddens us men and women. This brief and beautiful project as yet must be home for awhile, the anchorage of our heart." That's a real liberation. But this liberation is ultimately a liberation into the problematic of all liberated positions. The brighter we are, the quicker this is liable to dawn on us. And if we avoid the stupefactions of a seductive culture, this liberation into life's unsystematic, this problematic of all liberation, this conviction that that's the way things are is liable to be permanent. Now to be sure, we make penultimate decisions and resolutions on the way. Otherwise, we couldn't live. We say, "I can do this better than that. This realm of discourse is more appropriate for my endowments than that, and this shall be the operational theater of my life." And we can indeed become so involved in these penultimate answers to ultimate questions and become so seduced by the busyness within an operational life that we can mask the question from our attention or anesthetize our trouble within it. But something like that seems to me to be the present position. It is not the characteristic of a university student entering now to be told, or to be invited to suppose, that here is a guaranteed procedure whereby solutions to big problems can be found. Life in the university is rather an introduction to a life in the world that must get on with some tasks and construction and approximations and delights for which there are no guaranteed solutions. The university lies in its teeth if it assumes there are.

Indeed, it may be true that the whole history of our Western culture is a massive and complex version, played out on a big field, of the child's game "Button, Button, Who's Got the Button?" Look at what has happened. Many hands over the history of our culture have held what they supposed for the moment to be the answer to man's problem, or the way to the answer, or the kind of thoughtful labor or procedure which could bring guaranteed solutions. One can quickly review in his mind some of these hands who've held the button. They constitute in their dedication and in their labor our common Western tradition. Think of the haunting music of Dante, in which he beheld all things: "To be completely in the hand, you see, and bound together by the love that holds the sun in heaven and all the other stars." And then the button passed on to Bruno and Nicholas of Cusa and Galileo, to the writers of the Enlightenment who wrote discourses on the human understanding, and they helped engender Bacon who said, "Let us put aside the puerile speculations of the philosophers and let us live steadily among things." Now, some centuries of living steadily among things did not support quite the same exuberance that Bacon could bring to that prospect. And the button passed on in the great nineteenth-century historian who envisioned the possibility of so systematic an understanding of historical process that men should be supplied with a guide to life. It really hasn't worked out. And the present custodians of the button are making, to be sure, their considerable contributions to our life. They're also making a remarkable contribution to the problematic. I quote only one, Professor Bridgeman of Harvard, who says, "We now know enough to know that there is no necessary connection between the thoughts in our minds and the way things are." This liberation, then, is not a liberation into secured solutions, or the way to them, but into lifelong residence among the problematics of all liberation.

And finally, the second question: what is a moral stance appropriate to, indeed required by, that position if this be the way things are? By a "moral stance" I mean something more than merely intellectual; I mean a totality posture in the midst of that circumstance, something that Mr. Robert Oppenheimer meant when he said, "Style is the deference that action pays to uncertainty." What do I mean by "style" or a moral stance? Whatever that style might be, let it be suggested from this place, which has its own tradition of life's problematic. Let it be suggested primarily from here, and not wait for the dean of the college, to say that these days will require an order of moral courage and an order of moral sophistication that perhaps no other generation has had to bring to this task. And instead of speaking elaborately about this, I end with what I think a beautiful illustration:

Effort and Serenity

The year is 1066, which one sardonic teacher of history has said, "That's the only date we can be sure of on the entrance exam." The date is 1066. It's the time of the Norman Conquest, which is usually reported to us in the high school books in the vulgar language of a great success. But the real Norman story is otherwise. And remember how, according to the history, the *jongleur* on that day was a man who sang the greatest of all French epics, *The Song of Roland*. The text in that battle song is not a song about Roland who conquers, or thinks he can conquer, or who whips up the confidence in his followers that they shall conquer everything. The ballad text, the *Chanson de Roland*, is the song of Roland, the man of courage, who was not the conqueror, the man of courage in the midst of the unconquerable. There is a modern version of that text, done by Mr. Scott Moncrieff, and the introduction to it was written some years ago, of course, by Mr. Gilbert Chesterton. I want to read to you the paragraph taken from the introduction, in which he summarizes for us what he thinks to be the moral character of the poem:

> That high note of a forlorn hope of a host at bay and a battle at odds without end is the note upon which the great French epic ends. I know nothing more moving in poetry than that strange and unexpected ending. That strangely inconclusive conclusion: Charlemagne has established his empire in quiet, he has done justice, and he sleeps upon his throne with a peace almost like that of Paradise. Just then appears to him the Angel of God crying aloud, that his arms are needed in a new and distant land, that he must take up again the endless march of his days. And the great king tears his long white beard and cries out against his restless life. And thus the poem ends, with a vision of war against the Barbarians, and that vision is true. For that war is never ended, which defends the sanity of the world against all the stark anarchies and the rending negations which rage against it forever, and the grass is yet green on the graves of our friends who fell in it.[7]

Courage, then: courage in the unsolved, steadfastness in a life whose problematical character is a pattern and not just a phase—that is the kind of courage in which is fused both the vision of faith and the right function of a university. And that you may see the situation, know that you are not alone in it, find it possible to gain that courage—this is your university's tough and affectionate wish to you on the first Sunday of the term.

7. G. K. Chesterton in George Saintsbury, *Song of Roland*, translated into English verse by Charles Scott Moncrieff (New York: E. P. Dutton, 1920) xii.

The Nimbus and the Rainbow

1966

In this sermon the preacher ponders the familiar story of Noah, the deluge, and the rainbow. Once he has commented on the long history of the legend in the history of religions, he moves quickly to a more original and thoughtful question: that of the relationship of a favored person and a blessed creation. The nimbus or halo rests upon the head of the saints and patriarchs. The greater sign, the rainbow, spreads above the entire theater of God's creation, which in this sermon is symbolized by Lake Michigan and the city of Chicago. The whole panorama of grace is witnessed through the eyes of a creature named Noah, and now through our eyes as well. In this brief affirmation of God's care for the earth lay the seeds of a succession of rich meditations on the grace of creation and, ultimately, theology's engagement with ecology.

WE ARE ASKED TO reflect this morning upon the Old Testament lesson that was read in our hearing a few moments ago. The story is in the book of Genesis, a fairly long one, indeed, four chapters, and only the ending of the story was read. But you have only to hear the words "Noah and the ark" to cause the mind to recall the earthy, delightful, and even fantastic details of that long account. And it is, of course, precisely the details which constitute their resource in the story, which make it so hard for the sober reflections that are proper to a sermon to get past the details. For those details have engendered a long tradition of quite legitimate humor, to which certain contemporary entertainers in our day

The Nimbus and the Rainbow

are making their considerable and hilarious contribution. There is simply no point in being prissily academic in a protest against the incessant bubbling up of humor which has always been occasioned by the story of Noah and the ark. To be thus blue-nosed and academic about the point is a lost cause, because the primeval stuff of hilarity is *really* there. And too much sobriety about that would keep anyone from getting *to* the point. In other words, one has got to relax and enjoy the humor so that, having relaxed, we can get to its essence and its soberly theological message. The image is simply too strong and too juicy to deal with this story any other way. Imagine an old man, over 600 years we are told, presiding over a large family and a floating zoo, for a period of over a year, and all of this in a small boat. The children's books and the humorists are quite right. The problems of organization and sanitation must have been formidable.

But, when the amusement is over, the substance of the story is still there, and that substance constitutes an important element in Jewish religious faith to this day. The story, the name, the obedience of Noah, lived on to inform the daughter religious community, the Christians. Something comes to utterance in this story, and I'll ask, "Is it possible that the substance can again be excised, restated, and the ancient religious plenitude of it made freshly available for contemporary wisdom and right action?"

Paul Tillich—whose sermons are a fresh memory for many of us on this Memorial Day—Paul Tillich taught many of us to tread softly before the mystery of historical meaning and the profound complexity of the modalities of the transmission of all historical things. Every effort to impose upon the reality of historical knowledge a single way of knowing is the mark of the humorless and therefore immature mind. The university exists, indeed, for the annihilation of such innocence. Let us ask then, after the substance of this story by several steps: Where did the story come from? How was the form of the older story transformed by the community whose book Genesis is? And what is the proposal about God and man and the world to which the episodic momentum of the story drives us?

First, where did the story come from? Knowledge of the origin of the story is important because only so can one attend to such later transformations as constitute the point of the story in the Scripture version. In the Babylonian story, which certainly stands behind and shines through the biblical one, the tale of a great deluge illustrated a more fundamental belief. Namely, that all of life exhibits a struggle between chaos and order. Now here, and now there, one or the other of these is in the ascendancy, but the battle between chaos and order is an incessant one. And it is water, particularly, in the Babylonian story. It is particularly water at the flood which is the agent and is the principle of chaos. Turbulent, all-encompassing, irresistible, and confusion-making water is the principle of chaos.

But this origin is to be known only in order that we can now attend to how the myth is managed in the Scriptures of Israel. What a community does with the story is a kind of paradigm of how, in fact, myth becomes history, history becomes a matrix of faith, and faith engenders action. What the community did with that story was to unfold into huge new dimensions of meaning the older tale. The community did this in roughly three ways. First, the older story had nothing to do with humanity. The struggle between chaos and order is there depicted as going on above men's heads and out of their hands. These two mighty principles endlessly fought it out in timeless eternity. Second, the older story had nothing to do with, or to disclose about, history. Its scope and its terms do not focus upon or turn about human historical life in all of its unfolding pageantry. And third, the older story had nothing to do with will, choice, acceptance or rejection of a possibility. Neither God nor man is really involved. That is to say freedom, the mark and the burden of the human, is simply not in the old equation.

Observe now the transformation, and in it observe how myth becomes the matrix of faith. The pattern becomes personal. The eternal fixity of principles becomes the historical openness to freedom. In this story God is the actor in a completely human symbolism. He sees. He hurts from what he sees. He resolves to do something about what he sees. And he makes a proposal to a human being—a particular human. Not just to humanity, a principle, but a proposal to a man. The man's name is Noah. This man is, as it were, Søren Kierkegaard's "existing particular individual." The man's name is known to us, and the names of his man-begot sons are given.

Second, the ordeal in this transformed story is not timeless and indeterminate. It has limits, and the limitation of the action is set by the Initiator of the action. One little instance of that, in the symbolism of the detail: The waters rise, we are told, as the fountains of heaven are opened. But the waters do not rise absolutely to the vault of heaven; [they rise to] fifteen cubits above the highest mountains. Fifteen cubits above the highest mountains is a lot of water, but it is not absolute water. There *is* a limit, and the Actor who turns it on is presented in the story as the Actor who turns it off.

The Nimbus and the Rainbow

And third, the whole action in the transformed story is drenched in decision. It is volitional, through and through. God, for the evil imaginings of men's hearts, decides upon the deluge; and Noah, a man, in an act of will responds to a proffered possibility. Each has his responsibility. And the covenant at the end of the story is an announcement of that responsibility, a monument to it, and a celebration of it: "While the earth remains, seedtime and harvest, cold and heat, summer and winter, day and night, shall not cease."

Now how shall we understand the rhetoric of the good rhythms of the given? Save to suppose that the scope of the covenant of grace is here presented as identical with all that is? The scope of the covenant of grace is made not simply with this or that man, or with this or that people, but all that is—nature and history. And each man in his place, in his private and societal knot of decision—over it all bends the covenant of God.

Reflect then upon what that covenant and the grace which it includes, what that might mean for us, and require of us. And I think we get to that by piercing through the image of the rainbow, which is the sign of the covenant, and comparing the rainbow with that other biblical figure of incandescence, which is the mark of the presence of God, but which has a quite individual form and locus—the halo, or the nimbus. Observe that between these two, in their difference and in their sameness, there is a kind of lure of the symbolic, which suggests more than is said. For whereas the nimbus is the sign of the precision of grace, the rainbow is the sign of the theater, the scope, and the plentitude of grace. The nimbus encircles the head of a person, to say that here is one who heard, who trusted, who accepted, who dared what he trusted, and became by grace a kind of personal incandescence of a response to grace. Mary, for instance: "My soul magnifies the Lord, and my spirit rejoices in God my savior, for he has regarded the low estate of his handmaiden." This listening, this acceptance, this daring to be the vessel and to bear the burden of grace.

This, in Christian art, is always signed with the sign of the nimbus. But the rainbow is the sign of the scope of grace. The great story in Genesis does not end with a man, Noah, encircled by a nimbus. It ends with a kind of cosmic nimbus from God, bent in incandescence around the whole creation. And God said, "This is the sign of the covenant, which I make between me, and you, and every living creature that is with you, for all future generations. I set my bow in the clouds, and it shall be a sign of the covenant between me and the earth." It is here being said to us, the life of history and the life of nature are not separate, but the life of nature has been drawn into the destiny of man's decision as history. The processes of both, and the outcomes of both, are drawn into the crucial alembic of the decisions of man. A man, Noah, could listen or deafen himself. He could obey or not obey. Because he listened and obeyed, a little island of responsibility and care floated once upon the surface of chaos.

It is not required, I think, in this company, to spin out the signed depth of that image. We are hemmed in by problems whose solution demands such an evaluation and use of human beings and events and things and nature in its structure and process, as this legend sets forth. What this legend says about man's responsibility for the earth is exactly, in other language, what the *Bulletin of the Atomic Sciences* is saying month after month. The bow of God's promise and power and grace is, for instance, over the city. Absolutely, according to human decisions, the city can become a theater of grace, in which humanity can be most richly realized, or it can become a humanly intolerable hell, a stifling intersection of procedures for industrial process, and in Chicago's instance, for conventioneers' frivolity. Or, the bow of possibility is over Lake Michigan. How that magnificent givenness shall go is absolutely according to level of evaluation by which we regard it. It can remain a kind of gracious counterpart to the crowded city, a space that is open, seeming illimitable, always clean, and always there. It exists to modulate the fevers and the foolishness of crowded lives in a city. Or it can be turned over to sewage and the waiting algae. From symbol to evaluation to decision is, in the history of culture, not always a clear line, but it's always a line. And human beings can do what they will to one another in our time. It is now possible, for the first time, for humans to do with the earth what we choose. Humans can do with or against one another. They can do for or against the fecund earth, the clean air, and the clean water. And then, the level of their evaluation, as to what they will to do, becomes the pinion upon which the future really turns. The present cadre of radical theologians, with their appeal to a holy secularity, are not really repudiating transcendence. They are only relocating, domesticating, and making it vivid. They are simply announcing its presence and power and promise where the ancient story of Noah proclaims it always was, and where the Christian assertion of an incarnation acknowledges its residency.

A halo, then, for Noah! His obedience to God and the year he put in deserves one. But beyond the halo, the story talks of the glow of the holy over and within the evil—the problematic, always a possibility within and alluring before chaos and the sweat. Is that perhaps what the bow means? That is the bow of which the story speaks that may have been in Hopkins' mind when he wrote:

> *The world is charged with the grandeur of God.*
> *It will flame out, like shining from shook foil.*

Or when again he said:

> *I say that we are wound*
> *With mercy round and round*

Suffering and Splendor

1973

Romans 8:18–30

In this sermon Sittler weaves together his reflections on the method of biblical interpretation with the message of a particular text. The faith expounded here is clearly a matter of trust in the midst of life that has already seen the splendor of God's gracious promise but not yet face to face. In the interim between the already and the not yet we experience suffering. To express this eschatological tension Sittler employs the notion of "tautness," a favorite image of Sittler's in which lurks the interplay of law and gospel, judgment and grace. The sufferings of life, both personal and cosmic, are located within this tension; our own experience is part of the experience of the whole creation.

TWO WORDS, AND IMPORTANT ones, were different in the New English Bible. Because I studied that version in preparation, I wanted to begin by calling attention to those two changes. The NEB uses the word "endurance" rather than the word "patience." And the second change is that it uses the word "splendor" rather than the word "glory."

The lectionary system under which most of us grew up and with which most of us will exercise our ministry has many advantages and you are aware of these. But it also has some disadvantages, and we are commonly not so aware of these. The chief disadvantage of the lectionary system is that it asks us to preach bit by bit what did not come into existence bit by bit, but as an organic whole. In fact, that kind of preaching is particularly difficult when its matter is one of the epistles of Saint Paul. What redaction criticism does to make clearer the setting of particular pericopes in the gospels, it cannot perform with the same effect with the organic epistles of Saint Paul. They are already in the form, or very close to it, with which the early church heard them. Pericope preaching exclusively is a kind of invitation to the mind systematically to cut up into pieces what did not come to us cut up into little pieces. The ideal way to preach from Romans, then, would be to preach the entire argument of the entire epistle at a single sitting. The difficulties of this I shall not expound, but the problem in that, nevertheless, is not diminished by the recognition of it. The problem is, it simply will not do to dribble out in little pieces what the writer counted upon in the massive argument of the Epistle to the Romans, to make its point to us by the internal counterpoint in which each word in the epistle receives illumination from every other word. And, therefore, to take the bits and pieces is an embarrassment that can only really be overcome by acknowledging the character of it, and reading each bit in the light of all the rest, understanding that *anything* that Paul says has as its proper commentary *everything* that Paul says.

For instance, in the first section which is assigned for our meditation this morning, the lesson speaks of the sufferings that we now endure. And these sufferings that we now endure are compared with the splendor as yet unrevealed which is in store for us. And because *anything* that Paul says requires as context *everything* that he says, suffering and splendor belong together. They, as it were, mutually define one another in the whole of the Letter to the Romans. And when we take them apart the precision which they have when thus run together is somewhat dimmed or muted. For "suffering," in Paul's use of the word, is never episodic. Christian suffering is not occasional pain which may come and go. Suffering, in Paul's understanding, is fully explicated, for instance, in the beginning of the sixth chapter of Romans and in the third chapter of Philippians. Suffering, for Paul, always specified an inescapable *tautness* of the Christian life. Tautness in the life of the Christian believer is not an occasional thing, but the constant, never relaxed, steady condition of the life of faith. Suffering is not something that happens to us, in Paul's understanding, but is something that constantly characterizes the Christian life and is an internal component of the Christian life. And it comes from this: before God we see enough never again to be without a lurking remembrance of what we have seen, that is, the splendor; but what we see remains a dimmed beholding which, in finite time, never becomes the absolute clarity that one longs for. The suffering of the life of faith is therefore of the character of faith, not an episodic interruption of it. One can neither forget nor can one fully pass into possession of what the vision of the glory reveals. This is the substance and the dynamism of what Paul means by "suffering."

Remember that the word "splendor," here in the lesson in the Revised Standard Version interpreted "glory," means the light that the holy gives off. "Splendor" means that alluring beckoning of the promise of the glory of God. It's exactly that which lighted the face of Moses, that which enshrined the transfiguration story in the gospel, that which shimmers throughout every intersection of God and man on his pilgrimage through life; and it shown in the hearts of them that walked to Emmaus. Therefore the "glory," the "splendor"—they mean the same thing.

Now ours is an eschatological existence between a seeing that cannot be forgotten and, nevertheless, a living of one's whole life with that unforgettable memory that can never be wholly grasped. This is the interior climate of the Christian life, and this is what Paul means by "suffering." That suffering is not only characteristic and internally constitutive of the life of faith, it is also the story of all history, all nature, and all theological reflection. That is why the dimensions of this existence between suffering and the splendor are not only characteristic of the believer. That is, its residency is not only within the amazing hot privacy of personal life, although it is there. But it is also, as Paul says in this passage that follows, characteristic of everything in history and everything in nature too.

The entire created universe waits with eager expectation. It groans in every part of it. It waits for—as in the pangs of childbirth—it waits for the dawning of the splendor. To "wait" and to "hope"—these words play back and forth now in Paul's usage. To wait *is* to hope. And to hope in the Scripture is always to wait. And hope, then, is, as it were, the precondition of the splendor. The suffering is the precondition of our understanding of it. This suffering, this passage says, this suffering characterizes all that is. If all that is, then, according to Paul, is caught up in this hoping, waiting, suffering, all is also included in the splendor. Anyone who would dismiss the vision of Pierre Teilhard de Chardin as a gaseous dream—when he explicates the meaning of the glory, the splendor, the destiny of all things in terms that are universal—anyone who would dismiss that, or restrict the presence or the operations of the grace of God as opening all things toward the splendor of himself, had better come to terms with this enigmatic but perfectly clear statement in which the whole creation is involved both in the suffering and stands undisclosed before the splendor. But now, and only now, are we ready for what Paul says about hope and of God's Spirit.

Of those to whom the Spirit has been given, Paul writes, we have, he says, been saved, but only in hope. Now to see, he says, is no longer to hope. For why should a people hope for that for which they see? But if we hope for something we do not see yet then, in waiting for it, we show our endurance. Paul is saying to us that hope is the steady, the lasting, the never-to-be-surpassed character of faith. Faith moves within hope. It never moves out of it. And to wait is the fundamental gesture of the mind and the heart that hopes.

"Blessed Assurance," the title of an ancient hymn, is always given within the context of "blessed endurance." There is no "blessed assurance" which is of a character that can transcend or get above or do away with or fill with the internal glory so that we shall not have to understand the Christian life as "blessed endurance." Impatient piety would like things to be otherwise, but genuine piety knows that it cannot be out of line. And now follows the paragraph about the Spirit—how the Spirit comes to us. Paul says that the Spirit comes to us, but never in such a tension-obliterating way as to make slack, or reduce the tautness of, that very *spannung* (span) between splendor and suffering which is elaborated in the previous paragraphs. Now this is hard for us to take. It's hard for us, particularly in these greedy, carbonated, charismatic days, for it *is* a kind of spiritual greediness that wants in our day to have a special delivery torrent of Spirit that shall enter our lives in order to give us blessed assurance and permit us escape blessed endurance. It's the spiritual greediness because it wants from God what God gave neither to Paul nor to Jesus before him. The Spirit, we read, comes to our aid in our weakness. Now notice that the Spirit never transforms that weakness *out* of weakness. The Spirit, rather, sustains us in it, nurtures hope within it. How beautifully Paul speaks of this in relation to prayer. It's no accident, I think, that he illustrates this endurance in hope by using the illustration of the life of prayer, because we are often tempted, understandably, to believe that somehow in prayer, if anywhere, we ought to achieve a kind of communion with God in which the tautness between suffering and the splendor should be at least for a moment relaxed; and because it is not we sometimes talk about our own prayer or think about it in terms that are filled with guilt.

We sometimes forget how different is the way Paul speaks about prayer and the Spirit in prayer here from the polished elegance and fluency of our sonorous public prayers. For observe, God himself as Holy Spirit *is* the pray-er in our prayers. God himself is doing the praying—even in the stumbling, inarticulateness of our prayers. We read [that] God who searches our inmost being knows what the Spirit means, and God's Spirit pleads for God's own people in God's own way. Which means that when, in our praying, we cannot achieve the ecstasy of Saint Theresa, or the ascending to the holy that would seem to characterize the life and hymnody of Saint Bernard of Clairvaux, there is nevertheless a huge consolation here, because God's own way, as we read, of shaping us to the likeness of his Son to which this paragraph points—God's own way may work exactly within the guilt and stumbling of our own prayers. Do we perhaps read this properly when we suppose that that we pray at all may be a prayer more consonant with endurance and patience than a praying that pleases itself by the sonority of its relaxed fluency? That we pray at all even in the inarticulate groaning that Paul talks about is the kind of God's own way of praying which cannot be escaped if we live always and inescapably between the suffering and the splendor.

This pericope ends with words which point to, but do not really unwrap, a vast mystery. For we read that "God called those he foreknew, and those he foreknew he justified," and so forth, and I would suggest that nineteen centuries of exegetical sweat, including that of Calvin and Martin Luther and Karl Barth, who have tugged at the seals of this mystery, have not greatly unwrapped it. In fact, Paul himself in this passage does not unwrap it. Even Paul stands within the mystery of foreordination. He does not lay his hands upon it. He does not attack the mystery that is enclosed in those last verses about the mystery of God's knowledge which he had of us before we were, and which is called "foreknowledge of God." Paul does not continue the argument. He knows, as it were, when he's had it. He simply breaks it off. At the end of this paragraph, Paul passes from mystery to doxology, from astonishment to praise, from acceptance of the mystery to adoration of it. "What," then, "shall we say to these things?" And he says nothing to these things at all. He simply begins the last passage. Finally, he says, "What shall we say to these things? If God be for us, who can be against us?"

Three on Romans 8 (Sermon 1)

1975

Romans 8:31–39

It is very much like Joseph Sittler to explore exhaustively a single passage of Scripture, drawing from it not only its clearest teaching but its less obvious implications for the church. In this, his first in a trilogy of sermons on Romans 8, the preacher unveils his path-breaking theme of the Christian's responsibility for the care of the earth. The world of nature, he says, and human nature along with it, is incomplete and still unfolding. With uncharacteristic anger he unpacks the Pauline image of a creation in travail, in labor, waiting (and hoping) to be born. His trenchant comments on the reckless drilling for oil are prescient reminders of ongoing violations of God's creation.

THE INTRODUCTION TO THE sermon this morning is the first of what I hope to make a three-part consideration of this tremendous eighth chapter of Romans. This introduction ought to be of some comfort to many who have difficulty penetrating all the meanings of the Bible. I know because in forty-five years of preaching I have calculatedly ducked this text. I always found it possible on this Sunday to preach either on the Gospel or on the Old Testament text and consequently have not come to terms with this immense, meaningful lesson from the eighth chapter because I was not certain I had a good grasp of what it means. That should

Part 3: Sermons

be of some comfort because many people may think, "Well I don't understand this very well, but the pastor has been trained in biblical studies and knows all about it." Well let me assure you, in many instances he doesn't! But it belongs to the magnificence of the Holy Scripture that meanings may resonate in great depth through a lifetime of reflection—and even a lifetime of study does not reveal everything about them.

There are levels within levels and wheels within wheels. Think, for instance, of the great passage from Isaiah, when old Isaiah says, "there was no beauty that men should desire him," "we hid as it were our faces from him," "the Lord hath laid upon him the iniquity of us all," and "by his stripes we are healed." I know the meaning of the surface statement, but the interior resonance of meaning that comes out of those mighty metaphors—a lifetime does not suffice to unfold them. Or think of other statements in the Bible. There's a passage from Luke that still haunts me. Jesus is speaking about children: "And I say unto you that in heaven there are angels who always behold the face of my Father."[8] What is he saying here about the nature of new, fresh, and unspoiled life? What's being said here in a metaphor about child life? I do not certainly know that, but it is of the magnificence of Scripture that what we do not fully comprehend remains to haunt.

In studying Scripture, one stands, as it were, in the same situation that the poet John Keats did when once he wrote to his brother Tom, "A huge and alluring vision strides always just before me." That's true of any serious inquiry into any profundity. This groping after language with which to enclose and stop and make clear what is fundamentally ineffable is like the quest of the beautiful fairy princess in the child's fairy tale. One gets a glimpse that lets him never forget but never comes close enough really to grasp. So it is when we come to this great chapter in Romans, where I think it is fair to say that never in the history of literature has such a group of enormous notions, concepts, powers, been compacted in so short a space. Therefore, I have taken the liberty of my last three regular weeks with you to attend, in a fresh way, to Romans 8. I begin with the lesson that's given us today.

Now, having said that a thing is in some ways inscrutable, I shall not try flat-footedly to unscrew it. If the thing is really not fully clear, then let me not deny my preliminary affirmation and talk about it as if it were. But some things in the statement here are not fully obscure either, and

---

8. A paraphrase not from Luke, but from Matt 18:10.

you may wish to have the text in front of you from the insert, because this is no easy business.

The first statement which is quite clear is that, in the understanding of the apostle, this first great Christian preacher whose material we have in the New Testament—in the understanding of Paul, nature is not complete. The world is in motion. Things are yet to be unfolded that have not yet occurred. Now we know from observed fact that that is true of nature. Every element and process and structure in nature—this is not a religious judgment, it's a purely scientific judgment—every element, structure, combination, in nature is always moving toward profounder complexification. It always seeks to transcend itself. It is never content to be static in its situation. It is always to be arrived at. That's true of everything from viruses and bacteria, to the structure of the human brain. The whole creation is in movement. It's moving toward something. Now the metaphor by which that something is vaguely indicated does not open itself absolutely to our conceptualization. But the point is clear: man is imbedded in nature and shares nature's lack of fulfillment—the incompleteness. It has the shape of a bud, tightly folded, but aeon after aeon, it opens and opens and opens. This is not the old idea of "progress." One has only to look around to see how primitive man dealt with nature, how the American Indian lived on this continent, and then read the announcements about what the land developers are doing, to know that progress is a very dubious notion. But *we* have done this; nature hasn't. Nature in itself, and man in some aspects of his being, is still unfolding. It's an uncompleted and unfulfilled world.

The second thing that is relatively clear is: this is not simply a law of nature. Now the scientist may regard it that way, and has a legitimate right to do so. But the religious, specifically the Christian point of view, following Paul, would say, "And God has subjected it in hope." What does that mean? It means God did not give us a finished job. He did not in the creation present us with a static world, with all things in immutable place. God has subjected it in hope. And the very words "in hope" mean—and in the Hebrew the phrase "to wait" and "to hope" are the same verb—it means that things have an interior possibility which God both plans and is drawing toward some ultimate unfolding.

And the third relatively clear thing in the lesson—*relatively* clear—is that we are related to this process. Humanity is not to be set over against nature and understood purely as conscious, awareness, a dreaming and concept-making creature that is pure intellect. No. Man's life is deeply imbedded in the root, in the ground of nature, just as the leaves on that plant back of me are imbedded in the ground in that pot. Thus the whole creation, in the beautiful figure, the whole creation *and we ourselves* are groaning in travail, waiting. The picture here is not only of an untroubled opening toward God's fulfillment, but a tumultuous and a painful opening, so that the episodes that we might regard as being disruptive of the human community may be the groaning of nature and history to bring out a future better, a future justice. I recall when our late undistinguished vice president went up and down the country talking about, of all things, the weakening of the moral fiber of the American people. What he called "the weakening of the moral fiber" was riots in the streets, disruptions in society, and the screaming of people who had been systematically deprived of a decent humanity. There is a groaning and a travailing, but it brings forth a better child, so that all troubles are not negative, all disruptions do not necessarily require the FBI. All *dis*orders are not against a better order. But the coming into birth of the better often involves the groaning and the travailing of the less good. The respectable static will always be pained by the emerging better. The whole creation and we ourselves also are subjected in hope, waiting.

Now, if these three things be quite clear, I don't want to go on to say any more about this passage, because this passage is part of a great speech about the nature of the Spirit of God, which is the whole chapter. And to that we want to get next week.

But does this lesson convey on a very practical level to us? I'm convinced it says many things, some of which I'm sure I do not understand. But of the many things that our fathers in the church felt it was saying, one is indicated by the context of the other lessons given to us this morning. The psalm has to do with the earth, the green and fecund earth, and the joy that man should find in it and the care he ought to have for it. Thus it says something about the groaning and travailing of nature here, with which I now want to conclude this reflection.

I begin with a proposition I ask you to think about: when it comes to the really important issues, the visionaries of this world are more practical than the self-pronounced practicals. Practical people, in the long run, foul up the situation regularly. The practical people of this world know that there is a lot of cheap meat for dogs and cats available if they chase down the last of the remaining 300 sperm whales in the oceans of the world. And the practical men of affairs are busily destroying them, with the result that soon there will be no more of what the psalm called that

Three on Romans 8 (Sermon 1)

"great Leviathan in whom God delighted." Soon there will be no more because it is practical to get the most meat at the cheapest price. The practical people of the world, the Peabody Coal Company, certainly applaud our president's veto of the regulatory bill for regulating strip mining. The practical men know we have to have energy, and we've got to have it in a hurry; the easiest, quickest, cheapest way to get it is to rip off the topsoil and jerk it out of the earth. The practical men of the world who write the advertising for Gulf, Phillips, Sun, and Exxon have not said a word to admit what they know quite clearly (they are not stupid). They know there is a lot of oil under the earth, but no matter how much there is, it is a finite amount. But they act, and say in effect, "Just give us more money to pump it faster from more places and to get it quicker from where it is to where it ain't, and we will solve our energy crisis." That is one of the stupidest remarks ever made by a sane mind; that we solve the problem of a non-replaceable resource by using it faster. Now as regards these realities, this is not a religious man dreaming in Romans 8. When he says the whole creation groans in travail waiting—now watch it—waiting for the revealing of the sons of God, can that possibly mean that a son of God, a serious son of God, really means what he says when he says, "The earth is the Lord's and the fullness thereof"; that he really means what he says when he reads, "And God put this man *Adam* in the garden and said, 'Tend it'"? Now the practical man means, "Develop it." And the word "developer," as it is presently used, has nothing to do with tending or enhancement. What "development" commonly means would be the same as if I would call a rapist the "developer" of womanhood. The whole creation—and we too—groans in travail, waiting for the disclosure. Or could it be waiting for the sons of God to begin to act like the true children of God?

Now, finally, will you, along with this dreamer in the just, dream of this: what might it mean if 80 to 90 million nominally observant Christians and Jews in the United States of America really believed what they said? Suppose that in private reflection, behavior, and in familial practice, we really believed that the rape of the earth is not only irrational, impractical and stupid, but blasphemous.

Suppose we really believed it?

Three on Romans 8 (Sermon 2)

1975

Romans 8:31–39

Sittler typically circles around a text, introducing key words and concepts and digressing from them, only to return to them with a greater depth of insight. He follows this method in his treatment of the Spirit in Romans 8, paying special attention to the telling power of the little word "therefore."

SOME TEXTS PRESENT THE single question and some present a double one. That is, some texts are quite clear, and the point of the sermon is simply to urge people to understanding, that is, to stand before that clarity and do what the text says. But there are other texts—and the eighth chapter of Romans is filled with them—there are other texts in which one has a double problem. The language is so compacted and the images are so rich that one must first of all undertake the unpacking and the clarification of the several layers of meaning in the text, and then ask what we are to hear and obey. So in our consideration of this text this morning, this enormous passage, Romans 8 verses 1–18, it were folly to suppose that one could in a short sermon deal adequately with even a piece of it, but I want to take the resonance of the word "the Spirit" as it happens all through that text, and ask you to reflect with me upon how that word works in this particular text. Now I suppose we would agree that there is

Three on Romans 8 (Sermon 2)

no word in the vocabulary—the common vocabulary, or in this Christian vocabulary—which is in our day more confused or subject to dismaying inadequacies than the word "the Spirit." There are those who declare that the Spirit is a kind of private pipeline to God—that it is possible to have inputs of the Spirit which, in an ineffable, mysterious, and supernatural way, grant to the blessed children of that gift a relation to God that is not available to the common run of humanity. There is not an ounce of evidence in the Bible to defend that—that the fundamental word about the Holy Spirit in the Scripture is reserved for a spiritual coterie of the especially gifted. And there is no evidence that that is now or has ever been the case. The power and the enthusiasm of the Charismatic movement in our day has legitimate aspects which cannot be denied. But that movement, as it relates to the doctrine of the Spirit, could only gain by being enlarged to the size of this tremendous chapter.

So I begin to take you into that chapter by observing the first word, which is a piece of characteristic Pauline connective tissue. Time and again in his letters Paul says, "Well then . . . For this cause . . . If, then . . . ," which usually means that something has been said before to which a reply is now to be made. This chapter begins on an upbeat "Therefore!" Now it makes no sense to try to answer what lies on this side of the "therefore" without knowing the argument to which the "therefore" is the apostolic reply. What lies just back of the "therefore"? Well actually, the whole first seven chapters of Romans, but I will try to compress it into a single statement. It comes to a concentrated statement in the seventh chapter, where Paul, reviewing the situation of mortal, finite, sinful man in the midst of a world that is filled with evil, with demonic power, and, for all men, death. Out of that depth, Paul cries at the very end of the seventh chapter, "O, wretched man that I am, who shall deliver me from the grasp of this death?" Now that has often been understood as an eruption out of the deepest level of Paul's exquisite conscience. It is no such thing. There is no evidence that Paul had an exquisitely sensitive conscience at all! He could say, "As before the law, I am blameless." Paul did not take it lying down when people accused him of being worse than other people. What, then, can he mean—"O, wretched man that I am"? He means something we all know, knowledge of which does not depend upon exquisite sensitivity and moral consciousness. He means that, good or bad, fairly righteous or not so righteous, we are all within the grip of three structures, three mighty structures that are transpersonal, everlasting, and universal.

The first of them is the fact of evil. In our deepest cells, even the devout, the pious, the sanctified, those on the way to glory, know that evil in this life is always a power we fight against but never destroy. It's a thing that dogs the step of the pious with a more seductive evil than it does with the open sinner—the structure of evil.

Second, we live in the midst of demonic forces. When the epistles talk about principalities and powers, they don't mean simply the obvious rottenness, nastiness, and aggressiveness of the world. They mean that there's something tending toward destruction. There is a negativity. There is a *no* in the midst of all the *yeses* of this world. How shall one be delivered from that?

And third, he says, "O, wretched man that I am, who shall deliver me from the grasp of death?" We can sing pleasant songs about it and create soothing language about "passing away"—which is a particularly sloppy term. We can do all kinds of things to mask it, but we all move toward death. Who shall deliver me from the grip of *that* structure that stands as the terminus of all life?

When Paul says, "Therefore," he's not talking about private piety. He's not talking about the little evils and sins or even the major ones that lay waste life. He's talking about the vast structures that imprison finite man within an infinite dream. Now he begins this mighty doxology in Romans 8: "Therefore, brethren, there is now no condemnation." He piles the whole thing up and sweeps it all away with a gigantic gesture: "There is no condemnation because of one thing." Now the one thing to which Paul points is nothing less than the fact that God, who created this world, who knows this world in the depth of power of all these structures, entered into all of them and went down under the worst of them. And he came through and out of them alive! There is therefore now no condemnation if any man be in Christ Jesus, and Christ Jesus is but the name for that action whereby God became the hell of this world, this life, and this imprisonment and was not thereby destroyed. If you, therefore, are in him, your open, pathetic, destructibility to these forces is now hidden in the life of the one who was not destroyed by these forces. There is *therefore* now no condemnation. And when in the lesson Paul talks about being free from the law, he's not talking about statutes. What he means here by the word "law" is used to mean those structures—those structures of periodicity, permanency, of destructiveness. You are free from these if you are in the Spirit. Now what can he mean by "the Spirit" when he uses "the Spirit" here in relation to Jesus, to God, and to the Christian life?

Three on Romans 8 (Sermon 2)

I want to get into that by asking you to reflect with me upon a statement a student of mine once blurted out in class, when he said, "If God is not enough God for everything, he isn't enough God for anything." That statement was disclosing a typical modern mood, in which the student knows that a person has his roots biologically, geologically, and historically in everything that is. We are not merely crawling *Homo sapiens*, as it were, scuttling across the surface of the world. We are *of* the world; we were produced by it. And therefore any notion of God that comes to us as a private word whispered into our individual ear—"Buck up, old boy, I'm on your side"—is not enough. The only salvatory God is the God who's got the "whole world in his hands." If he somehow is not the God of everything, he is not an adequate God for my anything, no matter what that anything may be.

Now as we look at this text further, we find out that the Spirit, the Spirit which is the power of God whereby we are inserted into that victorious life of God—that Spirit is spoken of in many ways, but let me refer you to that way we just said together in the Nicene Creed. Here, in the year 384, the church made a statement of its confession. Now that seems away back and very early to us, but the church was already quite old—as old as the American Republic is, and older. A mature church said, "And I believe in the Holy Spirit, the Lord and giver of life." Now if you grasp that, then you're very close to what the Bible means by "the Spirit of God." Watch: The Lord's Spirit breathed over nothing and something was. Or, when something was made that was there, but only latent and not alive, his Spirit breathed into and it came alive. Therefore, "the Spirit" in its profoundest sense means God's creative action whereby there is a world, the creativity of God which is identical with life itself. Now this is not life in some aesthetic, philosophical sense, but plain biological reality: there are cells, there are organisms. I want to refer to three little things that constitute persuasion—not proof—a sort of analogy to what the Creed points to when it says, "And I believe in the Holy Spirit, the Lord, the giver of life."

Some weeks ago I read a little book by Dr. Lewis Thomas, who is a clinician and investigator at the Rockefeller Center. He called the book *The Living Cells*, and in one of the eloquent little chapters he discusses the apparent indestructibility of the process of biological life; that biological life does not go to waste but goes on. He uses the amazing word "unnatural": "There is something unnatural to a biologist. There is something unnatural about human death." Unnatural that life should cease at the moment of biological or physiological death—that is highly unnatural, says the biologist.

The television program *NOVA* delves into the fundamental operating concepts and ideas of the natural and physical sciences. In a program on astrophysics, scientists from Cambridge spoke of the discovery in about the year 1200 of a gigantic new galaxy which is known as the Crab Nebula. It can only been seen now with instruments, but its emission of power is so gigantic that the energy emitted from the Sun is 1/40,000th of the energy emitted by this nebula, which is invisible to the naked eye. But in another four billion years it will collapse upon itself with so vast a mass of life that out of sheer pressure it will then re-explode and a new galaxy will be born. *The Lord and the giver of life.* Think of it in big enough circles.

I had a neighbor several years ago who was an investigator at Argon National Laboratory, the atomic research site west of the city, and one day he said to me, "You know the bacteria are growing inside the reactor." Inside the reactor with incredible heat and dreamlike destructive power, with atom-splitting capability, he said the bacteria are doing their old thing on the inside of reactor. When, therefore, we are led here into the phrase, "There is no condemnation, because by the law of the Spirit of life, in Jesus." That phrase refers to the displacement of the absoluteness of the old structure. They're still there. We die. We know evil. We do evil. We know the demonic. But their ultimate power has been destroyed. "The law," in Paul's term, is the mighty structure of the life of God which came and was illuminated in Christ. If that is true, then there is another side to the whole story of human, finite existence. When we baptized a child this morning, that sacrament of the church represented the insertion of every new arrival into that lifecycle, into that story of no condemnation.

The second verse in this passage is the one that I call special attention to: "If the Spirit of him who raised Jesus from the dead dwell in you, you also shall be raised with him." The Spirit, then, is not simply something Jesus occasionally felt, or even extraordinarily felt. The Spirit that raised Jesus from the dead means that something greater than the dead is the life of God, and it goes in, through, and under all dying. So the power of the Spirit is nothing less than the power that raised Jesus from the dead. Now when I hear some people talk about the Spirit, and say, "I get the Spirit at occasional, important moments of my life, and when I don't know just whether I should buy this or that kind of a washing machine, I ask God's Holy Spirit to give me a tip-off," I have to wonder. This is a banal reduction of God's power and the majesty of Paul's statement into ridiculousness. If the Spirit of life in Christ Jesus that raised him from the dead reign in your bodies, you too shall be raised with him. And therefore the Christian hope of eternal life (and it's never a proof) is not an unreasonable one. And the text finally refers to that when it says, "The Spirit"—that's with a large "S"; the Holy Spirit—"The Spirit bears witness with our spirit." Now, not *without* our spirit, or not against our spirit, but the verb is, that the Spirit bears witness *with* our spirit. Our own spirit, as it were, is open toward this possibility. As one paleontologist says, "All living things move toward transcending themselves." That's true of every level of life including the human level. All living things move toward the trend to go beyond themselves. And that self-transcendence may be that in our spirit which, as it were, is open to hear the promise and to believe the promise and trust it. Dylan Thomas writes to his father, "Old age should rage at close of day / Do not go gentle into that good night / Rage, rage against the dying of the light." What is it within humanity that doesn't need to be reminded to rage against the dying of the light, which knows that there is something that transcends itself, which has a dream-like capacity to envision another possibility?

Now to that possibility, Paul writes, "There is, therefore, now no condemnation," because what our spirit dreams as possible, the disclosure of God in Jesus Christ declares as action.

Three on Romans 8 (Sermon 3)

1975

Romans 8:31–39

In the final sermon in his trilogy on Romans 8, Sittler illuminates the difference between belief as a body of information and belief as the act of believing. It is, he says, the dangerous and open-ended act of living in faith—believing, waiting, hoping—that throws us into the arms of the God who is always "for" us. These postures of faith, however, should not be limited to the popular view of religion as absolute inwardness or absolute knowledge, for believers are always deeply implicated in nature, history, and our own "cussedness," which means that we can never know God the way God knows us.

THIS IS THE THIRD of three Sundays in which we're reflecting together upon that enormously compacted passage, the eighth chapter of Paul's Letter to the Romans.

Two Sundays ago I called attention to this: that in old Christianity, in the biblical faith, in the history of the church, that which characterizes our contemporary religious mood was almost unknown. And what is that? It is the notion that Christian faith, or indeed *any* religious faith, is a matter of absolute inwardness, intense privacy, or intense individual belief. This certainly does characterize religious thought and feeling in our day, but I do not find it in the catholic tradition or in the Bible. Meaning

Three on Romans 8 (Sermon 3)

is indeed personal—the personal, the inward, the individual, is indeed a rich and immeasurable realm of meaning—but ultimate meaning is not and cannot be personal, because my person is not identical with reality. I come from a mighty universal process called "nature." I live in that which transcends my individual life, called "history." I have a long past, even as a biological organism, and move to an indefinite unfolding future as a biological organism. Therefore, any attempt to identify sufficient meaning with privacy is not only futile, but it works against the very tradition we are here to glorify.

Now the second step we took was to look at how the Letter to the Romans puts that. When Paul talks about faith and love and trust, how does he reach out for a metaphor big enough to handle the bigness of it? He says, "The whole creation . . ." The *whole creation* is a work of God that signifies the presence of God. And then he spins the orbits of the fundamental terms of faith—he spins these in the same dimensions as the whole creation, historically and naturally.

Now we come to the last part today of the Letter to the Romans, where, having built up the great story of how, into the futility, obscurity, and partial meaningfulness of human life, God has come with a clear, personal word in the form of his own self. He came among us in flesh and blood. And while we see always through a glass darkly, we *do* see. And therefore, having built up the argument, Paul now comes to this last, awfully condensed, even confusing and difficult passage. And I want to lead into it today. I can do no more.

The mood is clear among us that having religious faith, or belonging to a religious community, or taking the great central terms of faith seriously is a highly private affair. It has nothing to do with truth—the way things really are. It's a completely individual thing. It's sort of like stewed prunes. They're okay for people who like that kind of thing, but there isn't much chance that they should evoke universal gratification. The cathedral at Chartres, the Vatican, and Augustana Lutheran Church—these are roofs that shelter the idiosyncrasies of a few people who are disposed to like that kind of thing. Now you know if that were really true, the Christian faith would have had it long ago. The only reason there still is a continuing tradition—in partial eclipse at the moment, but hang in there, it's been that way before—the only reason there is a Christian tradition, whose symbols still constitute not only some meaning, but complete and absolute signals of meaning for millions of us, is because we never made it simply a kind of analgesic for privacy, a kind of aspirin for solitude, or a kind of Ben-Gay, as it were, for hurt in the gut. There has always been an effort to understand Christian faith in terms of "We believe it because it's true." Because it points to that which constitutes deeper understandings of the nature of human life: Transcendentality. Cussedness. Sin. Communion. Reality. Therefore, in the end of Romans, Paul moves into this deeper understanding and utters three terms that could be the subject of this sermon: believing, waiting, hoping.

Now notice how Paul deals with them. He lays out the story and the program of the Christian tradition and adds, "Now we must trust in this." "Trust" in the New Testament is really the same word as "to do believing." Let's look at that word. The word "to believe" is both a substantive and a verb. As a substantive, it means the substance in propositional form of what it is you say you believe—the Apostles Creed, the Nicene Creed, the Westminster Confession, the Catholic Baltimore Catechism, or the Augsburg Confession. These are statements of what people believe and have believed. Now it's necessary to make such statements, and we think they are true and adequate statements in their time and situation. Now that's "belief" used as a substantive. It's used that way even more banally by the college admissions offices when they used to ask, "What is your belief?" And they expect you to say Methodist, Baptist, Presbyterian, Roman Catholic or something or other. Well, that refers to a secondary aspect of belief. But "to believe" means to believe what you believe: to "do believing" all your life in your head, in your heart, your feet, and your hands, with your whole action, what it is you say you believe. Belief as a substantive for many persons has becomes a kind of soggy lump of unexamined propositions they heard their father say. "And I believe in the Holy Spirit, the Lord and giver of life." We say it solemnly every Sunday, but if you believe your belief, then you won't look at the processes of biology, geology, ethics, or running a city in the same way. If the Lord is the giver of all life, and he does this through the Spirit, then the Christian cannot turn ethics over to the professors of ethics, or politics over to the politicos, or war over to the military, or the meaning of life over to the psychologists and the sociologists and the philosophers.

Now, what is the fate of believing in this world? In this life, in time and history, are we ever related to the object of our faith, God, in such a way that we can say, "Now I know it absolutely, I've got it cold, the argument is complete, the logic is infrangible, QED, there is a God and he is thus and so, and what he wants me to do I can read as clearly as I can read the telephone book, or even clearer"? No. We never have God that way.

Three on Romans 8 (Sermon 3)

God has us absolutely, embraced in judgment, but we never grasp God as we are by him grasped. We see through a glass darkly. Paul refers again to the phrase which he used about nature and said, "And we too who have the first-fruits of the Spirit groan inwardly with an anguish too deep for words that cannot be uttered."

Anyone who's been a pastor in a church or has called upon fellow members of a church in anxiety or desolation or death knows that this believing has always got to skate on the ice of faith at every moment in life. At the death of a child. The death of the aged we can deal with better, but the death of children has always been one of the most horrible things to try to understand under the agency of a good God. Ivan in *The Brothers Karamazov* never solves it. In fact, he says, "If that's the kind of God you've got in this world, I respectfully hand him back the ticket." Paul adds a second word: we have this faith, we have this action of God toward humanity, whereby God does not leave us alone, but we wait.

It's interesting that in the Hebrew language—which Paul knew—in the Hebrew language, "waiting" and "hoping" are the same verb. The root of the verb is exactly the same: "to wait" and "to hope." What can it be to live one's whole life in waiting upon God, when the God in whom you trust, but whose actuality you cannot logically or empirically certify? Well may I say, whether we like it or not, or wish it might or not be otherwise, that is the way it is. And it is like never to be other. Evidence of this is the magnificent history of the Jews. Something strange about the Christian community: we almost never mention the Jews except during Holy Week, and then as the "rascals" of the story. But the whole magnificent history of Judaism, 6000 (at least) years of it: waiting, waiting, waiting. Some of you have read Eli Wiesel's marvelous stories about the Jews of central Europe in the Second World War, of the millions of Jews who, waiting upon a God against all the evidence, walked with the ancient prayers of their fathers into the gas ovens. The history of Judaism is the richest commentary I know upon the meaning of the word "to wait" upon God in the Bible.

And the third word Paul uses here: Then do we wait, but we do not wait simply in a vacuum. We wait in hope. If a man sees that for which he hopes, for which he waits, then he doesn't have to hope. He *sees* it. But he said, "If we see not that for which we hope, then do we with patience wait for it." Now having said these things, Paul has tied himself up in a kind of knot, and it's rather humorous, if I may say so, to watch him try to get out of it, and very elevating to see how he does come out. He says, "If God is like that, if God be for us, nothing is really against us." "Well then," he asks himself apparently, "how does that really work?"

And there you get those tangled sentences that have sent theologians up the wall for nearly two thousand years, in which he says, "He calls us his sons. If he calls us, then he must predestinate us, because if he's God he must know everything. And those whom he predestined, he also justified. And those he justified, he also glorifies." Well, that's a great apostolic ladder, but even Paul knows it isn't very clear. Even Paul knew he had a nut here he couldn't logically crack. And he got tired of the whole exercise. Because the next verse says, "What shall we say to all this?" You know, Paul was a pretty good theologian and he got himself wrapped up here in a kind of logical effort to understand the mystery of God and he did the best he could with it. He looked at the whole business and said, "No way." And with a sweep of the hand, he said, "What then shall we say to these things?" What he says is not another sentence, you observe; what he says is quite different.

He passes from doctrine to doxology. He goes from confusion to jubilation. He sweeps the things off the table, and goes from anxiety to adoration—the only possible step you can take when you come to the end of the logical possibility. What then shall we say to this whole ineffable fact that the God who acted in Christ and is trustworthy, even though we cannot understand the processes of his life and his dealing with us, and he remains often a mystery? "What shall we say to that?" And then he stops arguing and starts singing. What shall we say, he that did not hesitate to come into our situation himself? He may be trusted not to cast us off when the going gets rough. And therefore he says (and Luther loved this passage; so did the great J. S. Bach, whose death day we celebrate today in his great cantata *Denn Ich bin gewusst*), "What then shall we say to this? Now I am completely confident in life or death, that nothing in heaven or hell, none of the earthly powers or principalities that assault and make dubious, tragic, and ambiguous this life, nothing can really do me in, because nothing ultimately did *him* in, though he died at the place where I am done in." You see? Therefore, he says, nothing, nothing, and he adds up the whole score: "Nothing shall separate us from the love of God, which is in Christ Jesus our Lord."

Now as the eighth chapter of Romans ends with that great lyrical passage, so in a sense, do we end at least for now: To be a Christian is really not to know absolutely. It is not to have faith *absolutely*. Not the faith with which we are beloved—we shall never achieve that love. Faith, as Luther loved to say, faith is *fiducia*. It is trust. It is to stand with the evidence that the God who did what he did is to be trusted in all the obscurities and the darknesses of this life.

Maundy Thursday

1975

Joseph Sittler believed the best preaching happens musically. In his view, many composers and musicians might lay claim to the status of "Fifth Evangelist," including Bach, Palestrina, Buxtehude, and the author of "Christ Jesus Lay in Death's Strong Bands," Martin Luther. The preacher devotes much of his sermon here to the second stanza of that hymn. In the sermon he uses a student's innocent but profound question as the impetus for exploring Scripture, hymnody, poetry, and drama, all of it in service to the church's understanding of Christ's passion. The meaning of that act comes closer to music than common speech. The sermon ends where Luther's hymn ends—with a magnificent, if "mordant," "Alleluia!"

THE REFLECTION ON THIS Holy Thursday is directed not to a biblical text, but to the text of the hymn we just sang, which is a kind of summary of many biblical texts in the New Testament, and recollective also of the Old Testament. "Christ Jesus Lay in Death's Strong Bands" was written by Luther, and I call your attention particularly to the second stanza of it, which I want to use for our reflection tonight. But I begin by reminding you that Albert Schweitzer, who was not only a physician and a biblical scholar and theologian, but also of considerable gifts as a musician and musicologist, wrote a memorable paragraph about this hymn. He said, "Sometimes in the history of Christian thought and practice the pulpit has engaged in all kinds of theological fancies. But the ordinary people of the church who are represented by the voices from the choir loft kept right on singing the profounder understanding of the death of Christ." Now such a profound understanding is in that hymn, and I hope you recall, as it was played a moment ago, that marvelous final "Alleluia!" We're used to alleluias, and most of them dance and jump and are jubilant all over the place. Mozart wrote one that's so bouncy that it could have been used for an aria in an opera about boy meets girl. But the alleluia that ends this mordent, profound hymn is not like that. Schweitzer says of it, "This quiet, powerful alleluia announces that the pondering mind regarding the death of Christ has reflected on all possibilities, has known all mortal terrors, and knows that there is but one possible answer to the horror of life and the horror of death. And he knows that it is because God himself has entered into death. And therefore, he said, this great quiet alleluia."

The text of the second stanza to which I call your attention reads as follows:

> *It was a strange and dreadful strife*
> *when life and death contended;*
> *the victory remained with life,*
> *the reign of death was ended.*
> *Stripped of power, no more he reigns,*
> *an empty form alone remains.*
> *Death's sting is lost forever! Alleluia!*

It is sometimes the case that young children or adolescents blurt out what their more cautious parents or other adults are afraid to say or suppress. And one such blurting out happened in the confirmation class a couple of weeks ago, when one of the students said, "I don't get it. We keep on saying, 'Jesus died for us.' And I don't see how that makes any difference." Now we've all wondered about that too, but of course this one said it. "I don't see how it makes any difference. How could the death of a man back there, then, have anything to do with me now, up here?" Now tonight, by reflecting upon that hymn and the dramatic action that it describes, I should like to lead your reflection into the question the young person asked.

There are many ways in which the reality of things becomes clarified within itself and then finds a way to articulate what it knows or meets or beholds. In general, I think there are two large ways in which meaning gets across the chasm of incomprehension or lack of information—two principles ways. The one might be called the *propositional* way of the transmission of meaning, and the other could be called the *dramatic* way of the transmission of meaning. Now I want to get quickly into a concrete understanding of what I mean by those two ways, and not fuss around with abstraction.

In the first third of the nineteenth century, there was a British poet, William Wordsworth, who lived at Lake Windermere with a beloved sister, Dorothy. Now it would be a true proposition to say that his fear of Dorothy's death left William Wordsworth bereft, lonely, distraught. And that would be a true proposition. But Wordsworth was a poet, and not a logician. And what he said in two little poems is as follows. The one of them, very brief:

> But she is in her Grave, and Oh! / The difference to me.

You see, just as another poet said, "never seek to tell thy love," he didn't detail or retail the fundamental concreteness of his fear, but just the little cry, "and, Oh! / The difference to me." In another poem he writes:

> No motion has she now, no force;
> She neither hears nor sees;
> Rolled round in earth's diurnal course
> With rocks and stones and trees!

That is the dramatization of truth. By analogy, metaphor, and image, reality moves from its own interior substance to our own human hearts and minds.

The second illustration is not greatly different. You recall that in *Macbeth* Lady Macbeth, in order to advance her husband to the throne, with her own hands murders the king, Duncan. Then comes the moment of terrifying and horrible remorse—knowledge of guilt that cannot be assuaged by anything. Now a proposition would be, "Lady Macbeth knows immeasurable guilt." But Shakespeare didn't put it that way. He has a moment in the play when, in the eerie light of the dawn, Lady Macbeth looks at her hand and says, "Here's the smell of blood still: all the perfumes of Arabia will not sweeten this little hand, Oh, oh, oh!" (act V, scene 1). That is no proposition, but one gets the point.

The death of Christ, and the way the Scriptures talk about it, both in the reportorial part in the Gospels and in the reflection upon it which is the Epistles, and other parts of the New Testament—the death of Christ comes to us with its intended fullness and complexity of meaning. It comes only when we understand it dramatically. The propositions of Paul

Maundy Thursday

and others are not untrue, but the church has always known another way to talk of that death, and they used that other way before Paul or before the Gospels were ever written.

The theologians have tried by reflection to fill the gap between *that* man's death *then* and what it means for *our* dying life *now*. And they have done it in several ways. If you attended to the Old Testament lesson tonight, you heard the reading about God's liberation of his chosen people from Egypt and the Passover, the slaying of the innocent lamb, pure and undefiled—of how a death of the pure one somehow has an effect in constituting the faith of this people, generation after generation after generation. This very night in a million Jewish homes there will be the Seder meal and the recollection of the story, when the elder of the group asks, "Why is this night different than every other night?" The power of that image—of the pure one somehow undergoing an experience whose force goes beyond his own life and death, and is constitutive of meaning for all life thereafter—that comes through in the ancient Seder. The New Testament picks up the same theme: "O Lamb of God that taketh away the sin of the world." Now, theologically, there have been three or four ways, taken from the Scriptures themselves, in which believers have tried to say how the death of one effectuates the redemption of others.

The first is the notion of ransom—that Christ is a ransom paid to the powers of evil, the devil, and damnation to rescue all men from his grip. An ancient society that had the communal practice of paying ransom for the delivery of slaves understood that image. But to us it's an image that does so much damage to the doctrine of God that we seldom use it. What kind of a God is this who makes a quasi-commercial deal with the devil? The Bible is not wrong in using that image, but images sometime do not outlast the culture that shapes them. And that one has not fared well.

The second was a substitution—that Christ is the substitute for us. There is a profound sense in which that is true. When the Apostle said, "If any man be in Christ, he is there regarded by the Creator not in his own faulted and stained actuality, but in incorporation of the Lamb of God, pure and undefiled"—that's the meaning of grace.

And there's a third way of putting this, and there's New Testament substance to it, but somehow the church has never been satisfied with it. The third is that Christ is an example. Well, indeed he is—a towering and incomparable example. And the existence of a man exemplary in life, even unto death, somehow doesn't answer that adolescent question. That is admirable, that is good, that is even awe-inspiring, morally, aesthetically, humanly, but is it redemptive?

Now let's get to the final one, which Luther wraps up in this second stanza. But first I have to build in a little background: In this evening hour, we're not troubled by the morning limit on preaching, and I'm going to take full advantage of it. In the Old Testament there is a way of talking about God and man and the world that's very fascinating. Right in the first chapter, the big generic word for all men is *adam*. Now, *adam* is not a proper name. *Adam* in Hebrew means "mankind." Mankind, created of God, falls into temptation, celebrates his own identity and his autonomy over against his Creator, and breaks the divine connection. Now why it is that Christ in the New Testament is called the "Second Adam"? Because the drama suggests that all people identify themselves over against that which is ultimate and holy and good, and celebrate their egocentricity, and thus break the cords between themselves and God. Just as all human beings do that, Christ is called the "Second Adam" because God created another man, the second Adam. He lived not just in the paradisal garden of Eden, but he lived in the garden of Gethsemane. Just as the first Adam said, "Not thy will, but mine," so the Second Adam, in the second garden, was the right man who said, "Not my will, but thine." In other words, the figure of the Second Adam suggests that God, in human form, in the form of Christ, recapitulates the whole tragic error and overcomes it in his Second Adam.

Those of you who were in church last Sunday may remember the preface to the Holy Communion in which we said, "Who didst bring salvation unto man, whereby he who by a tree once overcame, might likewise by a tree be overcome." What were you saying? Just as the first Adam in the first garden was tempted by the fruit of the tree, so the Second Adam in the second garden, and among the olive trees of Gethsemane, played right, but the first Adam played wrong. The whole massive pattern of recapitulation and reenactment is the background of this picture of how Christ redeems. It's not just a solitary feeling that Jesus is my Lord, though that is right. Nor is it simply that into my isolation and privacy, by the gifts of the Spirit, I have a relationship to God that redeems me from the terror and the curse of both life and death, though that is possible and right. But an event in eternity that was before I was and will be when I am no more, an event that is trans-temporal and everlasting, has taken place. It will never *not* have been. The whole long record of man and God has

Maundy Thursday

been played over again, by the man of God's own choosing (in another phrase from Luther).

Now return to the hymn. Luther writes in this hymn, "Christ lay in death's strong bands." He doesn't speak of Jesus. He says life and death contended. The ultimate, last, final word to all human life is "death." We may say we do not fear death, and we lie in our teeth. We may create all kinds of analgesic ways to blunt the reality of death and evade its certainty, and the principal one is simple preoccupation with things that keep the mind from confronting it. Death is a horror. Luther says the fundamental meaning of the death of Christ is that into the solidarity of the human reality of death, the lord and giver of life, God himself, from whom all life precedes, entered, fought it out, and won. The whole drama of Jesus, who set his face to go to Jerusalem and steadfastly went to the cross, is not just one marked man being executed. God was in Christ not only reconciling the world to himself, but doing it with the heavy, bloody steps of that kind of an action.

In Northumberland from the eighth century comes a poem called the "Dream of the Rood." A rood is the beam across the front of a medieval church on which the cross is erected. The word sometimes means the cross itself—the rood. In the "Dream of the Rood," the ancient English churchman Cynewulf wrote a dramatic story which is so different than our usual theological picture that I want to give you just a line from it because it illustrates Schweitzer's word that the pastor may talk theological abstraction, and Mozart may dance to "hallelujah," but the common life of the church always knows better. In the "Dream of the Rood," there is a strange picture of the Christ as the "young hero." The young hero strips himself of his garment, and with young and bold and gallant steps he hurls himself upon the cross, thus in the name of all, to defeat death. Here is the kind of language that's closer to *Beowulf* than it is to Paul Tillich, but here's a kind of language which is very close to the New Testament, where Christ says that a strong man armed keeps us all in captivity. Ultimately, the captivity to finitude and death endures until a stronger one comes and breaks into the dungeon in which we are trapped, and we are liberated. So when Luther sings, "When life and death contended; / the victory remained with life," death is still there, but it is a form—the essence of death, that, as the Old Testament says, "in Sheol who shall praise thee," the awesome sense of nothingness. This is no more! An empty form no longer remains. His sting is lost forever, and therefore, when we understand that way of talking about the death of Christ, then we see that simply because it happened then, and not now, to another, and not to us, is really not an absolute objection to its truth and its reality.

You remember, now more than thirty years ago, when Britain was hurled to her knees, with Dunkirk behind her and the threatened invasion in front of her, how Churchill addressed the nation every week. I remember one of his speeches, in which he said, "Just as we recall our Saxon hero Beowulf, who fought the dragon, and just as in our English blood there runs the blood of Arthur, who against overwhelming odds, according to legend, unified this kingdom, and just as we recall the Battle of Agincourt when English yeomen met the mounted cavalry of the whole French kingdom, and drank to the glory of the realm out of the stirrup cup, the night before the battle, so," he says, "all that has ever been great in England becomes solidified in this, our finest hour." Now that's not just patriotic jargon. Here is a man who knows the solidarity of humanity. An event has taken place. Christians believe that the Second *Adam* represents God's dream for humankind; he overcomes the death of the first Adam, who spoiled God's dream for us. Therefore, against such a background we understand that musically powerful "Alleluia!" at the end of the mordent Lenten hymn.

Maundy Thursday

Christ Jesus Lay in Death's Strong Bands

1 Christ Jesus lay in death's strong bands for our of-fens-es giv-en;
2 It was a strange and dread-ful strife when life and death con-tend-ed;
3 Here the true Pas-chal Lamb we see, whom God so free-ly gave us;
4 So let us keep the fes-ti-val to which the Lord in-vites us;
5 Then let us feast this Eas-ter Day on Christ, the bread of heav-en;

but now at God's right hand he stands and brings us life from heav-en.
the vic-to-ry re-mained with life, the reign of death was end-ed.
he died on the ac-curs-ed tree— so strong his love—to save us.
Christ is him-self the joy of all, the sun that warms and lights us.
the Word of grace has purged a-way the old and e-vil leav-en.

There fore let us joy ful be and sing to God right thank ful ly
Ho-ly Scrip-ture plain-ly says that death is swal-lowed up by death.
See, his blood now marks our door; faith points to it; death pass-es o'er.
Now his grace to us im-parts e-ter-nal sun-shine to our hearts;
Christ a-lone our souls will feed; he is our meat and drink in-deed;

loud songs of hal-le-lu - jah! Hal-le - lu-jah!
its sting is lost for ev - er. Hal-le - lu-jah!
and Sa-tan can-not harm us, Hal-le - lu-jah!
the night of sin is end - ed. Hal-le - lu-jah!
faith lives up-on no oth - er! Hal-le - lu-jah!

Text: Martin Luther, 1483–1546, tr. Richard Massie, 1800–1887, alt.
Music: CHRIST LAG IN TODESBANDEN, J. Walter, *Geystliche Gesangkbüchlein*, 1524

Easter

"This Is the Feast of Victory for Our God"

1975

In this deceptively simple Easter homily the preacher uses a sentence from the liturgy as a vessel of the kerygma. Echoing Paul's mode of argumentation in 1 Corinthians 15, Sittler argues that if the resurrection of Jesus represents the victory of God, then our preoccupation with the eternal status of our bodies must be of secondary importance. Christian art has led us astray by depicting the resurrection with greater exactitude than any of the canonical Gospels dares to do. Sittler argues not only from the silence of the New Testament but also from the ineffability of music and the openness of being itself that God's victory is all-encompassing but indescribable.

For a brief and simple Easter homily, I want to propose that we reflect together upon the sentence which was the canticle that we sang in place of the *Gloria Excelsis* this morning: "This is the feast of victory for our God." I want to talk about that affirmation, that this *is* the feast of the victory of God, in order to make a single point that Easter is God's doing. The psalm has it very clear: "This is the day the Lord hath made, let us rejoice and be glad in it." Easter is *God's* day.

Now I want to make that clear because in the popular thinking of the church, and as one encounters the popular mind of the members of the church, as well as other persons, as to the fundamental meaning of Easter, a lot of secondary questions get cluttered up with the primary affirmation of the church. The meaning of Easter is often enclosed within secondary questions, such as, "What shall it mean to have eternal life?" "In what body shall the dead arise?" The same question they asked of Paul, to which he replied to the Thessalonians by walking around the question and not answering it.

In what body shall the dead arise? What kind of selfhood and identity shall I have in eternal life? These are inevitable questions, but Easter does not address the secondary questions, but asks you only to answer them in terms of the primary affirmation. "This is the feast of victory for our God." That is to say that if one is sure about God—that the power of God, the love of God, and the action of God is ultimately the victorious thing in all life, world, and history—if one is sure about that, then secondary questions about in what form shall we be eternally with God, in what body shall we rise, and so forth, these questions go properly into a secondary position. It's time that this be said very clearly by the church.

One of the reasons the question arises with such force is that all forms of Christian art have tried to materialize the meaning of the Resurrection, or the very actuality of the Resurrection, with far greater clarity than the New Testament does. The New Testament tells us *that*. It does not tell us exactly how, or why, or in what form. And therefore, I want to make the second affirmation, which Easter causes us to make. And that is that Easter makes the point very clearly that if God is victorious, and those who would question the love, power, and victory of God have actually been overcome by the raising of Christ from the dead, then our own questions of identity and of our own selfhood in eternity receive a certain clarity from that proposition.

Let's get at it this way: When we say, what kind of identity or what kind of selfhood shall I have in eternity, let us begin to reflect on that by remembering that selfhood is never an isolated thing. Even in this life, and certainly in the Christian life, the fundamentally egocentric notion that one's sense of consciousness, awareness, and fulfillment come from within oneself is a heresy. Every Christian knows that his or her selfhood is a community creation. Not only community, but community with all the other selves who constitute God's creation. Therefore, even in *this* life we are drawn out of the notion that the self is sufficient within itself. In fact, on the first page of the Bible, the effort of the self of Adam to be autonomous and sufficient to itself is not regarded as a good for the self, but as the annihilation of the self—a catastrophe, the heart of sin.

Now what does that tell us about the selfhood we shall have in eternity? Go at it a second way: has there ever been any person who did not know that the reality of his personhood is established by that possibility toward which his life is unfolding? I am not just what I am, but what I should imagine myself capable of becoming. I am not only the self I have or the identity I have, but that imagined fulfillment that even in this life allures me, but is never identical with what I become. The music Beethoven imagined is not identical with the music we have. His last quartets are a probing beyond music that anything on the written score discloses. The songs that people imagine are lovelier than any songs they sing. The possible that goes ever before me as a possible fulfillment, which I shall never achieve, is as constitutive of myself as the things that I achieve. Therefore, that which allures me, that possible which draws me, that promise which floats before me in terms of God's promise of eternal life, is even in this world constitutive of my selfhood. Therefore, when we say, "This is the feast of victory for our God," the important statement in the New Testament is not what kind of body shall we arise in, because even the body in which Jesus arose was not simply a resuscitated corpse that went into the grave, and the New Testament is quite clear that it is not the same: "We shall all be raised, but we shall all be changed." If, therefore, God is victorious, we should be quite happy to leave the secondary questions of "In what body shall the dead arise?" and "What kind of identity shall we have?" completely in his hands, knowing that any possible identity in eternity with God can be neither discontinuous with the selfhood in life, but must follow the line of our selfhood's tilting forward into a fuller selfhood in eternity.

There are certain verses from the New Testament which make this awfully clear. For instance, there is the verse in which Paul says, "If then you are buried with Christ, then are you also raised with him." And in Colossians he writes, "If then you are raised with Christ . . ." Notice the form of the verb. The form of the verb is not the future, "If you shall *someday* be raised with Christ," but it says, "If in your relationship to God through Christ *now*." If that has actually taken place, the resurrection is not simply an event in future time, but it is a word that characterizes that beginning of a process of the fulfilling of the selfhood that God promises to complete in eternity.

Easter

But notice "complete." It does not just begin beyond the grave. In the eighth chapter of Romans, the lesson says, "His Spirit bears witness." Now notice, not *against* our spirit, and not *without* our spirit, but "his Spirit bears witness *with* our spirit, that we are the children of God." Is it not the mark of the beginning of the fulfillment which resurrection means that I already know non-fulfillment in this life? The negativities of this present life are a kind of affirmation that in the victory of our God anything beyond our thoughts or dreams is possible. "Eye hath not seen, nor ear heard, what God hath prepared for them that love him." The message of the early church about God and Christ and the potential of human life in an eternity with God—that's dramatically put in a little incident in the book of the Acts with which I conclude.

Paul, preaching in Jerusalem, had offended certain parties among the Jews. They called upon the Roman officials who put him into jail. (We call it today "protective custody.") They put him into jail, and the poor centurion who was in charge of him didn't know what to do with this remarkable prisoner, and so he decided to send the case to a higher court in Caesarea where the king was. He sent a letter with the prisoner. He sent Paul accompanied by a hundred soldiers for his own safety to the king's court. The centurion Claudius Lysias sent a remarkable letter to explain to the king who this man was and why he was sending him to his court. The letter is one of the most beautiful insights into the reality of the resurrection in the early church, largely because it doesn't mean to be an insight. It's by the hand of a pagan. He says, "I, Claudius Lysias, herewith send you this man, because I'm stuck with him. He's been turned over to me by the Jews for safe keeping (or I've taken him) and it doesn't fall within my competence, and therefore I send him up to you." "Now the whole matter," he says, "has got to do with some strange religious quarrel among these strange people, the Jews. You and I as Romans don't dirty our hands with that kind of thing. We don't even understand it. But they've got a big hassle going on here, and the whole problem is concerning Jesus, who of course is dead. But Paul says he is alive."

The fundamental affirmation about the victory of our God comes, you see, from the witness of these people who knew what it meant to die, who had beheld what it meant for God's man, sent into the world, to undergo the tragedy which we have just celebrated in Holy Week, and then to know that his death was not his end—that he was still present with such power and that a community remembered and knew him. They also knew him to be constitutive of that community. "Paul says he is alive."

Part 3: Sermons

Therefore, the meaning of this day is not just about the death and the resurrection of the man Jesus, although that is the occasion, but it is the occasion for something even more ultimate: "This is the feast of victory for our God."

Passion of Christ

1977

Romans 8:31–39

In many of his sermons Sittler sought the irreducible core of the gospel, which inevitably led him to Paul's Letter to the Romans. In this sermon he finds that core in Romans 8 and Paul's assertion that God is "for" us, how radically for us the preacher explains at the very end of the sermon. Earlier he says that Paul is no "Jesus-ologist" and explains the apostle's relative silence on the subject of Jesus' earthly life by echoing the New Testament's assertion that we look to and through Jesus in order to see God and to discover God's claim upon our lives.

WE HAVE IN THE letters of Saint Paul the most primitive evidence available to us of what the earliest community thought about how God through Christ and his passion reconciled all people to himself. It's sometimes startling to recall that Paul lived and wrote and died before the earliest Gospel was circulated in the ancient church. There were no written Gospels when Paul wrote his reflections on Christ. That suggests that Paul's concern is always with God. It's always with, not Jesus, but through Jesus to what is coming to expression in Jesus. That's the reason I think that the word "Jesus" seldom occurs in Paul. It's either "Jesus Christ," which is a name of the role of this Jesus in the plan of God—Jesus who is Christ, the coming one, the Messiah—or it is "Christ Jesus." So that Paul's use of these two words in connection does two things.

This accounts for the fact that Paul is always concerned with the understanding of how this man called Christ—the one sent from God—discloses the reality of God. Paul is never a "Jesus-ologist." He's always seeing Jesus as the transparency through which, out of the obscurity of Jewish reflection, the reality of God becomes focused and clear. It also helps explain why Paul talks so little about Jesus at all. And very little of the teaching of Jesus. The episodic events of Jesus' life do not appear in the writings of Paul at all. He indeed may not have known many of them. We can recover from things that Paul does say, which later appear in the Gospels, elements of the tradition which might have been around before the Gospels were pulled together. But it's notable to remember that very little of the life of Jesus could be recovered from Saint Paul. So common an aspect of the church's adoration, for instance, as the virgin birth is apparently unknown to Paul.

Therefore we still confront the large problem in trying to get a clear reply to the question, "What is the testimony in the writings of Saint Paul as to the meaning and the force, the salvatory power, of the passion of Christ?" I found it very, very difficult to come up with a way to answer that or to speak of it tonight because of the great variety of the evidence. Let me try to get back of that and ask this question: can all the many ways in which Paul talks about Jesus Christ and our situation, and that which in his testimony God does in Christ for our situation, be caught in a sentence or two that is responsible to what seems to be the heart of Paul's encounter with God through Christ? Now that's a difficult thing to do, because Paul had a problem. As the first voice, at least the literary voice, to speak about Jesus Christ, he had a problem for which I can find an illustration.

Suppose there suddenly occurred in the Western world of written English a poet whose language, use of words, and way with images was so strange and startling as to cause people to say, "There has never been a poet like this before." No poet would believe that. Every poet knows that nothing is utterly new—that nothing is without roots in the earlier practice of any craft, whether it be poetry or the healing arts or education or engineering or what not. When, therefore, a brand new thing appears, everyone who is concerned with the thing at all tries to draw back the threads of it and peer through the various elements of it to ask, "Where in the old practice of this kind of thing can I find precedence? Where can I find something that might suggest something like this?"

For instance, when in the twentieth century a group of young poets started writing things which many older people said were not poetry at all, but which they insisted were poetry, and which critical opinion now admits to be poetry—when that happened, the critics all started looking back through Shakespeare, Milton, and Chaucer to find out whether they couldn't discover some little droplets of usage back there which they could collect enough of to make a cup full of evidence.

Now I think that's simply necessary in the operations of the mind, and thus my next point: Paul's crucial encounter with Christ was not an emotional, traumatic, guilt-laden thing. When Paul talks about what we call his "conversion"—three times he speaks about it in his own writings—there is not a shred of evidence that that was what we commonly mean by a conversion—a jolting, emotional, shaking, traumatic experience. The conversion of Paul was a thing at the top of his head, not in the middle of his viscera. What the conversion meant was this: he suddenly saw something that he had never seen before, in fact, had violently rejected looking at. On the way to Damascus what knocked him off his horse literally was the knowledge that the appearance in a vision, or some appearance of knowledge, whereby he saw that God is bigger than Paul had ever suspected he was. That the God of his fathers, Abraham, Isaac, and Jacob, was the God of the whole world, of all the people of the world. Paul's God of his own people through a Pharisaic tradition was too selective, too niggardly. The astounding, startling grace of this God, who draws his circle around all people, this was what really unhorsed Paul. It was a clarity in the understanding, not a disturbance in the emotional life, fundamentally. That accounts for Paul's radical change of direction, as evidenced by the fact that when he talks about his sin he never lists the kind of agenda that you and I could make all too easily about sins of pride and of the flesh and of lasciviousness and acquisitiveness and stupidity and sloth. Paul gives himself a very high score on all of these. He says, "I am chief of sinners," and notice what constitutes him chief of sinners, in his own eyes: "I persecuted the church of Christ. I refused to see the evidence right in front of my face, namely, that God has done a new 'end run' around the old line of Israel and the prophets."

Now when we see this, we come to the next problem. When a man has a new thing, as when the poet experiences a new way making poetry, he must try to find how that fits in somehow, how it adds up with all the predecessor events; so also good deal of what makes Paul's writing in the New Testament is not the favorite reading of the church-going

Part 3: Sermons

community, because as even a first-century man said, "Brother Paul is very tough." Well, indeed Brother Paul is very tough, but why? Because Paul had to take up all the great words in his previous faith: land, covenant, people, promise, propitiation, redemption, atonement, sacrifice. He had to pull that whole thing along with him and ask about that whole Jewish warehouse of religious and devotional conceptions, "Can Christ include it all?" So much of the epistles of Paul are taken up with a tormented, twisting intellectual effort to make these things somehow fit in with the great new thing, his encounter with God through Christ. It's not always a successful effort.

Sometimes Paul talks about Hagar in the wilderness in a kind of analogy that chases its tail around for 22 verses and really never does come off. Not everything can be poured into the new jug. And a good deal of what's very difficult about Paul must be forgivingly and patiently understood as a man who had a mind that would not rest until he turned every stone over from the ancient past, in order to see whether the things that crawled out from under it could be put within the new organization. Now with that characteristic of Paul on the meaning of Christ, let's get finally to the point.

In preparing for tonight, I found I had to lay aside big, classical, doctrinaire passages, one after another, as being too characteristic of the process I just talked about. Too propositional, too analogous, too loaded with ancient images and notions that it simply would not speak with a kind of directness an event like this calls for. And I've made the discovery—at least a discovery for me—that where Paul sings out most clear and clean and simple is when he's singing doxology. It's very interesting that the church was singing, apparently, before she was cerebrating. She made music before she made propositions. The truth of the gospel lies more in the congruity of images than in the verifiability of the propositions. When the church emerges out of the shadows of antiquity, we hear her with a song in her mouth.

You get one of those great doxologies of Paul in the lesson that was read tonight. Let's briefly attend to it. The whole of the Romans, up to the eighth chapter, is a gathering argument of enormous complexity, referential richness, at the end of which Paul suddenly, as it were, collapses under the weight of his own argument. And in the eighth chapter of Romans, beginning with the reading tonight, he says, "What then shall we say to these things?" And *these things* was, by that time, an enormous heap. "What then shall we say to these things?" And he says one, plain, simple,

Passion of Christ

but awesomely profound thing: "If God be for us, who can be against us?" He wraps the whole business up—his whole lifetime, as it were, of wrestling with how to fit the new encounter with God into his old devotion as a Hebrew born of Hebrew parents ("as to the law, a Zealot")—he wraps it all up: "If God be for us, who can be against us?" And the rest of the chapter you heard was the detailing of the ways in which God is for us and in the situations in which we may trust him—in distress, despair, tribulation, and so forth.

Now what did Paul mean by "for us"? When he said, "If God be for us," he points to Christ as the fundamental, in fact, the only crucial fact to establish that. Christ is the vehement, historical, present evidence that the God beyond proof, the God for whose existence we cannot even find a proof—that the God of faith is *for* us. If we acknowledge that as the church's affirmation, which we celebrate in the passion of Christ in the Lenten season, how do we account for what I've called the "awesome force" of that statement? May I wrap it up very simply by saying that the truth of that statement lies in its congruity with the human reality. Or, to put it another way, the shape of that statement that God is for us fits with an uncanny appropriateness into exactly who we are. I've sometimes used the analogy of the cruciform character of human experience, the sign of the cross, which is the sign of the act of God in Christ. That sign also describes the shape of our human existence. There is not a single affirmation which you or I make in our life by our work or our dedication which has not cost somebody a negation. There is not an accomplishment we have made for which somebody else has not paid something. There is no thought we think that does not generate its own ambiguous negation. There is no possibility of our accomplishment which, however noble and high, does not remind us in its accomplishment of the yet unaccomplished. There is no life which does not end in death. There is no unfolding which does not finally enfold again in death. There is no temporal unfolding in joy which is not also a temporal unfolding toward eternity.

Now if the nature of life is that way, is it any wonder that the God of all that is, the God of all creation, would come to humanity in a way that should intersect them in their reality? He had to become that reality, not just talk about it, tell us about it through psalmists, prophets, and apostles; that's why Paul can say, "this Son of God who loved me and gave himself for me," and in Philippians, "who did not scoff at the very notion of taking upon himself the form of our cross and becoming it, even unto death." So when, in these various little excursions into the testimony of the early church about the passion of Christ, we encounter this gigantic figure of the early church, Paul of Tarsus, I think it is not irresponsible to say one of the sentences in which we really get his fundamental testimony in its power and simplicity is in this one: "If God be for us, who can be against us?"

The Haunting Allure of Jesus

1982

Notwithstanding the particularity of this sermon occasion, it speaks at its core to the faith of all, not just to those graduating from Trinity Lutheran Seminary. A number of features stand out. First, he draws us into the evocative power of the language of the biblical text itself, reminding preachers by implication to play close attention to their own use of language and its potential "transmissive force." Closely related to that is Sittler's romance with the texts of Scripture as bottomless wells of meaning. Thirdly, we find here many clues to connecting with so many of today's young Christians who are captivated by the person of Jesus. Finally, the sermon illustrates that the skillful—not self-focused— sharing of ones faith journey sermonically can speak to the faith of the listener.

I WANT TO FULFILL a duty immediately. The president of our seminary in Chicago—a sister school—and the faculty thereof asked me to extend to all their colleagues in this faculty, to members of the graduating class, and to all parents and relatives of the same their warmest congratulations and friendship on this day.

Now it is endemic to old age for people to get nostalgic and to begin remembering. Part of it is they don't have much else to do! And if I indulge in some quite personal recollections at the opening of this little meditation, it will not only be in order to enjoy the recollections and hope you enjoy them too, but to lead into the one single and simple point I want to make in the main substance of what I have to say.

Part 3: Sermons

I indulge in these reminiscences because my roots are in this place. My early childhood, adolescence, and college years were all spent in central Ohio: in Columbus, Obetz Junction, Delaware, and Lancaster, where I go tomorrow to preach at the one-hundredth anniversary of the building in which my father was once pastor. My father was awarded his degree in 1898 by the predecessor of this seminary. I was, I am afraid, reluctantly awarded my degree in 1930 from Hamma Divinity School. I say "reluctantly" because I had a difficult time with courses in homiletics, because I could not find it possible to squeeze every text into three parts. So it is not only because of my roots in this place and my affectionate remembrances of childhood here that I recall the past, but it is because in remembering that I came to think of the kind of thing I want you to reflect upon with me this afternoon.

In carrying on those reflections in my mind, I began to reflect upon the kind of issue to which such reflections always lead. What is the nature of the transmission of the Christian faith? How did each of us come to it? Does not each of us have an interior story whereby in our youth we moved from the usual concerns of youth to a kind of focusing and solidification around the sense of vocation, whether it be to the ordained ministry or to making, as a layman, the general Christian confession? What is that strange, tangled, various, tumultuous, often ductile road—but not always recoverable—by which we came to the Christian faith? It was in the process of recollecting my father in this place, my own youth in central Ohio, my adolescent and pre-collegiate years at Lancaster, Ohio, that these reflections became enriched with a kind of immediate and recoverable concreteness, whereby I could begin to hone in on the issue I want to talk about.

What is the core interest, allure, secret, which draws us into this discipline of the Christian faith? As I thought about that, some elements of that symbiotic process came to my mind. Lest any of you tend to diminish the role of speech, consider this: before I knew exactly what was being said, or before I got very deeply into the substance of the readings of the Epistle, Old Testament, and the Gospel in my father's church, the alluring, haunting beauty of the language itself began to do its strange interior business with me.

I shall never forget the day at the end of World War I—I was then fourteen—when my father was asked by the local clergy to preach a memorial service for all the dead from our county. I recall the marvelous beauty of the passage he read about the lament of David over the death

The Haunting Allure of Jesus

of his son Jonathan. I recall the language of the Scripture, the marvelous rhetoric of joy and pity and indignation and judgment and grace and beauty. All these things are the kind of subterranean transmissive force which no one—no one—daring to speak of the great stories of the faith should neglect. That is the number one item: the language itself, a kind of substance delivered under the guise of gravity and beauty, the substance which, to the young mind, need not mean with clarity but draw with a kind of purity. The second thing I recall as I try to account for my own passage from an ordinary, as it were, adolescent pagan childhood (any adolescent who is not part pagan is not fully boy) is the stories of the New Testament, that is, the stories of the words and the deeds and the teachings of Jesus. Now I said that I was going to say a single and a very simple thing, and I proceed now with considerable brevity to do it.

Last summer Professor Krister Stendahl and I were asked by the president of the Iowa District to come for a four-day study conference. It was a moving moment on the third day when Professor Stendahl had finished one of his clear, substantial lectures on a New Testament problem, that a layman in the congregation asked Krister Stendahl, "How," as he put it, "did you get hooked on the Christian faith?" Now we all leaned back and expected from Stendahl a fairly long-haired description of the historical, conceptual, liturgical, familial path by which many of us came, and it was a great moment when Stendahl said, "My family were not church people at all and the only way I could rebel against the mores of my family was to go to church! And when I got to church, within six months I fell in love with Jesus." Now the very simplicity of that statement takes on power because it comes not from a simple-minded, sentimental man but from a very distinguished New Testament scholar, and therefore I want to say what I have to say around that simple phrase.

As I tried to discern the tangled history of my own coming to the Christian faith, my own study as a young seminarian of what of it I could learn, and my incessant digging away at the various aspects of Christian theology and history and liturgy and devotional life—as I tried to come to the very core of that, I ended up, as I was thinking of what I ought to say on this occasion, with a statement very much like Professor Stendahl. My whole life has been haunted by the reality of Jesus and I can say no wiser no more devout word to this class than to let that happen. Now let me detail it somewhat more in full. What do I mean, "haunted by the figure of Jesus"? [There are] two large aspects of that. First of all, [consider] the objective reality of Jesus insofar as we can recover that. Take one aspect:

the New Testament community greeted Jesus with all kinds of words, ascriptions, [and] titles, but what fascinated me when I first learned of it in New Testament study, and has not ceased to fascinate me to this day, is the way in which Jesus both wore and rejected the titles.

The community used the language of the hope of Israel to acknowledge the presence of this new thing—Jesus of Nazareth—and, as it were, they flung over him the garments, the rhetorical garments of their expectations. "He is the king." "He is the Messiah." "He is the son of David." "He is the son of man." "He is the son of God." "He is the anointed one, he that should come." The whole rich language of Israel's expectation of God's most mighty act was wrapped around Jesus. And now notice the interesting thing: Jesus never explicitly rejected nor did he ever explicitly adopt that language. He seemed always to acknowledge what the intention was of those who ascribed that kind of language to him, but he was never content to shrink the dimensions of his reality to the language of our expectation. This fascinates me absolutely.

We use the language of our expectation or the historical expectations all the way from Judaism through 1900 years. We use the language of our expectation as a kind of descriptive, ascriptive, christological language. Jesus himself lives within that language, but he always slips out and exceeds the nature and the intentionality of that language.

There was a certain woman, for instance, who stood before him, thrilled by the words that proceeded from his lips. She muttered—perhaps only to herself, but he heard it—"Oh, how happy your mother must be to have a lad like you." But with an abruptness, almost brusqueness, Jesus says, "Yea, rather, blessed are they that hear the Word of God and keep it." In every situation in which an effort was made to say, "Aha, now we know who you are, now we have the linguistic label whereby to pin the secret of your reality," Jesus seems quietly or openly to slip away from the confines of our own ascription and to affirm his own reality.

That is the objective fact which first caused me to use the strong words "the haunting figure of Jesus." The second is a much more subjective but no less legitimate fact of my own history. All my life, particularly since I have had the ordained obligation to preach and teach the Word of God, that haunting reality has not diminished. There has been no abatement in the allure of it. I find that, despite all the scholarship which has taken place between my seminary days and this moment, there is no abatement in the power of the haunting allure of the figure of Jesus. From Barth and Bultmann and Kasemann to the constructionist and the

The Haunting Allure of Jesus

structuralist and the deconstructionist and the existentialist, Jesus seems somehow to live. Each illuminates aspects of his reality but none of them succeeds in buttoning up a conceptual, descriptive proposition that includes the reality of Jesus.

I use an illustration which you who have studied here as the first class to have your entire formal training in Trinity Lutheran Seminary will understand. In the last four years have you pondered the overwhelming, the overflowing magnitude of the New Testament story—particularly the parables. I have preached, for instance, on the parable of the unjust steward for now fifty-two years. Yet I end up with the strange, exciting situation that I not only know that I probably have not reached the bottom of it, but I have come up with the interesting notion that there may be no bottom. What I am saying is that when we confront the statements of Jesus, this objective allure of his own escape from all confining ascriptions is matched by the subjective experience that every attack upon a parable of Jesus is a new raid on the inarticulate. So the parable of the unjust steward: "And Jesus commended this man for his prudence." He didn't commend him for his morality, but he did commend him for his prudence. The English word "prudence" is much too prissy for what the Greek word means. A better word would be "commended the man because he was canny." He was shrewd. He was a man who knew what the score was, and he acted in relation to it.

When I was first in seminary studies, I remember it was said to us by a teacher and by books that the parables have lasted through the centuries because they are marvelously concentrated little stories about the way things are. The longer I studied them, the more ridiculous that notion appeared. The secret of the parables is exactly that they are about the way things are not. They are stories that are attacks upon our expectations. They pull the rug out from under what we think the nature of things is. Every parable about the kingdom is not a kind of seconding of the obvious notion, but a voice of rebellion against the accepted notions of the God-man relationship.

So if I have one single thing to say to you young people who are entering the ordained ministry, it would be not to take too lightly what the church used to call "the mystery of Christ" and what I have called the allure of the figure of Jesus. This allure is not only something that I am theologically reporting or homiletically confessing, but it is something that comes straight out of my weekly work for thirteen years as a parish preacher. I had the sense of something which was bigger than I was and more compelling than my own sense of vocation. It almost rescued me from absurdity time and again! I had the sense of the allure of that strange figure just over my shoulder every time I sat down to prepare a sermon. This grave man, with all the pathos and the magnificence of his life, must not be betrayed. I must not talk nonsense about this man. I must not make jokes about him. I must not trivialize moralistically the awesome figure who in his death cried out, "My God, why hast thou forsaken me?" So I take that simple ending, that awesome ending, of Mark's Gospel, and make it a kind of symbol of what I have this day called the inexhaustible, the unshakeable, and the insoluble allure of the figure of Jesus. I do not know any way more honorably to discharge my responsibility to you.

Now may God bless you in your ministry.

Post-Easter Sermon

1983

John 21:1–14

Sittler uses the practice of long-range planning—today we would speak of "strategic" planning—as a metaphor for the human propensity to predict and hopefully predetermine desired outcomes. The walk of faith is not susceptible to such thinking. What discipleship requires of us in the unexpected circumstances of life—for Peter, the death of Jesus—is often baffling. We can only move forward in the tasks we know are ours, knowing God is with us, more often than not surprising us with a burst of grace for the way. God's grace is like a wild card! It pops up in our hand and we suddenly know the next move.

I ASK YOU THIS morning to reflect on the Gospel for the day. In the formation of the church year, the appearance of Jesus following the resurrection constitutes the focal point of the reflections of the whole period between Easter and Pentecost, but I want to get at a meaning of that Gospel lesson by a kind of strange and roundabout way, and I begin with an observation from a book of some years ago entitled, *The Human Condition*. The author says that in the various stages of development of a culture a certain way of acting becomes a certain way of thinking. And that way of thinking may prevent other and rival ways of thinking even from penetrating our consciousness. Now if this is true, and I think it is, is there a way of thinking that is characteristic of our time in the twentieth century which makes the message of this gospel lesson, the appearance of Jesus, which upsets all the determinate expectations of men—is there something in our way of thinking that makes it hard for us either intellectually or emotionally to suppose that that might be possible?

I think there is, and let me try to elaborate it with a very flat-footed and common phrase. We are positively enraptured with what we call "long-range planning." Everybody, if they wish to be really with it, has to be engaged in long-range planning. How did we get to this point in which our historical and emotional sense of humor got so atrophied that we could ever assume that long-range planning was ever a human possibility with any great chance of success? What do we mean by "long-range planning"? Why do we engage in it? Why does a generation, all the way from the Department of Mission in North America down to the Uneeda Biscuit Company, seem to be deeply engaged in long-range planning? With sober-knitted brows we sit around amid the awesome indeterminacies of human life and assume that present trends will continue, which they infrequently do. We are long-range planners. Why have we suddenly become so fond of that procedure despite multiple evidences that it has only a limited possibility of doing much good? I think it is because we have been able to envision a world, by virtue of experimental development in the natural and biological sciences, in which we are able to see and oversee facts in such a way as actually to predetermine outcomes in many areas of human life. We can know very well that certain conditions are conducive for responses on the part of ecological organisms, of biological organisms, the social organism, and we can to a limited degree manage this kind of thing. This is all a marvelous creative human endeavor, and it is good. No, the degree of our success in the scientific enterprise is not to be looked down upon, much less despised. It is the human act of creativity; it is a gift of God.

We look at the world and understand how it works, but our very success in this area of the transactions of the natural world has led us to suppose that the same kind of analysis which is operative there can be automatically translated over here into the historical, social, personal, emotional world, and with equal exactitude and facility. We ought to raise certain questions about that in the last few years; the babble of economic advisers is really a little strange. Reminds us of Harry Truman who said he wished he had a one-side-of-the-street economic adviser instead of one who would say, "On the one hand, Mr. President" and, "On the other

Post-Easter Sermon

hand, Mr. President." "Can't someone find me a one-handed adviser?" The problem of using the achievements of determination to apply all the way across the human spectrum to the indeterminacies of human life has led us into this love affair with long-range planning. I say this by way of background to the text we have today.

Peter and the sons of Zebedee, with a couple of others unnamed, are by the Sea of Tiberius, and the crucifixion of Jesus has taken place. Remember the evidence of Jesus' resurrection was not yet completely clear to Peter. He, at least in John's account, looked into the tomb and saw and heard nothing, and in confusion and bewilderment, he went back to his home turf around the Sea of Tiberius of Galilee. Can you in a sense intuit what must have been the situation?

Here was a man who must have been dismayed at the collapse of the great dream articulated by a noble and pure man to whom he had attached the hopes for the redemption of Israel. He was dismayed by the collapse of that whole enterprise. He was not only dismayed; he was bewildered because there were various statements about the outcome of this crucifixion, statements about a resurrection, that were not clear. He was dismayed, he was bewildered, he was frustrated and annoyed. Now, notice the very crisp and quick way in which the Gospel gives us this wonderful man, Peter. We know him so well from other vignettes in the Gospel. His vices were the other side of his virtues. What one would call "impetuosity" could with equal correctness be called "enthusiasm." He popped off often without thinking, but this quick, vehement, ardent love of his Lord is why he popped off, so we forgive him. His vices were but the underside of his virtues. He was impetuous, he was loyal, he cared, but here was a man who stood in bewilderment, confusion, and suddenly he said to his companions, "I'm going fishing."

Can you get a glimpse into what was going on inside this man, that out of such gravity he makes that ordinary statement? I have some insight into this from the common experience as a pastor for some part of my life. I noticed that when women are pregnant and about to have a child, in about the seventh or eighth month they get fussy, and I know my wife always started to wash the kitchen walls about the beginning of the eighth month. When a situation becomes both tough and intolerable and insoluble, what do you do? Grab the first decent possible thing to do and start doing it. Now Peter was a fisherman; he didn't know about the indeterminate future. He didn't know what God planned in the birth, life, teaching, and crucifixion of Jesus, but he knew how to fish. In the exasperation of the extraordinary, he reached for the reenactment of the ordinary. When you don't know what to do, you do what lies at hand. When you can't do the big, you go to work on the necessary little. So Peter said, "I don't know the answer to the big thing, but I sure know what I can do. Get out the boat; we're going fishing." And the others joined him.

John's Gospel delights in portraying something I want to point out. It takes positive delight in bringing into sharp intersection the indeterminacy of life and how God's grace intersects exactly at that point. Now that is rather a fat idea. Let me break it up. What I mean is that if we have the future too well put together, John's Gospel delights in seeing it collapse. If things are too well long-range planned, John's Gospel shows that the grace of God operates with a kind of humorous extemporaneity and upsets the whole well-built house. They go fishing and it wasn't a great success. They weren't catching anything and the figure of the Lord appears and said—they didn't know who it was—but a figure asked if they'd done very well, and when they replied, "No," "Try it on the other side of the boat." And that's very interesting because it is said that among fishing people the sign of the holy is often accompanied by an extraordinary catch of fish; that in the presence of something indeterminate the whole scene is turned around and so many fish. (There have been all kinds of cerebral sweat wasted on why 153 fish and, as a matter of fact, nobody knows. It was probably one of the sacred numbers in ancient religion.) Lots of fish, and they brought them ashore without breaking the net (and that's an interesting thing), and the story ends with Jesus appearing and the recognition first by John and then Peter. Later, with his typical kind of enthusiasm, Peter starts to put on his clothes. The Greek says that he tucked his garment up under a cord, which makes more sense than going into the sea with all his clothes on. He immediately went toward the Lord. Then the story ends with the incident on the seashore, but it seems to me that what this lesson is saying to us is something so strong, so beautiful, so graciously destructive of our tendency to believe that we can long-range plan our lives in such a way that there is no crevice left for God's grace to break it up, to break in.

Let me introduce this conclusion by reminding you of the beautiful little poem by Theodore Roethke—I will recall only three lines of it:

> I wake to sleep, and take my waking slow.
> I feel my fate in what I cannot fear.
> I learn by walking where I have to go.[9]

9. Theodore Roethke, "The Waking," in Roethke, *Words for the Wind: The Collected Verse of Theodore Roethke* (Garden City, NY: Doubleday, 1958).

Have you learned, as I have sometimes, by walking not where you long-range planned to go but where you just had to go? Has not strange grace sometimes struck you not along the path you wanted to take, were determined to take, were even prepared to take, but in one of the diverted bypaths you'd had no intention of taking, and there something gracious, good, opening, and creative happened? Think of the number of unplanned little ways in which our lives are thrown off their predetermined courses, in which the never suspected becomes the occasion of the freshly possible, in which things that you didn't think could be, became. "I learn by walking where I have to go." Now notice that Peter didn't know what he ought to do; he didn't know where to go; the path was unclear, the center of his life was pulled out like a plug, but he said, "There's one thing I can do"—and he did the obvious, clear thing that was close at hand—"I'm going fishing."

Just one more reflection: is not our disposition to assume that the shape of our lives, the enumeration of what possibilities there are, can only be long-range planned in the absence of a sense of humor? Anyone with a sense of humor, which, as Kierkegaard once said, is very close to the sense of the holy. The sense of humor, of the holy, sheds upon our lives a light by which we know that in a variety of life's plans there is never an absolute. Situations are never completely closed; circumstances never add up absolutely to outcomes. "I learn by walking where I have to go." This means that the grace of God is deuces wild. It doesn't play straight. It doesn't always come just by those occasions which traditionally have been the gracious kind. Grace is a surprise. We have just sung "Amazing Grace." What's amazing about it? Not only the substance of it, but the "you can't call it" character of grace. How many times in your life have you not met grace where you had no expectation of anything but another day? How many times has the unexpected completely reversed the expected, the wanted, and the chosen?

"I learn by walking where I have to go." And Peter said, "I go fishing."

Sermon on Memory

1986

A congregation's centennial celebration is certainly an appropriate opportunity for reflections on time. However, Sittler's reflections are profoundly spiritual and lacking in the indulgence of nostalgia. We sense God's gift of time as a flow of life having a future, a future implied in the life of the gospel that has marked the hundred years of the congregation. The discussion of the beatitude that follows, though apparently discontinuous with the reflection on time, is connected when we reflect on how the gift of blessedness unites the gift of a future with the call to responsibility for that promised future in the care of the earth. Lessons for the preacher are there in the example of Sittler's ability to penetrate language word by word and out of that small scale focus produce a large scale vision that invokes reflection on the full breadth of divine activity.

MY REFLECTIONS THIS MORNING will be in three parts. The first will be what one might call acknowledgements: the second, memory; and third, the meditation. First, acknowledgements: I want to acknowledge the joy I feel in being permitted to participate with you in this occasion, not only because it is for you a significant and a happy time, but because it permits me to spend several days with two of my oldest and dearest friends.

The second thing I ask you to reflect upon has to do with memory and the significance of it in the formation of our lives. I begin with an observation about which I wrote a little essay some months ago. The first time I ever saw a digital watch, I was angry. I was disproportionately angry—I mean, the presence of that new gadget called a digital watch shouldn't have made me that mad—so I reflected upon why the disproportion between the smallness of the watch and the bigness of my anger, and in the course of those reflections I think I got a hold of something important. The digital watch is a bad instrument because it's a liar—it doesn't tell the truth about time. The digital watch jumps. It's a jerky little thing, and when a minute is up, it jerks and the time is recorded on the little opening in the watch face. It makes time jerky, episodic—now you have it, now you don't. But time is not like that. On the old watch, you remember, the great minute hand slowly, slowly sweeps around the minute, and the hour hand creeps through the hours of the day and the night, and the slow and uninterrupted motion of the hands on the watch is a kind of honest representation of the way time is; time doesn't jump, it creeps. Time is not episodic; time is a kind of flowing. You remember the words of the great Isaac Watts hymn: "Time, like an ever-rolling stream, bears all its sons away; they fly forgotten, as a dream dies at the opening day." So that, there's something about the digitalization of life which is destructive of the true nature of life. It leads us to forget that time is a continuum. Time is a stream. It's not a series of unrelated episodes.

And there is a kind of infinite pathos in that too, because time only leans in one way. You can't go home again. Time leans irretrievably forward. This, that I call this "pathos of time," has been marvelously concentrated in an image in a little poem by the English poet of the turn of the century, A. E. Housman. He is remembering in his poem the days when as a child he used to go to the country fair in England, and those fairs are much like the country fairs we know in this county and remember, I suppose, with childhood delight. He says,

> When first my way to fair I took
> Few pence in my purse had I,
> And long I used to stand and look
> At things I could not buy.
>
> Now times are altered: if I care
> To buy a thing I can;
> The pence and here and here's the fair,
> But where's the lost young man?

So, this sense of time in its flowing, in the slowness, in the almost unrecognizable fragility of its multiple changes—this is an important fact that human life ought to recognize; and if we turn our life into a kind of jumpy, jerky series of separated episodes, we tend to forget and even to make banal the profound pathos of time in our life. Now, what is profound about it? What is profound about time—say the hundred years which has passed since this lovely old building was conceived and created? What is profound about it is this: time is not constituted by episodes. Time is not an event; it is an accumulation. Time is a kind of ever-flowing stream. It is a passage.

And if that be true, then we have thereby a hint or clue as to the importance and goodness of celebration. Why should you celebrate the hundred years in this old place where the Word has been proclaimed and the Sacrament administered? Why should life always be rich in remembrance? Why should we always think of the whence in order to have a direction for the whither? You see, if time is digitalized and chopped up into pieces then the most profound events and ponderings of life tend to be lost in the frenzied excitement of each passing moment. Remembrance is a quality that tends to pull life into an organic fullness. In remembrance I reenact, I recapitulate, I reach back and throw light upon my present by the illuminations that come from the past. In remembrance and recapitulation, I also gain wisdom and prudence to a living of the future, so that this idea that celebration should be honored on important occasions has a rich intellectual and personal good to deliver to us if we do them properly.

Now, the third element of my observation with you on this day is to invite you to a little meditation. Now that I can't read very well anymore, I often reflect upon texts about which previously I could read all I wanted, and find I have the possibility in darkness to reflect in a way that has a kind of depth to the light it reflects. As one man said to me once, "When you're partly blind you have to think more about less, and that's not altogether bad." Well, in thinking more about less, I have been pondering about a certain obscure text in the New Testament which I want to invite you to reflect upon for a moment. I say "obscure" text because the text is not only obscure, but is even obscure to the point of bewilderment, and it seems not even to be true.

The text from the Beatitudes, "Blessed are the meek, for they shall inherit the earth"—that seems simply to be untrue. Is it the meek who inherit the earth? Is it not, rather, the bold, the brassy, the aggressive, the go-getters of this life who seem to get a hold of things and run things? And yet, Jesus, who was no fool, Jesus, that truth-telling man, said, "Blessed are the meek, for they shall inherit the earth." What can that possibly mean? If a thing is said by a wise man and is not immediately meaningful, then we ought to peer into it and probe and try to find out what it means. And that is what I have been doing for awhile, and I ask you to think with me about the three words "blessed," "meek," and "inherit the earth." What do they mean?

In a modern translation of the Beatitudes in the New English Bible, and in other versions, it says in the Beatitudes, "Happy are the pure in heart . . . happy are the meek . . ." That's all very jolly, but that doesn't say what the Bible says. The Hebrew word for blessed, *baruch*, and the Greek word translated here "blessed," do not mean "happy." If we read "happy" instead of "blessed" we miss the point right off the bat. The difference is this: to be happy is, on the whole, a result of fortunate circumstances. Happiness is a very fragile and highly breakable thing. If my wife is well, and my children are doing well, and my own work is satisfying, and I can pay my bills, then you can say that you are a happy man, but all of that can change in a moment. Happiness is so fragile a thing because it can be blown to pieces by an unfortunate circumstance, by an accident, but illness, or death. Happiness is a good and it is a blessed thing, but it is not what the word "blessed" means. The word "blessed" is a profounder thing than happiness. The old Hebrew scholar Joshua Heschel said, "A Jew understands blessedness to mean interior joy in the presence of God." That is not destructible, but the fragility of happiness does not characterize the blessed life. In the Old Testament we read, "Blessed is the man who lives by the streams of water, the refreshment of God's Law, the Torah." Blessedness is solid-centeredness in God. It is the interior solidity of that which comes from God's gift, and his mercy, and is not vulnerable to the convolutions and the convulsions of our life. Therefore, we ought to read the passage, "Blessed . . . blessed are the meek," not just "happy."

Okay, look at the second word. "Blessed are the *meek*." Well, now, that's a problem too, because meekness for us is not a very admirable virtue or way of life. By "meek" we usually mean the pusillanimous, the weak, the shifting, the not very clear and precise and definite people, the people whose life lacks outline and focus. "Meek" tends to mean sniveling. Well, that's an unhappy word because the Greek word translated "meek" was all right in the sixteenth or seventeenth century, when our English Bible was done, because "meek" then meant something other. Our present notion of meek is not exactly what the word meant in 1611, when our English Bible was translated from the Greek text. I looked this up in the Oxford English Dictionary and was immediately illuminated.

The work "meek" in the seventeenth century meant, "They of a strong and gentle spirit." It means exactly the opposite of weak. It means strong, but a strength characterized by the gentleness of strength, not by the fierceness or ferocity or the violence of strength. So if you read, "Blessed are they of the strong and gentle spirit," then you get close to the original meaning of the text.

I had another little light thrown on this by reading it in the French New Testament. My grandmother grew up in Alsace, and she knew French as well as German, and she used to write us, as children, little French notes, and she always encouraged us to learn a little French because she said, "It's a beautiful language," which indeed it is. So, I looked in the French New Testament on this verse and with a kind of shock of delight read the translation in French. Blessed are the meek in "*Heureux les débonnaires.*" Any high school kids here in the French class will be delighted with me. *Debonaire*, what a word for "meek"! *Debonaire* in French means to have a kind of holy light-heartedness about life; not to take relative things to seriously; to take seriously only the absolute things and not get hooked on passing, relative values. Blessed are the *debonaire*. Blessed are they of a strong and gentle spirit.

Now look at the last word. "Blessed are they of a strong and gentle spirit for they shall *inherit the earth*." Now that's where the catch comes, because that doesn't seem to be the case. Exxon and Phillips Petroleum and General Motors didn't get that way by being meek, non-aggressive, and sniveling. They got that way be being tough, aggressive, grabbing every opportunity and getting as much as they could. But what can it possibly mean? Well, look at the verb. It doesn't say, "blessed are they of a strong and gentle spirit for they shall *own* the world," or "run the earth," or "get all the boodle," or "pile up all the power." "Blessed are they of a strong and gentle spirit, for they shall *inherit* the earth." Well, what's the difference between an inheritance and a possession—something you've won, own, gain? An "inheritance" is the name for something that comes to me as a surprise. I didn't own it. I didn't earn it. If my old uncle dies and leaves a thousand dollars in his will, that's an inheritance. It's mine by the sheer gift of my uncle, or whoever. It's a surprise and it's a delight because I did not earn it. "Blessed are they of the strong and gentle spirit, for they shall receive the earth as a gift." Suddenly, you see that perplexing verse opens up like a flower.

What might it mean—and after I have finished, you think about this awhile—what might it mean in the days of corruption of the world, with foul waters and bad air, the misuse of the land, the rapacious use of God's gift of nature? What might it mean if we created a civilization of a strong and gentle spirit that dealt with God's gift of the world as an inheritance, as a gift? Suppose that we dealt with our environment with a strong and gentle gratitude, rather than an assault upon God's good earth. So that this apparently obscure verse, "Blessed are the meek, for they shall inherit the earth"—get it right: blessed (joyful in the presence of God) are they who exercise a gentle and strong obedience toward God's gift, for to them the world gives itself back with beauty, richness, and grace.

Therefore on this hundredth anniversary of this handsome old building, and in remembrance of the fidelity with which this congregation has, I trust, heard for so long the preached Word of God and received here the Sacrament—on this occasion let us, as we look forward to the endangered world of our nation in the next hundred years, know how important it is to change our manner, to change our way of life so that we do not live assaulting God's creation, but with a strong and gentle spirit deal with God's gracious gift of life and the good earth according to his commandment.

Postscript

The Last Lecture: A Walk around Truth, Eternal Life, Faith

1987

This lecture, delivered at the University of Chicago toward the end of Sittler's life, is a fitting postscript and a complement to "His God Story," with which we began. Familiar themes of the importance of language in the communication of the faith and the role of literature as a window to life are reiterated here. Sittler also offers an insightful reflection on the relationship of love and truth. His concluding thoughts on eternal life go beyond formulaic statements to engage in a probing engagement that illustrates again his characteristic readiness to ponder the mysteries of our faith.

I TOOK VERY SERIOUSLY the plan for these periods together, and when one asks a man what he'd really want to talk about if he had only about an hour to do it, then he shouldn't play. So I rifled my own reflections and tried to come up with what were the kinds of issues that have been perduring from my first inquiry until this very close to my last, and I came up with these three things which have been on my mind, literally, since I had a mind that was aware of the world at all: the nature of truth, what the Scripture means by eternal life, and the nature of faith. So instead of going at these one after another—because they all circle around a certain way of thinking and reflecting about the world and the way of organizing experience—I want to walk all around those three questions and hope that something coherent will emerge as we get on with it.

First of all, to be very old and have very bad vision does not have many benefits that I can think of, but one of them is that you are obliged to think more about less. As one gets old, the sensate world, the constant battering of impression, sensation, suffers a severe abatement—but that abatement is not altogether a loss. Because in the semidarkness and in the absence of many things that call for your awareness to spring now here, now there, one faces a situation in which the light of reflection is invited to do its proper business. For some years now, retired from Monday-Wednesday-Friday and Tuesday-Thursday schedules, I have had a lot of time and, in semidarkness, good occasion to reflect. I want to begin the reflection way out on the edge and move in toward the center of these issues.

I cannot think of a time when every question, intellectual, experiential, social did not end up with a linguistic question for me. That is to say, whatever reality is has from my earliest moment not been separable from language, from words. One of the benefits of age is that one is no longer in a hurry to find a solution to things, but is invited by solitude to figure things back to the finest tendril, to the very beginning of awareness, to be reexamined. As I think of how I came to be so fascinated with the linguistic reality whereby things announce their presence to us, I have tried to figure where that came from and when I got it. And I think I know, at least in part. I remember in grade school I had an extraordinary teacher, a large, round, obese, rosy, lovely lady who loved to quote little verses to us when we were children in class. She'd start the day with a nice piece of verse. And the first one I ever learned is banal, but it's the earliest one I can recall:

> The night was thick and hazy
> When the "Picadilly Daisy"
> Carried down the crew and captain in the sea;
> And the water must have drowned 'em;
> For they never, never found 'em,
> And I know they didn't come ashore with me.[1]

---

1. The first stanza from Charles E. Carryl, "Robinson Crusoe's Story." Reprinted from Louis Untermeyer, ed., *Modern American Poetry: An Introduction* (New York: Harcourt, Brace and Howe, 1919).

Postscript

I think I was thoroughly fascinated with the quality of language to not only point to, but create the thing which it then celebrated. I didn't intellectually think of it that way then, for I was too fascinated with the jingle, but from that moment on, I've been unable in what intellectual prowess I possess to separate the abstract ability of conceptualization—abstract thought and logic, philosophy—from the language in which they carry on their various enterprises. I think this reflective habit of finding a thing only capable of acknowledgement when it comes with an enticing linguistic character was developed for me at the beginning of this century when the English Bible provided a common language. That is simply not true anymore, and I could spend a lot of time lamenting the loss entailed by that; but to grow up in a time when the majestic sonorities of the English Bible were a part of the ordinary life of ordinary people in America is something for which I am very grateful. Coming from a tradition in which both the biblical literature and the old liturgical life of the church were very important, this affection for, and this invitatory character of language as a way to understanding, were early grooved in my mind and I want to give several illustrations of it.

I have taken certain things which have always been in my mind and asked, "Can you analyze what evokes admiration and sticks in the memory in such a way as to say, if it does that, why does it do that?" I take one illustration for those of you who know something about the great prayers of the church. On Christmas Eve the prayer that is common in the old liturgy of the church is one which I heard when I was very young. I heard every Christmas: "O God, who has caused this most holy night to shine with the brightness of the true light . . ." Why is that so compelling? One can take it apart and almost do an anatomical study of the "i" sounds: holy night, shine bright, true light. In the way the "i" sounds dance, and are like little Christmas tree lights, the language not only points to, and is celebrative of an object or an occasion or a remembrance or even a dream, but it also contributes to the reality of that to which it points with such vehemence that the reality without the language could not subsist.

We go on from there to the first of the big words I am struck with—not simply Pilate's statement that caused me to be fascinated with the term "truth," but a fascinating sentence in the New Testament, in the interview that Jesus had with Pilate. Jesus replied, "If you were of the truth, you would hear my voice." "If you were *of* the truth . . ." What might it mean, logically, philosophically, to be "of the truth"? The sentence does not postulate we have a certain body of truth, or that there is a certain body available, and if you work at it long enough and seriously enough you would be brought to the place where you would know the truth. No, that isn't what it says. The sentence suggests that there is something before the quest for truth, something more primal than the various ways to truth, or disciplines for gaining truth or describing truth, more primitive than that, in the phrase "if you were *of* the truth." Does the phrase perhaps (I have checked with my betters who know the Greek text, and the English is exactly what the Greek text says, so there are no tricks there) suggest that the phrase "of the truth" is a predispositional, preempirical, preinvestigatory tilt of the whole disposition of the whole person? You can be "of the truth" in the sense that you really wish that there should be a truth and that that truth could somehow evoke from you a kind of allegiance; that your relationship to truth should be one of affection, not just a function, that you should really love, will, resolve the truth—not just seek for or empirically pile up data and come to a conclusion that this is the truth about this or this or this. I leave the suggestion that to be "of the truth" raises a question about how we enter into a relationship with whatever is ultimate in life and is not simply a matter of information, or logic, or reason, or discipline. You can be "of the truth" and you can be one who is *not* "of the truth."

We can put another angle on that. I remember something I read in my early days in theological school, from Saint Augustine: "There is no entrance into truth, save by love." This entrance into truth is not separable from *caritas*, from *caring about* truth, *loving* truth—not loving it simply because of the functional use of it that may be opened up by more exact knowledge; that's another purely legitimate thing, but it is not what Jesus meant. "There is no entrance into truth, save by love."

Now the next step is one that further complicates the matter, I think. I find it difficult to use so ordinary a word for the very big thing I want to say, but I recall the fine lecture that Wendy O'Flaherty gave some months ago in this school which suggested the following to me. The aim of education, it seems to me, is admiration, which is another way of saying the same thing about truth. To evoke and to supply the gift of admiration for legitimate objects, it seems to me, is what a university is for. One can get the thing outside the institution, and most of what is valuable for me I have gotten that way, but simply to admire, to have evoked within you the kind of wonder at the variety, the majesty, or the delightfulness, or the silliness, or the randomness of things of this world, is what education must come upon, work to evoke and to cultivate, and finally secure. Jonathan

Edwards, with his wonderful statements about the primitive character in the development of knowledge of the heart's affections, as necessary to the refinement and disciplining of the mind in its higher conceptual practices, is all part of the thing I am groping to put into language. What I notice about the young people I still see a lot of is a kind of veneer of coolness which is fatal to a life of admiration. You know the attitude: "big deal." They can look at things which contain within themselves a great human depth or brilliance or beauty, and so incessant is the sensate passage of events in rapid order from day to day that they tend to become case-hardened about the marvels. The very gift of admiration becomes dulled.

All of this is by way of getting to the next theme, which is something everyone wonders about, but few people talk about openly. What is the nature of eternal life? What does the term mean? You may recall that it was in this university some years ago that Elizabeth Kübler-Ross, then having some relationship to the Department of Biological Sciences, made a national stir by a book in which she deployed certain fairly psychedelic images of life after death. There was a nationwide discussion of the whole matter. The discussion wasn't very important. It didn't turn up anything. But it did disclose that the moment you mention the phrase "life after death" people think, "Oh yes, that's what the Bible means, that's what the Christian tradition means by eternal life." It was when I became aware that that is *not* the case that I began these reflections which I want to share with you.

The particular phrase itself, "eternal life," is a curious phrase. It is so illogical as to be absurd and improbable. The only possible meaning of life that we can certify and use as a kind of negotiable term which we can all understand is that life is characterized by temporality, mortality, passingness, mutability. Life comes, unfolds, closes, and departs. That is the only kind of life we know anything about. To use the adjective "eternal" about life is really to make no sense. Yet Jesus, who made sense, used the phrase. The Fourth Gospel is loaded with it. I would suggest something interesting to people interested in theological language: that what the Fourth Gospel calls "eternal life" is the equivalent of what Matthew, Mark, and Luke call the "kingdom of God"; and that the historical term "kingdom of God," to be realized, to be envisioned, admired, sought for, received within historical existence—at least in most parts—does not point to a life after death as its primary reference. It has little to do with resuscitation, a rerun of the life I've already had, or reenactment, repetition, or everlasting and endless playback through all eternity. In fact, I would suggest that to understand the meaning of eternal life that way is not only irreverent, it is positively blasphemous. It would be to raise egocentricity to an absolute state to want to be oneself forever and ever; to regard being Joe Sittler through all eternity would be to raise the evil of idolatry to an absolute pitch. Therefore the notion of eternal life, it seems to me, is one which must be pondered. Can it possibly mean this: an unfolding into a participation in that which certifies itself to you as more than yourself, greater than yourself? Before, and during, and after yourself, it *is*. It is a participation in the depth of that Being which underlies all being, a participation in the primal source of all that is. It is active life in its temporality, qualified by eternity with such celebrative joy and vision as to deserve the phrase "eternal life."

With that kind of reflection on two terms, I come to the question, why, after all these years do I still make the catholic Christian profession? To put the question that way means I think I really shouldn't; that if I were really a smart fellow and had my eyes open in this world, and have not been rocked into lifelong somnolence by an unchanged childhood illusion, I really ought to know better at this age. Why do I still make the confession, "I believe in God the Father Almighty" and so on? Let me put the question in the largest possible way. I still make the Christian confession, the whole business, with vehemence, with a confidence that it is the truth, with a kind of happiness and joy—I make that confession because I think it is the most capacious story, the most capacious, congruent, cohesive, and fitting way to describe what I know about human life. As G. K. Chesterton put it, "I find as I grow older that the spoke of dogma fits into the hole of experience with eerie exactness."

That's exactly what I mean. The story of creation—coming into existence with a kind of wholeness, integrity, and then somehow or other with an alienation, cleavage, dividedness, a long journey in the wilderness, lostness, a call to return, a divine Creator of all things becoming our situation in order to address us where we are—this story seems to me to fit the reality of human experience with a kind of exactitude which evokes from me constant surprise and admiration. When I talk about the actuality, I do not mean "churchy" actuality, or a pious actuality. My life has not been concerned with piety or church all the time, by any means. I mean everything from Aeschylus and Dante, the Middle Ages and Shakespeare, and Saul Bellow and Richard Wilbur and Joseph Conrad and Hemingway, *Moby Dick*. I've tried to sail the seas of Western literature as widely as I can; so when I talk of human experience, I don't mean that little drop of experience that is my own existence. I mean that multiplication of humanity that literature affords, that opening of oneself to the great confessional which is fiction and poetry and history. That human experience seems to me to present a kind of contour of temptation, idolatry, ambiguity, majesty and misery, delight and despair; and the Christian story, which comes to its intellectual explication or expression in the great creeds, fits that with an eerie exactitude.

Why, generation after generation, do novels and other works of art come out with titles from biblical stories? Consider *East of Eden* or the poetry or narrative literature that comes out of one aspect or another of a biblical kind, like Thomas Mann's "Joseph" novel. Robert Penn Warren's introduction to one of the editions of Joseph Conrad's tales contains a memorable paragraph that ends his discussion of Conrad. He says Conrad was ultimately skeptical about truth, beauty. He knew the transiency of all things human, the deceptiveness of everything in human life. These values, he said, that Conrad talks about, they may be illusions, but for Conrad these illusions are infinitely precious. The search to maintain and sustain them constitutes our deepest humanity, which may be the only truth of which we are capable.

If these things which I call "truth" are only illusions, to live with these illusions is better than to try to live without them. They evoke from us a deepening, a broadening of our humanity, a growth of that fundamental pathos which constitutes our human life; hence they make the most that can be made out of the human creature and therefore may be "of the truth."

About three months ago I had a couple of hours with a man of mixed gifts but remarkable personality, William Sloane Coffin. He said, "What we gotta do from now on is to be vehement as hell about the perfectly obvious." And I think he was right. The perfectly obvious is that the scattered life, which does not admire and is thus not drawn toward anything better than episodic sensation, which has no center, no value toward which it is drawn, is self-destructive. You can't bring it off. To live with take-it-day-by-day, get-what-you-can, get-on-with-your-career, is a fateful way to live and won't in the long run work. I think that is perfectly obvious, and I don't think you have to be a confessing Christian to see that that is the case.

Faith is a kind of response to the allure, the allure that resides in every living thing, every occasion. I do not reject the notion that some kind of eternal residency with the Eternal is a hope of the Christian tradition.

But I cannot fill it with content. The New Testament does not try to. "Eye hath not seen, nor ear heard, what God hath prepared for those who love him." It's interesting that Saint Paul tried on one occasion—two really, but one remarkably unsuccessful occasion—to answer the question, "In what body shall the dead arise and in what form will they come?" Well, he said, "There's one flesh of fowl, and one of fish, one of animal . . ." He tried a bunch of not very good analogies and he saw where he was getting, which was nowhere, and he quit. And then, after the end of his writing career, in the Epistle to the Romans, he has one smart little sentence: "If we live we are the Lord's; if we die we are the Lord's; therefore, living and dying, we are the Lord's." Period. And that's exactly what the New Testament says, and what the Christian faith promises as a Christian hope: that is, if God is the Eternal One, and if one be in him in faith and participate in the eternal, God does not die. What does that mean for me? I don't *know*. But it could mean nothing ill.

The usual language for life after death is a language which I find depressing: reenactment, eternal recapitulation, a living with one's adorable selfhood forever and ever. Don't you have any ambition? Charles Hartshorne, the metaphysician formerly of this university, said in an essay called "The Abiding Presence" that "in the mind of God we shall never not have been." That is an interesting way to suggest what to me is a way of pointing to the hope of eternal life. It's enough.

Index

American Lutheran Church, 129
Aquinas, Thomas, 67, 205
Arnold, Matthew, 68
Association of Evangelical Lutheran
    Churches, 129
Auden, W.H., 22
Augsburg Confession, 30–31, 274
Augustine, Saint, 65, 69, 82, 122,
    194, 198, 318
Aulen, Gustaf, 99
Ayer, A.J., 136

Bach, Johann Sebastian, 88, 169,
    184–88, 196, 205, 276, 278
Bakken, Peter, 7, 9
Baltimore Catechism, 174
Barth, Karl, 19, 21, 91, 162, 260, 300
Beatitudes, 23–24, 310–11
Bellow, Saul, 320
biblical authority, 115–127
biblical interpretation, 5–10, 134,
    138–38, 150, 161, 165, 167,
    239, 25
biblical imagination, 159–71
Bohr, Niels, 142
Bonhoeffer, Dietrich, 194, 197
Brontë, Charlotte and Emily, 16
Brunner, Emil, 21
Bultmann, Rudolph, 135, 148, 162,
    300
Buxtehude, Dietrich, 186, 278

Calvin, John, 24, 47, 76, 192, 260
Cappadocians, 194
Carryl, Charles, 306
Carson, Rachel, 26
Cassirer, Ernst, 139
Chaucer, Goeffrey, 293
Chesterton, Gilbert, 117, 171, 209–
    11, 241–42, 249, 320
christology, 27–37, 65–72, 92, 105
    and ecology, 7–10
    and preaching, 38–48
Conrad, Joseph, 16, 177–78, 320–21
Cummings, e.e., 25, 206, 233

Dante Alighieri, 15, 125, 141, 248,
    320
Davenport, William, 83
Deissmann, Adolf, 19, 179
de la Mare, Walter, 165
Dibelius, Martin, 19
Dodd, Charles Harold, 93, 223
Donne, John, 225

Eastern Orthodoxy, 9, 13, 65–66,
    107, 131, 155, 218
Ebeling, Gerhard, 148
ecology, 7, 78.104
    See also christology and ecology
    of faith, 104–10, 170, 250
    of preaching, 198

323

Index

Edwards, Jonathan, 318–19
Einstein, Albert, 125
Eliot, T.S., 22, 237
environment, 9, 76–80, 106, 110, 313
ethics, 3, 9–10, 50–62, 92, 112, 176, 242, 274
Erasmus, 246
eternal life, 107, 271, 287–88, 315, 319–22

faith, 5, 9, 13–17, 22, 28, 31, 34, 40–43, 46–48, 51–62, 71–72, 81, 105–12, 139, 143–48, 160–75, 181–82, 191, 210, 229, 231, 239–52, 257–59, 272–77, 295–99, 303, 315, 322
    active in love, 9–10, 107, 126

Galloway, Allan, 65
glory, 34–36, 41, 47–48, 62, 71, 77, 131–32, 204–5, 236–41, 256–58
gospel, 17, 19, 21, 42, 45–48, 50, 53, 78, 81, 96, 111–13, 154, 167, 170, 174, 196–97, 231, 294,
    and law, 50, 113, 133, 189–91, 195, 215, 256
Goethe, J.W., 141

Hall, Douglas John, 11–12
Harrington, Michael, 143
Hartshorne, Charles, 322
Hawthorn, Nathaniel, 16
Hemingway, Ernest, 320
historical-critical method, 6, 29, 30–31, 134–35
Homer, Paul, 176
Hopkins, Gerard Manley, 48, 68–69, 230, 241, 255
Houseman, A.E., 52
humility, 5, 10, 108, 112

imagination in preaching, 172–83, 198
imago Dei, 44
Irenaeus, 65, 67

John XXIII, Pope, 124
justification, 29, 47, 54, 189
justice, 11, 56–59, 66, 98,109, 112, 182, 198, 219, 240, 245–46
    and love, 61–62
Keats, John, 16, 120, 222, 232, 262
Kierkegaard, Søren, 39, 176, 307
Knox, John, 162–63
Knubel-Miller Lectures, 5, 112
Kroner, Richard, 173
Kűbler-Ross, Elizabeth, 319

law, 4, 53, 60, 64, 81, 109, 190–92, 267–68, 270, 311
    and gospel, see gospel and law
    public, 62, 79
Lawrence, D.H., 240
Lightfoot, Robert Henry, 93
liturgy, 13–15, 17, 21, 79, 81, 167, 197, 286, 299, 317
logos, 3, 32, 35–37, 176
love, 4, 8–10, 36, 48, 51, 54–62, 72, 81–82, 107, 109, 118, 122, 136, 153, 174, 205, 210, 216–20, 273, 276, 287–89
    and truth, 315, 318
    see also, faith active in love
    see also, justice and love
Luther, Martin, 5, 7, 31, 39, 42–43, 54, 81, 109, 113, 131, 133, 139, 189, 194,196, 227–28, 260, 276–77, 278, 282–83
Lutheran Church in America, 115
Lutheran Church-Missouri Synod, 129
Lyman Beecher Lectures, 104

Mann, Thomas, 321
Maxwell, Clark, 125
Melville, Thomas, 16
Miller, Alexander, 55
Milton, John, 164
ministry, 21, 84–87, 89–94, 100, 108, 137, 144, 301
    of the laity, 97–100, 231
Moltmann, Jürgen, 9

nature and grace, 8–11, 27, 54,
    66–69, 72, 75–83, 88, 107,
    174, 181
Niebuhr, Richard, R., 21, 85, 161,
    163, 165
Niebuhr, Reinhold,, 21

Oppenheimer, Robert, 108, 248
Origen, 194
Otto, Rudolph, 204

Palestrina, Giovanni Pierluigi, 169,
    186, 239, 278
Pannenberg, Wolfhart, 2
parables, 214–35
Penn-Warren, Robert, 321
Pius XII, Pope, 124
prayer, 21, 88, 111, 118, 204, 241,
    259–60

Rahner, Karl, 27
Reformation, 30, 33, 46, 67, 81, 134,
    185
repentance, 61
Ricoeur, Paul., 6
righteous, 54, 245, 267
righteousness, 191, 219, 245
Roethke, Theodore, 43, 306

sacrament(s), 28, 30, 56, 67, 96–97,
    192, 270, 310, 313
Scripture, see biblical authority and
    biblical interpretation
Schrödinger, Erwin, 142
Schweitzer, Albert, 278–79
Shakespeare, William, 15–16, 121,
    125, 137, 156, 280, 293, 320
simul justus et peccator, 59
spirituality, 5, 106, 109, 111–12

Stendahl, Krister, 299
Stevens, Wallace, 22
Stewart, James, 93
style, 108–9, 179, 248

Ten Commandments, 53–54, 242
theology, 2, 4–5, 7–8, 11, 28–31,
    35–37, 44, 69–70, 75, 80–82,
    87–88, 111, 129, 142–43,
    162–63, 168, 171, 196, 225
  and ecology, 9–10, 26
  of the cross, 5, 112–13, 194
  for preaching, 84, 88, 104–5,
    109, 112, 159–61, 165–66,
    194
Thomas, Dylan, 52, 271
Thomas, Lewis, 269
Tillich, Paul, 21, 251,283
Toulmin, Stephen, 142
Trinity, Holy, 27, 46–47, 75, 77, 81
Troeltsch, Ernst, 134

Via, Dan O., 144, 224
Von Weisäcker, Carl, 142
Vööbus, Arthur, 34

Walther, C.F.W., 189
Westminster Catechism, 203
Westminster Confession, 274
Wiesel, Eli, 275
Wilbur, Richard, 22, 73, 201, 203,
    320
Wiley, Basil, 160
Wordsworth, William, 280
World Council of Churches, 6
  Faith and Order Commission, 9,
    20–21, 27, 46, 71, 107, 166